What the Bible Says About...

Child Training

2ND EDITION

by
J. Richard Fugate

Published by
Foundation for Biblical Research

All Scripture quotations are taken from the
Authorized King James Version, New Scofield Reference Bible

WHAT THE BIBLE SAYS ABOUT ... ™ CHILD TRAINING

2ND EDITION

2nd Edition Copyright © 1996 by
J. Richard Fugate
Publisher: Foundation for Biblical Research
8319 Parkside Ln
CITRUS HEIGHTS, CA 95610

Printed in the United States of America

ISBN 1-889700-13-4
Library of Congress
Catalog Card Number:
96-61914

This book provides Biblical answers for parents' questions about:

- How to be successful parents and thereby receive God's promised blessings.

- How to set standards and train up a child in the way he should go.

- How to teach a child according to his stages of growth.

- How to understand and control a child's negative behavior traits.

- How to express true love to your child.

- How to identify and conquer a child's rebellion.

- How to punish a child justly and in love.

- How to produce a well-adjusted, self-confident, moral, young adult who is prepared for a successful life.

CREDITS:
Edited by Dr. Myron Yeager
Footnotes by Dan Carlen
Cover Art by Jonathan Chong
Cover Insert Art by Bart Lindstrom
Inside Illustrations by Melissa Evers Corwin
Typing & Proofreading by Phyllis Carlen
2nd Edition Typesetting by Christine Korecki
2nd Edition Proofreading by David J. Korecki

WHAT THE BIBLE SAYS ABOUT... ™

is a series designed to present the systematic development of the Bible as it speaks on specific subjects. All study was performed under the principle of 2 Timothy 2:15 *Study to shew thyself approved unto God, a workman that needeth not to be ashamed, rightly dividing the word of truth.* All referenced passages have been studied in depth within their context from the original languages of Scripture. Word studies have been performed on each word that pertains to this specific subject. Much of the research used in the writing of this book was performed by the Foundation for Biblical Research. FBR is a nonprofit corporation that is dedicated to the discovery of the exact meaning of Scripture and the fully substantiated presentation of that meaning.

The opinions, illustrations, and applications given in this book represent years of practical experience in child rearing as well as the result of many personal hours of Biblical study. The author accepts full responsibility for these opinions, illustrations, and applications. To God alone be the glory for the Biblical information revealed herein.

FOREWORD

This book is an unique coverage of the vital subject of child training. In a day when most information is based on man's constantly changing opinions and his limited observations, it is exciting to see the objective truth of God's revelation presented. This truth is information by which man can live his life with the confidence that he is right. It is also truth that will produce predictable results when properly utilized.

There is an explosion of information today, much of which is false or unverifiable. Man desperately needs an accurate and reliable source of information that will provide beneficial and verifiable results when used. The Bible provides that source. When an intensive investigation has been honestly performed and a specific subject has been systematically developed from the Bible, the result is dependable information by which man can successfully live his life. This book is the presentation of just such a subject. It was developed on the basis of more than 1600 hours of Biblical research. The information provided is not just another man's opinion; it is based firmly on the Word of God.

2 Timothy 3:16 *"All scripture is given by inspiration of God, and is profitable for doctrine, for reproof, for correction, for instruction in righteousness,"*

FOUNDATION FOR BIBLICAL RESEARCH

Forward To The 2nd Edition

In the twenty years since What the Bible Says About...*Child Training* has been available, it has become the manual for training children in the Biblical manner. *What the Bible Says About...Child Training* has sold over 250,000 copies worldwide; it has been translated into Spanish; and translation rights have been granted for Polish, French, Hungarian, German and Russian editions. It has also become an integral part of many college Family Life courses; and it is a foundational element of the home schooling movement nationwide.

There have been fourteen printings during these twenty years, but a revision has never been required for a single chapter. However, the author has heard comments over the years from a number of parents which indicated that certain amount of clarification was needed. Additionally, as in any issue where only white and black information is set forth, humans sometimes become extreme in their practice and in not balancing their expectations. For example, because many parents began to apply the principles taught herein with dramatic and immediate success, they expected their children to become totally trained without proper consideration for each child's natural immaturity. A child of four is still a four-year-old and can only reasonably be expected to be the best trained that a four-year-old should be, not to be held accountable for being a little adult.

Therefore, this 2nd edition will attempt to discourage any possible imbalance of application by providing author notes as needed for each of the chapters. It will also better illustrate the various principles as they are presented. The notes will be in the form of a personal discussion with examples provided where needed and will be located directly after the original chapters. It is hoped that these notes will not detract from the absolute Biblical truths being presented in each chapter, but only enhance the reader's understanding and protect him or her from any possible misapplication.

Psalm 119:105 *"Thy word is a lamp unto my feet, and a light unto my path."*

J. Richard Fugate

TABLE OF CONTENTS

INTRODUCTION

What the Bible Says About . . . Child Training is a study designed to help parents to better understand their role and to discover the mechanics for successfully raising children. To accomplish these ends this book will carefully define parental accountability, authority, and responsibility. It will also describe the nature of a child and explain his Biblically defined stages of development. With these principles firmly established, the book will present the Biblical system for training children.

This system is divided into two distinct phases, **controlling** and **teaching**. The control phase is the establishment of the parents' right of rulership over the will of the child. When parents can control their children, they have laid the necessary foundation for the fulfillment of the Biblical commandment for children to obey their parents. The teaching phase can only be accomplished by parents who have first trained their children to obey. This is because, before a child will receive the instructions of his parents, he must first respect their word; and before he will respect their word, he must first become obedient.

Colossians 3:20a *"Children, obey your parents in all things;"*

Children will not accept instruction from those whom they do not respect. The Biblical commandment for children to honor their father and mother is fulfilled when children respect their parents enough to accept their advice and instructions of wisdom.

Ephesians 6:2a *"Honor thy father and mother,"*

Parents who utilize this system consistently from the time their children are very young have God's guarantee of success. It is possible for even those parents who have failed in training their child during his early years to gain control and still produce an obedient and respectful child.

Isaiah 55:11 *"So shall my word be that goeth forth out of my mouth; it shall not return unto me void, but it shall accomplish that which I please, and it shall prosper in the thing whereto I sent it."*

What the Bible Says About . . . Child Training is unique in that the subject is handled solely from the Biblical viewpoint. The author accepts the Bible as absolute truth and as infinitely superior to any human system of thinking. There has been no attempt to modify God's Word to make it compatible with human philosophies, psychology, sociology, religious views, or public opinion. God's Word is accepted as is, without human adulteration. The Bible is also accepted as living and powerful information that is as relevant today as in the day when it was first revealed.

The reason the author absolutely accepts the Bible as the best source of information for man is explained in Appendix A. **Every reader should study the explanation of this premise before beginning this book.**

It is not necessary to be a Christian to understand or to utilize most Biblical information on child training. Information on the institution of the family is available to all humanity. However, only a Christian who is mature in the Word and empowered by the Spirit of God will be able to train his child *"in the nurture and admonition of the Lord."* (Ephesians 6:4b).

The need for clear guidelines for parents to be successful in child training is dramatically evident in our society today. Many parents have virtually no control over their own children. This lack of control is evidenced in many ways such as: the flagrant disrespect shown even by very young children; intense parental frustration; and the inability that Christian parents have in training their children into young adults who accept their parents' standards as their own.

Beyond the purpose of this book, to produce successful parents, is the hope to restore our nation. God intends for mankind to live in harmony within a national entity, under law, in marriage, and in working and business relationships. When parents fail in properly training their children, every other institution within that national entity disintegrates, and eventually the nation itself is destroyed. We are now experiencing the destruction of the Western Civilization. Not only have the past few generations been unable to attain God's general purpose to live in harmony, but few individuals have been able to find specific purpose for their very existence.

It is the author's prayer that this book may begin a return to God's Word for the information that will enable mankind to find God's purpose for life. The results would not only be the restoration of our civilization, but also the glorification of God.

What the Bible Says About . . . Child Training is a logical presentation of the systematic procedure found in God's Word that can be utilized by parents in first controlling their children and then teaching them to reach God's intended objective. This system of child training has been used by thousands of families with dramatic results, thus providing the proof that testifies of all truth— IT WORKS!

AUTHOR NOTES TO THE 2ND EDITION

Testimonies

I think I have come to the end of my search for a *complete* system of discipline and child training for my family. Dr. X and Dr. Y are great, but after reading your book, I can see that psychology is not "where it's at" when it comes to getting children to be obedient.

I know your system is 100% correct and I see the difference in my children already.

Ron & Mary Tangeman — OH

I'm almost scared to realize how very wrong I might have gone in doing things my way. I can verify so many of the principles you present by my own growing up!

Nancy Bethea

I thank you for giving me the courage as a parent to take full control until they can control themselves. The children aren't perfect, but they are growing so nicely in the Lord and I am SO thankful! I have friends who talk about teenage rebellion as "normal," but I'm not planning on this.

June Faucette — VA

It has been a blessing to watch my boys mature and to know that I am being obedient to the Lord by following His instruction.

Paul & Debra Reimer — OH

We respect you for maintaining a strong Biblical view despite views of modern humanistic child development *specialists*. Since I am an elementary school major and my sister is a child development major we are very aware of the difference between the two.

We have found that not only has our children's behavior improved, but so has our relationship with them. As we continue to see the success of raising our children God's way, our confidence is built that we are doing the right thing.

Thank you for what we believe is going to change the course of family history as we teach our children self-discipline, self-control, and the truth about life and God's Word and the reasons why.

Erin Relph & Lisa Bisson

It has been my mainstay for decision-making in the thousand little gray areas of child behavior. It has helped more than pastoral counseling, more than my $45/hour Christian psychologist, more than Dr. X!

Ginger Garbacz — TX

The following article is reprinted by permission from the author and from the Teaching Home Magazine, August/September 1991:

The "Justwaits" — Biblical Child Training
Produces Unusual Children

When our first child was born, my husband and I began to meet a new group of people–the Justwaits.

Adjusting to the joys and challenges of new parenthood, we were inexperienced and naive enough to believe literally that the scriptural guidelines for raising children would work! Our new friends, the Justwaits, were quick to set us straight.

Our first encounter with this "family" began at our daughter's crib. Gazing at our infant sleeping so peacefully, our Justwait friends would comment, "She's so precious, but just wait. . .!"

"Oh!" we would laugh, pretending to understand the implication. The Justwaits never completed this sentence, so we assumed that it was something all parents understood. This group was comprised only of experienced parents, so they must know something frightening that we had yet to learn.

However, we plugged doggedly on, choosing for our parenting manual God's Word, instead of the magazines and books written by the "experts" that the Justwaits recommended.

When our daughter began to crawl, we believed she was old enough to obey when we said "No," for her own protection as well as our family's peace.

"Babies have to have freedom to explore. You'll stifle her creativity by not letting her touch the things she wants to," my Justwait relative explained to me patiently as her own 2-year-old screamed through the house and pulled all the knobs off my stereo.

In spite of all the good advice we received from our Justwait friends, we clung stubbornly to the idea that "foolishness is bound up in the heart of a child, but the rod of correction will drive it far from him" (Proverbs 22:15).

As our daughter neared her first birthday, we met some close relatives of the Justwaits — the Oh-You're So Luckys. They began to appear as our child became old enough to exhibit some of the traits we had worked constantly to develop. When she obeyed instantly and came to sit quietly by my side at a relative's home, my relative sighed, "Oh, you're so lucky. *My* kids are so hyper they will never sit still!"

This was the same relative whose "creative" 2-year-old had dismantled my home on several occasions. She was also a Justwait whose children had been in day care from 6 weeks of age. As my mind flashed briefly to the long hours of cuddling, storytelling, singing Scripture songs, and consistent, loving discipline, I wondered if "luck" had much to do with it. But it is difficult to tell these things to a Justwait.

As our daughter grew, she became more of a joy to be with. She certainly wasn't perfect, and neither were her parents, but our home was a place of fun and learning. She knew the limits from the earliest age and the penalties that always followed the crossing of those limits. We were continually amazed at the effectiveness of God's Word when applied quickly and consistently.

When we tried to explain our family lifestyle to the Oh-You're-So-Luckys, they brushed it quickly aside. We soon learned that Oh-You're-So-Luckys don't like the implication that we reap what we sow. They enjoy the belief that all parenting is basically the same and equally effective as long as everyone's happy.

"Oh, we never spank," my Justwait friend explained one day when she saw the thin dowel rod we used. "Experts are now saying that hitting children makes them violent. We use more intelligent ways to reason with our children." As I glanced to where her children were screaming hysterically and throwing rocks at each other, I had to agree that we would not want these children to become more violent!

When our daughter was 2, our good friend Julie Justwait came to visit with her 5-year-old son, Jimmy. Julie had always been a source of friendship and a fountain of advice. Since her child was older than mine, we both conceded that she knew more about child-rearing. Before we could begin our visit, Jimmy proceeded to throw toys at the furniture, scream insults at his mother, and when finally banned to the other room, screamed, "I hate you!" until she looked at me and sighed, "Oh, just wait . . ."

My daughter sat in wide-eyed terror, huddled next to me on the sofa during Jimmy's display of "self-expression." Her eyes were asking, "Can he do that, Mommy?" Was this behavior inevitable in growing children? Was this a "phase" my child would also go through and one which should go unchecked?

Suddenly I knew the answer. *No.* Raising children is not a "shot in the dark and hope for the best" proposition. God has a strict plan for raising children outlined in His Word if people like the Justwaits and the Oh-You're-So-Luckys would only put it into practice in its entirety.

Now we also have a son who is presenting us with a new set of joys and challenges. He is completely different from his 4-year-old sister, as God designed him to be. But we believe the same commands and promises apply to his training as they do to our daughter's.

The Justwaits will always be there with plenty of warnings and advice. And quite often we meet an Oh-You're-So-Lucky, usually when our children are with adults behaving themselves as we've diligently taught them to.

We smile and thank them for the compliment and continue in our "old-fashioned" way of training our children according to God's Word, which for us includes home schooling.

But I must admit that I, too, have now become a member of the Justwaits.

When I see a new mother committing herself to staying home and raising her child by God's Word and a father establishing himself as God's leader in the home, I admire their beautiful child and tell them eagerly, "He's fun now, but just wait . . . it gets even better!"

Lea Ann McCombs
Claremore, Oklahoma

Section ONE

THE PARENT

Chapter 1

WHAT DO I DO NOW?

So you are the father or mother of a child who is dependent on you for support, protection, and most of all guidance. All parents must realize that the physical ability to have children does not automatically qualify them for the task of properly training children. Therefore, what do you do now? This chapter outlines the dilemma most parents face in raising their children.

Being a parent today is a difficult and often bewildering challenge. There are so many conflicting theories about child training that even the reputed "experts" disagree with each other. Everyone has his own opinion on how children should be raised. Prior to the late 1940's, this confusion didn't exist. Old fashioned child training methods were passed down from generation to generation. But, in 1945 the new psychological approach became popularized by Dr. Benjamin Spock's book, *Baby and Child Care*. This book sold nearly one million copies the first year, and about thirty million copies to date (second only in sales to the Bible). This means that more than one-third of all parents over the past fifty years have had this book; and many of them have followed its advice religiously. Dr. Spock taught parents not to inhibit (restrain) a child, but to give him freedom to be himself; and not to use physical punishment (chastisement) in disciplining a child, but lovingly reason with him instead. A steady stream of books and magazine articles have carried that message of behavioral psychology forward to the present day.

To add to the parents' confusion about proper child training has been the religious teaching on love that equates Christian grace and love with tolerance of even wrong doing (permissiveness). We need to examine the issue of Christian love from the Biblical viewpoint to determine its proper use in child training. First, let's see what Biblical love **is not**:

- It is not love to raise a child who lacks self-discipline and is therefore guided by his or her lusts for attention, food or drink, sex, play and entertainment, wandering, loafing, or seeking to gain something for nothing. Which of these lusts have hampered your own life? Do you wish you would have been better trained in self-discipline?

- It is not love to train a child not to be responsible for his own actions and not to accept the consequences of those actions. What has it cost you as an adult to have blamed others or justified yourself for your own mistakes and failures? Would you have progressed further and sooner in your life had you been trained to be more responsible as a child?

One of the benefits of this book will be the clarification of how parents can demonstrate true Christian love to their children by a balanced and responsible exercise of their authority. It will be demonstrated that when toleration of wrong behavior is applied to the raising of children, it results in an overly-permissive approach that produces tragic results. Distinction between the **attributes** of love and the **practice** of love needs to be understood, and then kept in mind throughout our study :

- The attributes of Christian love are expressed in I Corinthians 13:4-7 and Philippians 2:1-4 as being patient, kind, not easily provoked, merciful, and humble — all which Christian parents would desire to emulate. However, these attributes in no way nullify the equally important attributes of righteousness and justice. For example, a righteous government can not apply the attributes of patience, kindness, or mercy to law breakers. In the practice of proper government, justice can not be served by a tolerance of criminal activity. Governments must uphold righteous law for a stable condition to exist within a nation.

- Likewise, parents are to provide for and comfort their children; but they are also required to set and enforce righteous standards for them. The practice of Christian love in parenting is exercised when parents combine the righteousness of setting legitimate standards for their children with the justice of fairly punishing for disobedience. It is in a child's best interest to learn right from wrong as well as to develop self-control over his self-centered nature. Loving parents will therefore train a child for his own benefit. This training process will require personal sacrifice on the parents' part, and that is even further demonstration of true Christian love in practice.

John 15:13 *"Greater love hath no man than this, that a man lay down his life for his friends."*

When righteousness and justice are practiced according to God's principles in the training of children, there will be a balance for our responsive love; and then incorrect and unsuccessful extremes will be avoided. Parents can be firm in setting and enforcing righteous standards without being tyrannical or abusive. They can sacrificially give of themselves on behalf of their children, but still not give in to the demands of an immature child.

WARNING: Let's face the truth, most parents don't evade training their children properly because they "love" them so much. It's because we parents from previously untrained generations are self-centered, lazy, and lack the character to handle conflict with our children. We will stand by and allow our children to raise themselves, rather than sacrifice our time or our emotions for their benefit — i.e., to love them. Perhaps committing yourself to truly loving your children **before** reading this book is your first step to successful child training.

You can begin to see why knowing how to train children is a challenge today. We have the remnants of old fashioned child training; the new humanistic behavioral psychology methods; and a wishy-washy, luke warm tolerance of all things. To top these opinions off, we have a multitude of Christian books on child rearing that give forth a wide range of personal advice and opinions. Many of these books lean heavily on the theories of behavioral psychology rather than on the principles set forth in the Bible. Others intermingle elements of psychology with Bible verses and/or the religious concepts of love, thus adding to the general confusion. A few even attack specific Bible verses in an attempt to justify their personal positions!

It is no surprise that mass confusion about child rearing exists. About the only thing the reputed "experts" do agree upon is : "there is no set pattern for training children." In other words, they say that there is no one, right way to parent. Many of these "experts" have taken the position that parental use of any physical discipline constitutes child abuse. This has caused conscientious parents to question their right to discipline their own children. With advice like this, it is no wonder that the past several generations of parents have turned to their own understanding for their best guess on child training.

These parents develop a system of child training consisting of a mixture of the confused information available. It probably contains some behavior modification, some non-Biblical love, and the use of force when all else fails. This system will produce great instability for both children and parents as the parents over-compensate from one extreme to the other. As a result the parents exist between ineffectiveness and guilt; while their children exist between frustration and anger.

Without any clear system, parents will default to the trial and error method — the hope that the second child will benefit from the mistakes made with the first, that the third will benefit from the mistakes made with the second, and so forth. Some parents believe they can be successful by simply avoiding the mistakes they think their own parents made. The question for all parents who are raising their children on their own opinions is this: how do you know when your system is correct?

As a parent, you have only one chance with each child. You spend a major part of your life raising a child, and all that effort can seem painfully wasted unless there are positive results. Are you satisfied that you know how to handle that one chance to the benefit of each child? Have you considered the cost to your children and to yourself if you fail to train them properly? These are awesome questions that every parent must face.

What is the answer? Is there a system for child training that can end all of this confusion? Is there one that you can know for sure is correct and that can be utilized to obtain the right results? Yes! This book sets forth the only system for child training given in the Bible — a system you can use with confidence in becoming a successful parent.

I John 5:14 & 15   *"And this is the confidence that we have in him, that, if we ask any thing according to his will, he heareth us; And if we know that he hear us, whatever we ask, we know that we have the petitions that we desired of him."*

AUTHOR NOTES TO THE 2ND EDITION

Encouragement

The reader would do well constantly to consider God's grace while studying this book. You will learn things that you will wish you had known before. You may discover mistakes you have made up to now. But, God will consider your past as *"forgetting those things which are behind"* (Philippians 3:13b) and deal with you and your children on the basis of what you do with the truth in the future. He will also deal with your future child training errors in grace. We all grow incrementally in both understanding and application. Commit yourself to Biblical child training and call upon God to empower you to do His will.

Chapter 2

GOD'S PROMISES TO PARENTS

Based on the premise discussed in Appendix A, we know God has provided information in the Bible that parents need in order to train their children. God's Word also promises that those parents who follow this truth will receive blessing, while those who do not will receive cursing.

The blessing in training children is realized in the joy and peace experienced by parents who faithfully utilize God's truth during the training process. This blessing will be realized as the parents are able to observe the results of their training throughout their children's adult life. Parents do not normally recognize most of these blessings while the child is being trained. The joy begins when well-trained children become teenagers and then move into adulthood.

Can parents really experience joy during their children's teen years? They not only can, but should, for it is during the teen years that the results of child training, good or bad, become self-evident. While children are young and tightly under external control, they will normally conform to their parents' standards. However, when they become teenagers and choose to do what is right on their own, they reveal the results of good parenting. Parents can experience true happiness in receiving the promises of God's Word when their children have been well trained.

Proverbs 10:1a *"A wise son maketh a glad father,"*

Proverbs 23:24 & 25 *"The father of the righteous shall greatly rejoice, 1 and he that begetteth a wise child shall have joy 2 of him. Thy father and thy mother shall be glad, 3 and she that bore thee shall rejoice." 4*

Proverbs 29:17 *"Correct thy son, and he shall give thee rest; 5 yea, he shall give delight unto thy soul."*

Proverbs 31:28 *"Her children rise up, and call her blessed; her husband also, and he praiseth her."*

God's Word often contrasts wisdom with foolishness. One who acts wisely is one who utilizes truth in living, while the fool is one who goes his own way in ignorance or in rebellion. The previous Bible verses promise great joy and happiness to parents who raise a wise child. In the Proverbs 31:28 passage, a mother is shown to receive special honor as her children grow up and bless her. What a contrast to the conditions in our civilization today in which the mother is neither respected in her role nor appreciated for her teaching.

The present condition of our nation demonstrates how far our people have deviated from the truth of God's Word. The Bible is not out-of-date, we are still reaping the cursing that results from man's failure to utilize God's truth. Parents who resort to a human system of child training will miss the blessings promised by God and receive instead the natural consequences of cursing for ignorance of, or disobedience to, truth.

The Cursing

Proverbs 10:1b *"a foolish son is the heaviness [6] of his mother."*

Proverbs 17:21 *"He that begetteth a fool doeth it to his sorrow; [7] and the father of a fool hath no joy."* [8]

Proverbs 29:15b *"a child left to himself bringeth his mother to shame."*

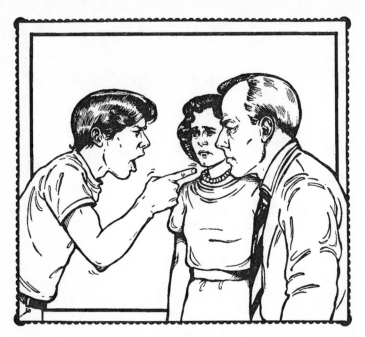

These verses give a clear description of what parents will experience if they fail in training their children. The heaviness that the mother will feel in raising a foolish child is the weight of sadness and extreme sorrow. She will even experience shame from raising a child who is sent off to face life without being properly trained. The father of a fool (one who rejects both God and the truth of God's Word) will also experience sadness and a lack of internal happiness.

These examples of cursing for parents reveal the sorrow and heartache they experience as their child rebels in his teens and early twenties. This cursing continues as the parents observe their child experiencing intense pressure as a result of his attempting to live a selfish and willful existence. They see his self-centered attitude affect his education, career, marriage, and family — eventually destroying what could have been a productive life. Thus the children themselves become the instruments of cursing to their own parents.

Many thousands of parents today are observing the failures of their grown children with this kind of sorrow in their hearts. Perhaps nothing fosters more grief in good, moral parents than seeing their children totally rebel against everything for which those parents stand. For those of you who have already experienced this sadness through your grown children, we sorrow with you. This book has been written to assist parents in avoiding the pain you have suffered. Appendix B, "Hope for the Failing Parent," may be of some comfort to you.

Training children is not a hit-or-miss proposition in which the parent has no control. It is not that some children just turn out okay while others may not. There is no such thing as a "bad seed." Although a child could conceivably reject all attempts to train him properly, he would have to choose against what he clearly knows to be right. Eventually, the one who rebels against good child training is likely to return to a productive life after a period of rebellion.

God has provided His truth to enable every parent to receive blessing rather than cursing. It is the responsibility of each mother and father to seek this truth and then to apply it in training their children. Even if you have failed miserably up to now, you can still affect your child's future by committing yourself to God's way. It ordinarily takes a full nineteen years to raise either a fool or a wise child. However, it is possible (with God's grace) to reverse twelve or thirteen years of fool raising and to start a child on the right path within the remaining six or seven years. To accomplish this feat will require an understanding of and a commitment to God's viewpoint on child training.

Properly training a child is the maximum expression of true love that a parent can give their son or daughter. No amount of material benefits parents could ever give a child can take the place of truly caring enough for him to train him. If you really love your child, train him; you and he both will receive the blessings that are promised by God.

AUTHOR NOTES TO THE 2ND EDITION

Our children are now 37, 34, and 32 (December, 1996). The joy my wife and I have experienced from seeing each of them consistently apply God's Word to their lives, and in the training of their own children, exceeds any human happiness we have known from anything else in our lives. Each adult child has experienced his or her share of tribulation: ill health, death of a loved one, deprivation, painful relationships, and shattered dreams. However, they have all acted maturely, i.e. taken responsibility for their own actions, accepted their own consequences, and depended on God to deliver them through their pressure-filled trials. Two of our children experienced a brief period of seeking their own way— following their own opinions. Eventually, they each willingly turned their lives back to God. Praise Him!

God's grace exceeded His promises in our family's case. Our oldest child was already nine when Virginia and I were saved. None of our children had the head start of Biblical child training, church, or Christian education during their very important formative years. But, my wife and I committed ourselves to God and to following His Word after our salvation, and He was faithful and fair to our children.

Over the years, I have spoken to thousands of concerned parents and a particular question often arises: "Is it really a promise from God that our children will turn out okay if we properly train them?" Some Christian authors have denied this concept. Please note that it is not just Proverbs 22:6 *"Train up a child in the way he should go: and when he is old, he will not depart from it."* that indicates a guarantee. All of the other passages cited in this chapter warn us that young adults are the products of their upbringing. It seems very clear to me that parents who raise their child to be a fool (one who rejects God's Word in living his life) will reap the promise of cursing. Equally clear is the promise that training up a wise child, who honors his parents as well as God's Word, will result in blessings for both parents and child.

Exodus 20:12   *"Honor thy father and thy mother, that thy days may be long upon the land which the Lord thy God giveth thee."*

Ephesians 6:2 & 3   *"Honor thy father and mother (which is the first commandment with promise), That it may be well with thee, and thou mayest live long on the earth."*

I have never known of a child "going bad" who was raised by a Christian father and mother who both practiced: a right marriage (father in leadership, mother in support, both operating in love and justice), and; correct child training principles (with a proper balance between controlling and teaching). On the other hand, I have met a great number of young adults who have paid a terrible price because their Christian parents failed in properly training them. Some of these young adults have been delivered by God's grace from not being trained and now understand the source of their problems. Each and every one of these restored ones are now committed not to repeat their parents' mistakes.

My prayer is that parents who read this book will commit themselves to: train up their children in the way they should go.

FOOTNOTES

[1]   Hebrew, *gil* "rejoice;" used to denote primarily the overt expression of joy "to leap for joy" (Proverbs 21:1; 31:8; Psalm 35:9 etc.). Here the verb is used twice for emphasis and intensity meaning "greatly rejoice." (Foundation for Biblical Research, "Child Training," Austin, Texas, 1979.)

[2]   Hebrew, *sameach* "rejoice, glad;" used to denote internal happiness or joy (Psalm 16:9; 33:21; Proverbs 13:9, 23:15 etc.). (Ibid.)

[3]   See footnote #2.

[4]   See footnote #1. However, here the verb is used normally without the added emphasis of being repeated.

[5] Hebrew, *nuach* "to set at rest, quiet rest" (of mind). (Ibid.)

[6] Hebrew, *tugah* "grief, heaviness, sorrow" (Psalm 119:28; Proverbs 10:1; 14:13). (Ibid.)

[7] See footnote #6.

[8] See footnote #2.

Chapter 3

PARENTAL ACCOUNTABILITY

God has entrusted you, as human parents, with His creation of life. You would not have your child if it were not for the will of God.

Job 33:4   *"The Spirit of God hath made me, and the breath of the Almighty hath given me life."*

The fact that God has entrusted you with His creation makes you accountable to Him for this gift of life. God, as a responsible Creator, has a purpose and plan for everything that He creates.

Psalm 127:3   *"Lo, children are an heritage from the Lord; and the fruit of the womb is his reward."*

"Children" and "fruit of the womb" refer to the physical results of human reproduction.[1] The phrase "heritage from the Lord" refers to the source of the child's soul life. Children are physically a product of the parents, but God is the source of every child's essence of life. The word translated "heritage" from the Hebrew means "an inheritance which is not given according to hereditary rights, but is a gift from the freewill of the donor." [2] In other words, your child is a gift from God.

You might ask yourself what your purpose was in having children. Did you actually consider how or why you would raise a family? Most of mankind have not even discovered the purpose for their own existence, much less the purpose for their children. Man generally is not a responsible creator and often finds himself a parent without either planning or purpose for his children. After having children, parents begin to envision how the children will turn out when they are grown. They hope that their children will become well adjusted, moral, educated adults. However, little thought is given to the attainment of these results.

God has a plan and purpose for each child. Each child is a life from God that is placed in a specific family as a part of that plan. God has set children under their parents' control for approximately one-third of their lives. Unlike animals that raise their young for only a few months, children are dependent on their parents for an extensive training period. Animals need to receive training only for their physical existence, but a child requires training for his soul. Therefore, parents are responsible to train their children according to God's standards.

Children Are to be Trained by Their Parents

Deuteronomy 6:6 & 7   *"And these words, which I command thee this day, shall be in thine heart; And thou shalt teach them diligently unto thy children, and shalt talk of them when thou sittest in thine house, and when thou walkest by the way, and when thou liest down, and when thou risest up."*

Ephesians 6:4   *"And, ye fathers, provoke not your children to wrath, but bring them up in the nurture and
admonition of the Lord."*

Proverbs 22:6   *"Train up a child in the way he should go
and, when he is old, he will not depart from it."*

If you, as a parent, really desire the best for your children,
you will observe these commands to train your children.
Training requires that you teach them and that your
teaching is accepted. But, before your child will receive
your instructions, he must first honor your position.

Children Are to Honor Both Their
Father and Mother

Exodus 20:12   *"Honor [3] thy father and thy mother, that
thy days may be long upon the land which the Lord
thy God giveth thee."*

Ephesians 6:2   *"Honor [4] thy father and mother (which is
the first commandment with promise),"*

Both the Hebrew and Greek words translated "honor"
mean "to honor, revere, or have great respect for someone." Children are commanded to honor both their father
and mother. Parents are to receive from their children the
respect due their position. Many parents may not consider
themselves worthy of honor, but they still hold the God-
given position of ruler over their children. They may feel
themselves under-educated or unsuccessful in every other
area of life, but as parents, they are to be respected.

Neither a father nor a mother should ever allow disrespect
to be shown toward his or her position. They have the
right to rule because God gave that right to parents, not
because it is one they have earned or deserved.

As a parent, you hold a key position of authority. And, God holds every parent accountable for how he or she trains up each child He has entrusted to them. Therefore, it is necessary for you to understand thoroughly the principles of authority so you can accept and function successfully in that position.

AUTHOR NOTES TO THE 2ND EDITION

Teaching Honor

A child begins to notice something different about his Mom and Dad soon after birth — they are **humongous**! Even when he begins to stand up and teeter a few steps, Mom's and Dad's faces are still several child lengths above him. What a great beginning for parents who need to have their child's respect for effective training. The child already accepts his parents' position above him and is ready to be taught.

Parents can instill the concept of honor (respect for their position) by requiring the child to speak to them and others courteously. Please, thank you, yes and no ma'am (or sir), excuse me, and may I, should be taught and required as early as a child can say them. He should also be taught always to answer when spoken to and to look at you when you are speaking. As soon as possible he should be taught not to yell at you from another room, never to enter a room talking, not to interrupt an adult conversation (even on the phone) unless it is an emergency; to watch where he is going; not to rush through a door ahead of adults; to show respect for all elderly and smaller children, and kindness for animals. Allowing a child to playfully hit, tease, run from you; or play argumentative games such as: "Yes, you will." (parent) "No, I won't." (child) "Yes, you will." "No, I won't" teach disrespect and eventually will lead to an all out challenge of the parent's authority.

Requiring respect from a small child will begin the parent/child relationship with his honoring his parents. To the extent parents act maturely throughout his childhood, they will keep that respect. If they act immaturely: break the same standards they teach, break promises, fight with each other, admire or laugh at the wrong doing of others (like entertainment), steal, lie, curse, or divorce, it confuses and saddens the child tremendously. Eventually, and with much pain, he loses the respect that was so easily instilled. Parents need to understand that how they live their lives will affect how their children will respect them in their teen and later years. However, all parents have a God-given right to require honor for their position at all times, even if they have tarnished their child's respect for their person.

FOOTNOTES

[1] Hebrew, *ben* (pl.) "sons" and *peri* (sg.) "fruit, offspring" (singular in number, used collectively). (Foundation for Biblical Research, "Child Training.")

[2] Hebrew, *nachalah* "possession, property, inheritance," with regard to Psalm 127:3 "a portion, share" assigned by God. It denotes an inheritance not according to hereditary right, but in accordance with the free-will of the giver (i.e. the Lord). (Ibid.)

[3] Hebrew, *kabed* "be heavy, weighty;" here used in the piel stem denoting honor with respect to persons (Judges 13:17; 2 Samuel 10:3; Exodus 20:12; Deuteronomy 5:16). (Ibid.)

[4] Greek, *timao* "to estimate a fixed value," and thus used for "honor, revere." (Ibid.)

Chapter 4

PRINCIPLES OF AUTHORITY

Authority! Here is a word that all rebels hate. Authority is a concept that causes a negative response in those who do not understand its proper meaning and use. Recent generations almost react as if they had been programmed against even the legitimate use of authority. A general attitude exists today of distrust and disrespect for all positions of rulership. The misunderstanding of God's principles for authority, added to experience with authoritarians who have truly misused their power, has caused many to reject the concept altogether. Some parents have abdicated their role and have withdrawn from even the proper use of authority.

We need to study the principles of authority so that we will not be deceived into a programmed response against the very system God has established for our freedom. First, we will look at the definition of authority. From that definition we will study some characteristics of God's authority and determine the principles for human authority.

Authority means "the right to rule; the power to act,

decide, command, and judge." [1] It is the right to set policy, the rulership to command subordinates, and the power to administer judgment to those who disobey the commands or to reward those who conform.

At first glance, it may appear that authority is unbridled power which can be used to oppress those who are in subjection. Although it is true that there are, and always have been, those who abuse the power of authority, these exceptions do not change the principle. The power of authority is not without controls or limits. God has established rules and boundaries to govern the use of all authority. Even more importantly, God is always in control. He has the position and the power to enforce His will over all other authorities.

God is the Ultimate Authority

Psalm 47:2   *"For the Lord Most High is awe-inspiring; he is a great King over all the earth."*

Psalm 83:18   *"That men may know that thou, whose name alone is the Lord, art the Most High over all the earth."*

The word translated "most high" is a title, and is only used in Scripture for God. [2] This title of "most high" is never given to a member of the human race in his role as ruler. It is a title to describe God's absolute position of authority. He is the Most High. There is none other above Him with any right to rule.

Daniel 4:34b   *"I blessed the Most High, and I praised and honored him who liveth forever, whose dominion is an everlasting dominion, and his kingdom is from generation to generation."*

This passage recognizes the extent of God's rule. There is no end to the reign of God. His timelessness strikes a sobering contrast to the insignificant period of time in which any human authority can exercise rulership. God is always in control!

Psalm 115:3   *"But our God is in the heavens; he hath done whatsoever he hath pleased."*

Romans 9:20b & 21   *"Shall the thing formed say to him that formed it, Why hast thou made me thus? Hath not the potter power over the clay, of the same lump to make one vessel unto honor, and another unto dishonor?"*

God is the Creator. He has the right to rule whatever He creates. In other words, He has the total right to rule His creatures according to His will.

Daniel 4:35   *"And all the inhabitants of the earth are reputed as nothing; and he doeth according to his will in the army of heaven, and among the inhabitants of the earth, and none can stay his hand, or say unto him, What doest thou?"*

"And all the inhabitants of the earth are reputed as nothing" is a relative statement. It establishes a relationship between God's absolute position of authority (right to rule) and mankind's position of authority. Nebuchadnezzar, the speaker in this verse, is king over a mighty kingdom, and he is saying that even as king he has no right to say to God, "What are you doing?"

The conclusion from these verses, and many others on the subject, is that God as the Creator has the right to set the policy for all His creation according to His own will. He has the ultimate position of rulership above all the creatures whereby He may direct their actions. He also has the power to administer justice; in other words, the power to punish evil and to praise good. Since ultimate authority belongs to God, any legitimate right to rule must be delegated by Him.

No Authority Exists Except As Appointed by God

Romans 13:1   *"Let every soul be subject unto the higher powers. For there is no power but of God; the powers that be are ordained by God."*

The Greek word translated "power" means "authority, the right to decide or act, ruling or official powers." [3] God commands every individual to place himself willingly under the positions of rulership that exist above him. How do we dare do this? We can submit to our authorities because the verse then states that no ruling power exists except through God. Every position of authority is under His control. The verse continues by stating that all existing positions of rulership have been established by God. The word translated "ordained" means "to place, station, appoint or determine someone into an official position over others." [4] It is the Greek word from which the theological term "institution" is derived. God has instituted all existing positions of rulership over His creatures to carry out His will and to administer justice to those under their rule.

Principles of Authority

1. God is the ultimate authority. As the Creator, He has the right to rule His creation according to His will. God also possesses the absolute power to administer justice to all creatures.

2. God has established institutions such as government, marriage, and parents for the orderly administration of His plan.

3. Each institution ordained by God has been

arranged with definite positions of authority for the orderly function of that institution. Each institution is independent from every other institution and is directly accountable to God. Government is not a higher institution than marriage or parents. The head of a family answers directly to God as does the government leader. Both the king of a country and the father of a family are equally and independently responsible to God.

4. The one who is in the position of authority of an institution has the right of rulership over the subjects of that institution. This right to rule may be exercised **only** over those within an individual entity of that institution. If you are a father, you are the person in the position of authority over only your own family. You have no authority over any other family and no other father has any authority over your family. Each entity of a particular institution is independent of every other entity.

5 Every person is subject to one or more of these institutions at all times. For example, every individual is subject to the government, but a wife is also subject to the husband in the family.

6. God's Word gives specific boundaries for the power of each institution. Each position of rulership has defined limits in the extent of its authority. The boundaries include those who are subject to the authority, as well as the extent to which they must submit. For example, government has the right to rule only within individual national boundaries. Government has no right to administer justice to other nations (except in self-defense) or to exercise authority over other independent institutions, like parents or marriage (except when moral law has

been **clearly** broken). For another example, a
father has the right to rule his own family, but even
his authority has certain limitations as established
by God. A father does not have the right to make
his son steal.

God could always control any individual who oversteps his
boundaries, but often allows such a one to remain in his
position of power to discipline the people or to test those
under his rulership. The fact that evil kings, evil husbands, and evil fathers exist is not God's fault. All evil is
the invention of Satan or the result of man's sinful condition. But, *"we know that all things work together for good
to them that love God,"* (Romans 8:28a).

Each human institution has been established by God for
the protection and blessing of those within that institution. When functioning properly they maintain order
within a nation. The various institutions provide a diver-
sification of power which helps to restrain evil leaders
from possessing absolute control. Historically, all evil leaders have always attempted to destroy the separate institutions and establish themselves as the absolute authority
in place of God. Only God is capable of ruling through the
multiple institutions because of His all power, all presence, and all knowledge.

Any problems concerning authority are not the fault of
God's principles, but are due to man's failure to function
properly according to God's Word. You need to understand
thoroughly the issue of authority because, as a parent, you
are in one of these positions of authority. As a parent, you
answer directly to God. Therefore, you need to know the
areas of your accountability, the boundaries of your rulership, and how to handle properly your responsibilities.

AUTHOR NOTES TO THE 2ND EDITION

Anti-Authority Problems

Do you resent the concept of authority? Are you a father or a mother who detests being in the position of telling your child what to do, and especially of punishing him or her for not obeying? If you were the child of a truly abusive (unfair and/or excessive) parent, it's understandable that you might want to avoid your Biblical role. You may fear expressing the same anger to your children that your parent did to you. In reaction to your fear, you would probably go to the extreme and ruin your children with the passive abuse of permissiveness. I suggest that you study the next section on the child to see how desperately they need your mature guidance in directing and in restraining them. God will help you deal with your sin of anger once you forgive your parent, and thus prevent them from continuing to influence you still today.

Only those who are not under their own authorities resent the concept of true authority and, therefore, can't be a good authority themselves. Guilt of their own rebellion prevents them from properly exercising authority over others. Wives, if you reject your husband's authority, you will either be tyrannical or permissive with your children. You will probably find yourself trying to over-compensate for his manner of child training. The stricter he is, the more permissive you become, or visa versa. Men, if you set your opinion or practice above God's Word (reject God's leadership), you also will be an improper authority for both your wife and children. It's surprising that people don't see that the failure in their marriage and parenting comes from their own rebellion.

Proverbs 16:18   *"Pride goeth before destruction, and an haughty spirit before a fall."*

Proverbs 29:23a   *"A man's pride shall bring him low,"*

I have never seen a person who refused to submit himself to proper authorities — government, parents, husband, bosses, coaches — who could ever function in a leadership role with proper balance. He is either arrogant in his leadership, or fearful of exercising his authority.

No matter what the reason is for an anti-authority attitude, God has the solution for any sin including pride. Every parent must honestly face and deal with this issue **before** they can be effective in training their children.

FOOTNOTES

[1] *The Compact Edition of the Oxford English Dictionary, (1971), s.v.* "authority."

[2] Hebrew, *'elyon,* "high, supreme" from the verb *'alah,* "go up, ascend." (Foundation for Biblical Research, "Child-Training.")

[3] Greek, *exousia* "authority;" those who are in a position of authority "officials, governments" (Romans 13:2; Luke 12:11; Titus 3:1). (Ibid.)

[4] Greek, *tasso* "arrange, put in a place;" here referring to the authorities being "instituted" (or arranged) by God. (Ibid.)

Chapter 5

PARENTAL AUTHORITY

God has established the institution of the parent as one of His ruling authorities on earth. To this position has been delegated both the right to rule children and all the power necessary to succeed in training children according to God's plan. This position is the direct agency through which children are to receive ruling during their childhood. That is, it is through this position that each child is to receive protection, direction, and instruction.

Whomever God places in the position of being a parent is accountable directly to God for how he or she rules. This position can be occupied by the natural parents, by a remaining single parent, or by whomever else God has placed there, such as a relative, guardian, adoptee, stepparent, or foster parent. Whoever occupies the position is held accountable by God as much as the natural parents would have been. It is important to realize that one who marries a remaining parent has accepted full parental responsibility before God.

Because of God-granted parental authority, parents have the right to set their will above that of their children and to command them to follow their rulership. They also have the power to administer justice and to punish for disobedience, or to reward for conformance to their commands. To what extent may the parents enforce their will on their children?

Children Must Obey Both Their Father and Mother

Colossians 3:20a *"Children, obey your parents in all things,"*

The word translated "obey" from the Greek language is a command and means "to hear and obey." [1] In other words, this passage says children must do what they are told. This means that a parent's word is law for children. You may never have considered yourself to be someone who has the right to create law, but as far as your child is concerned, **your word is law**. If your child is disobedient to your word, he has broken the law you have set for him. Your children are to do what you tell them to do.

Even though this command is addressed to children, parents, as the ones who are in charge, are accountable for its fulfillment as long as the children are under their control. God always holds the ones in authority responsible for the actions of those under their rulership. The parents are accountable to God for the obedience of their children. A parallel to this principle is that God has commanded man not to commit murder, but He has given government the responsibility and the power to administer the judgment of the death penalty. In the same way, God has given parents the power to enforce the child's compliance to obey his parents *"in all things."*

The boundary for parental authority is more extensive

than that of any other institution. This is true because the parents' right to rule includes the power to force obedience to their will in all things. No other institution is given this much power. The subjects of other institutions are to submit to their authorities, but the child is commanded to obey his parents. The basic difference between the Greek words translated "submit" and "obey" is that submission appeals to the attitude of voluntary acceptance of authority, whereas obedience is compliance with the authority whether the subject wills to or not. [2] Parents not only have the right to rule in all things, they also have the power to enforce their child's unwilling compliance to their commands.

Parental authority delegates to parents the right to rule the children under their control. No other institution or person has rulership rights over children. Neither society, school personnel, nosy individuals, nor even other institutions have any authority over children. The parents' power over their children is accountable to government only through God's laws concerning incest, injury, and murder. Parents are directly responsible to God for any other misuse of their authority. There is no such thing as "child rights" sanctioned by the Word of God. The child has only the God-given right to be raised by his parents without the intervention of any other institution.

When a government begins to misuse its authority, it goes beyond its boundaries and begins to undermine parental authority. The tendency then is to make the child responsible to the state rather than to the parents. Historically this has occurred many times with tragic results. The governments of such nations as Sparta, Hitler's Germany, and Communist Russia all usurped the parents' role. Currently, parental authority is being undermined in America through compulsory public education, child advocacy agencies, and child abuse laws. Parents must not allow government to usurp their authority in those areas in which God holds the parents alone accountable. For example, parents have the explicit instructions in the Bible to teach their children information consistent with God's Word. The institution of government has no such instructions and therefore has no authority above the parents to teach children contrary information. In fact, no instructions can be found in the Bible that grant authority to government over children in any area except that of upholding the parents' position of authority.

God honors the value of parental authority so highly that He instituted laws for government to protect the parental authority from internal revolution by the child himself. Rather than government being an agency to do the job of parents, it is actually to be the agency to enforce their position. Instead of invading the family and taking away the responsibility of the parents over the child, government is to ensure that parents are not prevented from doing their job. Children are not to be allowed to revolt against their parents.

God's Protection of Parental Authority by Government

Matthew 15:4   *"For God commanded, saying, Honor thy father and mother; and, He that curseth father or mother, let him die the death."*

Exodus 21:15   *"And he that smiteth his father, or his mother, shall be surely put to death."*

Exodus 21:17   *"And he that curseth his father, or his mother, shall surely be put to death."*

Deuteronomy 27:16a *"Cursed be he who dishonoreth his father or his mother."*

Proverbs 30:17   *"The eye that mocketh at his father, and despiseth to obey his mother, the ravens of the valley shall pick it out, and the young eagles shall eat it."*

Three important principles are revealed in these verses:

1. Both father and mother are considered equal in their role as parents.

2. God will not tolerate flagrant disrespect of parental authority by children. The death penalty was to be administered to any child who made a practice of overt disrespect by hitting or even cursing his parents. Of course, parents were not given the right to take their own child's life. The institution of government alone has that power. However, the parents were required to testify against such a child.

    Deuteronomy 21:18-21   *"If a man have a stubborn and rebellious son, who will not obey the voice of his father or the voice of his mother, and that, when they have chastened him, will not hearken unto them, Then shall his father and his mother lay hold on him, and bring him out unto the elders of his city, and unto the gate of his place. And they shall say unto the elders of his city, This, our son, is stubborn and rebellious. He will not obey our voice; he is a glutton, and a drunkard. And all the men of his city shall stone him with stones, that he die. So shalt thou put evil away from among you, and all Israel shall hear, and fear."*

    As you can see, God is very serious about children being obedient. These verses were given to the nation Israel, but the principle still applies that

God will not tolerate disrespectful or disobedient children. Drastic as it may seem that God would institute the death penalty for a child, it was for the protection and benefit of the nation itself. If a child is raised to adulthood who disrespects and disobeys his parents, he is not likely to respect either the national laws or even God. The mere existence of such a law would itself act as a deterrent to its being needed. Few, if any, parents would fail to train their children to be obedient knowing that if they failed they would have to testify against them for the death penalty. Likewise, few children, knowing what the penalty was, would be openly rebellious to their parents.

3. If a rebel escaped the death penalty, because either the parental or governmental institution failed in their responsibilities, God's Word warns of direct judgment to the child, the parent, and the nation. (1 Samuel 3:13 compared to 1 Samuel 4:10-18 and Proverbs 30:11-17.) America has been experiencing this type of curse over the last several generations. Wars, drugs, and violent death have been the way of life for youth in our nation for many years. Much of this carnage can be directly attributed to untrained youth.

In conclusion, cursing is the consequence of the rebellious child, the one who is un-trainable. For the child who learns obedience and who honors his parents, God has promised the blessings of peace and prosperity.

God's Promise of Blessing for Children

Ephesians 6:2 & 3   *"Honor thy father and mother (which is the first commandment with promise), That it may be well with thee, and thou mayest live long on the earth."*

Exodus 20:12   *"Honor thy father and thy mother, that thy days may be long upon the land which the Lord thy God giveth thee."*

The promise of long life had many facets of blessing in the day these words were given by God to man. Long life meant no violent death from war, disease, famine, or wild beast. It was a promise of death at just the right time. Long life was also a promise of physical prosperity since there would be more time to accumulate wealth in live-stock, land, and children. The promise in the Old Testament declared that this long life would be lived *"in the land which the Lord your God gives you."* This land was the promised land of milk and honey, again an idiom for physical prosperity.

The child who honors his father and mother will be pro-tected throughout his adult life by God's promise. In addi-tion, when a child follows his parents' instructions, his prosperity is increased even more.

Proverbs 3:1 & 2   *"My son, forget not my law, but let thine heart keep my commandments; For length of days, and long life, and peace, shall they add to thee."*

We can again see the principle of truth as it applies to a child's becoming obedient and honoring his parents. When this truth is observed, the result is blessing; when not, the result is cursing. Parents who truly love their children will desire the best for them. These parents will see that their child honors them so he will receive God's promised blessing.

Parental authority is not without restraint. God, Himself, is responsible to His attributes of righteousness, justice, and love to deal with every child in a manner that is con-sistent with His character. We can trust totally that since God ordained the institution of parental authority, He will be fair and just to every child who is placed under each entity of this institution.

There have been, and will be, evil individuals who become parental authorities just as there are evil leaders in government. Those parents who misuse their authority fall under the direct judgment of God. God has a plan for every life, a plan that incorporates even the unfairness of this world. Perhaps the child who receives unfair treatment at the hand of his parents will be used by God because of that very pressure (see story of Joseph).

When we see a child receive what we consider unfair treatment from such parents, we must remember that God knows about the situation and is in complete control. We are only able to see a moment in time with our finite minds. Therefore, we should be cautious about interfering unless we know for sure that a child is being harmed or endangered.

As a human authority, you will make many mistakes even if you desire to be right and just. These mistakes can be from ignorance of what or how to deal with children, or they can be a result of sin. An authority does not have to be perfect in his rulership. Obedience and respect for the power of rulership is often learned from what appears to be unfair or incompetent leadership. Parents, you are the authority, both when you are right and when you are wrong. However, your humanity does not excuse the sin of abusing your child. Nevertheless, do not allow the fact that you are human and subject to error hinder you from meeting your responsibilities. God knew you were imperfect when He gave you a child. The recognition of this fact should make you dependent on Him, not cause you to avoid the responsibility.

AUTHOR NOTES TO THE 2ND EDITION

Step-Parents

One of the most common questions I receive at my live seminars comes from step-parents. They want to know how they can parent when they are not the natural father or mother. Or, they want to know how to deal with their spouse because he or she blocks them from parenting their child (or vise versa). Today: yours, mine, and ours is not a situation comedy — it's an unfortunate reality.

Dealing with the problems that result from second marriages is like trying to give advice to someone who jumps off a thirty story building and then wants to know how to prevent his sudden deceleration. The older the children are at the time of remarriage and the longer they have been living with only one parent, the more difficult it will be for an outsider to step into the missing parent's role. This factor should be the subject of several honest discussions prior to marriage (after both parties read this book). Will she allow him to use corporal punishment on her precious son? Will he insist that his possibly jealous daughter treats his new wife with proper respect? If both parties believe they are in **complete** agreement, they need to meet with the children to tell them how life is going to be. Even though the children have no say in either the remarriage, or in your joint commitment to train them according to Biblical principles, they do have a right to know what to expect. Better to know what objections surface before the marriage than after it is too late.

I do not recommend remarriage for anyone except for those who have been widowed or who have been divorced by a mate who has since remarried so that reconciliation is now impossible. If you divorced your mate, or if the one who divorced you has not remarried, you have no Biblical justification for remarriage. God's Word requires that you continue in your state — trusting in Him for your companionship, comfort, security, and hope. God promises to be a father to the fatherless, so I believe He gives the woman alone spiritual power to train up her children without a Dad — if she is totally committed to God.

The answer for those of you already in either a Biblically legitimate or an illegitimate step-parent role is to obey God's Word about child training. (The fact that your remarriage was not according to Biblical guidelines is now past tense. You still have a moral responsibility to your spouse and to all the children involved.) Study the book together, commit yourselves to practice Biblical child training consistently, tell the children of your decisions in no uncertain terms, and then follow through on your convictions (your children will test you immediately). May God empower you to keep your commitment for yours and your children's sakes.

Unified Parents

Matthew 12:25b "and every city or house divided against itself shall not stand."

Normally, a husband and his wife will share the role of parenting. It is imperative that they present a unified front to the children, even if they disagree. They can discuss their disagreements in private, but they must not ever undercut each other's decisions. The children need to know that each parent will back up the other.

FOOTNOTES

[1]   Greek, *hupakouo* "obey." Compound word consisting of the preposition *hupo* "under" and *akouo* "hear;" literally "to hear under," thus to obey what is heard (Ephesians 6:1, 5; Colossians 3:20, 22; 2 Thessalonians 1:8; 3:14). (Foundation for Biblical Research, "Child Training.")

[2]   Greek, *hupotasso* "submit, subordinate." Compound word consisting of the preposition *hupo* "under" and *tasso* "put in place, station;" literally "to place under," thus to submit to a position (Romans 13:1, 5; Ephesians 5:22, 24; Titus 2:9, 3:1; James 4:7; 1 Peter 2:13). NB. The distinction between *hupakouo* and *hupotasso is* that *hupakouo* emphasizes the strict following of verbal commands (mandatory compliance in action) regardless of personal willingness, while *hupotasso* emphasizes the attitude of voluntary compliance with the known will or position of another. (Ibid.)

Chapter 6

PARENTAL RESPONSIBILITY

This may be the first time you have realized that you are, and have the right to be, the ruler over your children. Since God has placed you in this position, you should function as one who has the right to rule. In other words, your children need to know that you are in charge. This means that you make the decisions, not the children. You are to decide when it is time for bed, what is to be eaten or not eaten, and what activities are permitted. These decisions belong to the parent until the child has been trained to make the **right** decisions himself. The parent even decides when and in what areas the child is allowed to make his own decisions.

Children need an authority figure. If parents, especially fathers, do not provide the needed leadership, their children will seek it elsewhere. Children desperately need someone whom they can follow and to whom they can give their allegiance. God has made their souls to respond to authority; therefore, they will find a replacement if the parents abdicate their position.

Without firm leadership in the home, children will find someone outside of the family who will tell them what to do. It should be no surprise that leaderless children respond to cults, such as the Moonies and the Jones groups, street gangs, or revolutionary movements. These counterculture groups all have one thing in common — they **demand** followership. They each provide strong leadership, teach and enforce rules, and set a purpose for the life of the follower. Dare we as parents offer less?

Contrary to the popularly accepted teaching of child psychology, your child needs a leader — not a pal, buddy, big sister, or big brother. Parents are authority figures and therefore cannot also be pals or buddies with a child who must become obedient to their rule. If parents rule well when their child is growing up, there can be a life-time of friendship between them and the grown child. However, even this can occur only after a child has been trained to meet his parents' standards.

Parents who have failed to train their children properly often identify a patsy to blame for negatively influencing them. Teachers, other children, TV, and even the church often receive this blame. However, God holds only the parent accountable for training children. Therefore, it is the parents' responsibility to control what influences their children.

Children may be taught things at school that oppose the teaching of their parents, but it is the parents' responsibility to determine where the children go to school and what they are taught. Children can be influenced by their peers, but it is the parents' responsibility to control with whom their children associate. Children are definitely influenced by what they see on television and other media, but it is still the parent who is ultimately responsible for choosing to what his child is exposed. Children can ignore what is taught in church, but it is the parent whom God holds accountable for a child's instruction in the Word.

Another technique of parents in attempting to avoid their responsibility is to pass the buck to God. This is done by telling a child who will not obey that God will punish him for his disobedience. Parents are God's chosen representatives of authority over children to teach about and administer justice. Parents cannot pass the responsibility back to God. God's Word tells parents that they are not only to tell their children what to do, but also to enforce obedience to their instructions. This is the parents' job, not God's. A child learns obedience to parents as a preparation for his obeying God.

Parents are the symbol and representative of God's authority to their children. The way parents handle their rulership is the way children will begin to think about God and all other authorities under God. Parents are in a very crucial position in the child's life. Let us look at how a child thinks. If he sees his parents are fair, then he will consider that God must also be fair. If his parents punish for wrong doing, then God will punish for wrong doing. If his parents care for him, then God must care for him. If his parents respect and obey God's Word, then he must respect and obey God. If his parents mean what they say, then God must mean what He says.

As a parent, you have the opportunity to mold the child's opinions about God, government, and his or her marriage relationship. A child who is required to obey his parents will come to respect their authority and will thus be prepared to submit to other authorities, including God's Word.

Being a Parent — Summary

We have seen that the Bible clearly defines the positions of the parent and the child. It also defines the consequences resulting from meeting or failing to meet God's standards. Let us review some of the major principles about parents:

- Blessings of great joy and satisfaction exist for both the father and mother who properly train their children, while the cursing of great sorrow is the consequence to those who do not.

- The soul life of each child is the creation of God, and God has a plan and a purpose for anything He creates.

- God intends for children to be trained by their parents according to His standards.

- Child training is dependent on the child's respect for his parent's position of authority.

- The principle of authority was designed by God for the orderly administration of His plan for mankind and is totally under His control.

- Parental authority is the most extensive of all institutions and includes the right to demand obedience from children.

- The parents' word is law to their children.

- Parents are responsible to raise obedient and respectful children.

- Parents are accountable to God alone for their rulership.

- Children who honor their parents are blessed with physical prosperity, whereas those who rebel in overt disrespect receive the cursing of a living death and/or a violent end.

- Parents must provide strong leadership for their children and stand responsible for their outside influences.

- Parents are the symbol and representative of God's authority to their children.

At this point, you may not know how you are going to obtain obedience or respect from your children, or exactly what you are to teach them. But, you should understand both your responsibility of rulership over the children and your accountability to God for how that responsibility is handled. You also may begin to see how much your child needs your rulership to protect him. Parents must come to understand that fulfilling parental responsibilities is the expression of their love for their children. In other words, if you love your children, rule them.

With this orientation to parental authority from God's point of view, we will next see what God's Word reveals about this child we are to train.

AUTHOR NOTES TO THE 2ND EDITION

Familiarization

"Parents are authority figures and therefore cannot also be pals or buddies with a child who must become obedient to their role." Parents must be careful not to sabotage their own authority. When parents become too familiar with their children (treating them as equals in decision making with adults, allowing them to use parents' first names in address, or allowing them to have preeminence in all adult conversations), they will loose proper respect for all adults. "Familiarity breeds contempt" is a true saying when applied to immature children. Untrained children are not meant to have an equal voice in family decisions, even about their own lives. Parents really are supposed to know more than their children about proper diet and dress, church attendance, manners, acceptable friends and entertainment, and a hundred other issues.

We don't need to go so far as the military's "no fraternizing with the troops" position. It is certainly beneficial that both parents spend time talking to, playing with, and cuddling their sons and daughters. Children need closeness from each parent, but parents need to recognize when the lines between play and over-familiarization have been crossed. When your child begins to give you orders, demands your exclusive attention, or talks back, it's time to back off and restore your position as a parent.

Parents who make their children the focal point of the home, rather than a participant with responsibilities, do them a great injustice. The children are raised to think of themselves as more important than anyone else. They are taught to believe that their opinions, accomplishments, and dreams should monopolize adult's time, even if they have to interrupt. They are taught to brag about themselves and their accomplishments; no matter how trivial. These self-centered children are certainly not being trained to: *"let each esteem others better than themselves."* (Philippians 2:3). Such children will grow up with the "me first" mentality of the past several generations.

Maintaining your position of authority does not mean that you never include children in discussions about certain decisions, especially when they will be involved in those decisions. For instance, when the grandparents are coming for a visit and decisions must be made on the sleeping arrangements and about who will perform which chores, it is a good time to teach planning and cooperation. For matters such as this, Virginia and I had a voting system that helped our children learn about the chain of command. We called a family meeting and I presented the decision that needed to be made. Each child was encouraged to offer suggestions and then we all voted. Granted, the voting was not equal: the three children each had one vote, Mother had four votes, and Dad had eight (keeping family order in tact); but each child was allowed to participate, make suggestions, and offer help. The children enjoyed this arrangement and, even when they were out-voted, they never felt their thoughts weren't considered. Our votes usually were unanimous anyway so there were no resentments when it came time for one of them to give up their bedroom to the grandparents, or when each one had special duties. Today's family would probably have the mother with two votes, the three children with one each, and Dad asking if it was all right for him to hear the decision.

Buck Passing

I don't know how many Christian parents I've heard trying to intimidate a little child with some threat that God is watching and may punish him directly for misbehaving. In doing this, parents are trying to escape the responsibility of parenting. They don't want to train their child or to punish for disobedience. They might as well use Santa Claus threats, like the heathen do to control their children's behavior. Using God as a threat is even worse. Never make God appear as a wrathful ogre!

Using a Child's Fears to Control

Some parents cruelly use a child's insecurities or fears against him: "You stay in bed tonight or the monster under your bed will get you." "If you don't come right now, I'll leave you in the store by yourself." "If you don't behave, I'll have the police come and arrest you." "If you don't straighten up, we'll have to send you to an institution for delinquents." Imagine these threats being given to a totally immature child who needs the firm hand of his parents to help him grow to maturity. Children treated in this manner are expected to parent themselves and thus pull themselves into maturity by their own bootstraps. This is absurd!

Should children fear their parents? They definitely should have a healthy fear of their parents' authority. They will also fear the instrument of chastisement, if it's used correctly. Healthy fear is one that protects one from harm — road dangers, high places, dangerous reptiles and insects, bad areas of town; and when you do wrong, authorities (God, parents, police, principals, coaches, and bosses). When children are raised without a proper fear of authority, they become like street ruffians with no respect for anyone or anything except raw force.

The Role of Father and Mother

Parenting is both a Father and a Mother responsibility.

Ephesians 6:2a   *"Honor thy father **and mother**"* (Emphasis added)

Colossians 3:20 *"Children, **obey your parents** in all things;"* (Emphasis added)

Fathers are suppose to give leadership to the family by setting the standards, warning the children about penalties, and delegating some follow-through to the Mother. Men generally have defected from their role as leader in the home, and especially from fatherhood. This has badly damaged the last several generations of child development. The 50 year absence of fathers who were secure with their masculinity and their role of leader, provider, and protector of the family as well as cherisher of their wife, has dramatically distorted the development of both boys and girls. As a result, the men of the past three or four generations have been raised either effeminate, or totally insensitive toward women. My book, *What the Bible Says About . . . Manhood*, was written to explain how Satan has destroyed manhood and, consequently, the family; and to call men back to their historical place of leadership before it is too late for our nation.

The mother also has a key role in the proper training of children. She assures that the father's standards are upheld in his absence; she maintains the peace and punishes for wrong doing in her presence; she sets her own law (Proverbs 1:8), but not contrary to her husband's will; and she enforces her own laws as needed. Unfortunately, if the father will not take the lead in the home and set or enforce the laws, the mother must set and administer right laws for the children (but not in front of the husband.) She must **never** push, badger, nag, or try to shame her husband into taking his responsibility.

I Peter 3:1 *"In the same manner, ye wives, be in subjection to your own husbands that, if any obey not the word, they also may without the word be won by the behavior of the wives,"*

She should continue to pray that God will cause her husband to see his role and take that responsibility for the sake of the children. I have known many wives who have quietly and faithfully prayed about their husbands neglecting their roles. Some of these women now tell of the miracle that has occurred in their "new" husband and children's father. Don't lose hope in God.

Section TWO

THE CHILD

Chapter 7

THE CHILD'S NATURE

We have seen what the Bible says about parents' responsibility to train their children in conformance with God's standards, their position of rulership, and their accountability to God for His gift of life — the child. Now, exactly who is this child we are to train? What in his makeup requires such extensive training? Why is the power of parental authority necessary?

To answer these questions, we will study what the Bible teaches about the composition of this creature called child. To understand children it is necessary first to understand the origin of mankind.

Mankind Was Originally Created in the "Image of God"

Genesis 1:26a *"And God said, Let us make man in our image, after our likeness;"*

God is perfect, and all His creation was perfect in its original state. Even Satan was perfect when he came into existence (Ezekiel 28:12b-15). At the time of man's creation by

God, man also was perfect in his humanity. Mankind began his existence in a state of blessing, but man (like Satan before him) chose to act contrary to the will of God. God expressed His will to man explicitly by His Word.

Genesis 2:17 *"But of the tree of the knowledge of good and evil, thou shall not eat of it; for in the day that thou eatest thereof thou shalt surely die."*

Man's subsequent, willful act of sin in transgressing the known standard of God caused a change in the nature of man. When sin entered into the world, mankind became a corruption of God's original creation. He became separated from God, subject to death, and under judicial sentence of the all-righteous God. Mankind then began to reproduce itself "after its kind."

Mankind Is Now Reproduced in the "Likeness of Adam"

Genesis 5:3 *"And Adam lived an hundred and thirty years, and begot a son in his own likeness, after his image;"*

Mankind no longer exists in the state of original creation, but has been altered according to the image of corrupted humanity. This state has been perpetuated through birth.

Romans 5:12 *"Wherefore, as by one man sin entered into the world, and death by sin, and so death passed upon all men, for all have sinned."*

Romans 5:18a *"Therefore, as by the offense of one judgment came upon all men to condemnation,"*

Ephesians 2:1 *"And you hath he made alive, who were dead in trespasses and sins;"*

The results of this fallen state are threefold:

1. Dying. Each member of the human race is born with a mortal, physical body (subject to physical death).

2. Dead. Each is born with his spirit separated from fellowship with God (in a state of spiritual death).

3. Damned. Each is born with a soul that is subject to the penalty for sin (eternal condemnation). It is in this condition that a child enters the world. Until a child becomes cognizant of sin, righteousness, and judgment, he is protected by God's law of accountability. Once a child becomes mentally accountable, his personal acts of sin vindicate the righteousness of God's judgment. (It is beyond the scope of this book to develop the doctrine of accountability.)

Each Child is Born with this Sinful Human Nature

Psalm 51:5 *"Behold, I was shaped in iniquity, and in sin did my mother conceive me."*

Psalm 58:3 *"The wicked are estranged from the womb; they go astray as soon as they are born, speaking lies."*

A child need not be taught how to lie, to be selfish, or to do wrong; these things come naturally. Every sweet, innocent, cuddly baby possesses within his flesh the constant temptation to fulfill the strong desire of sin. Under the control of sin, the child is totally self-centered; he wants what he wants when he wants it. A child wants to be fed what and when he wishes, to have the total attention of others, to play always, and generally to have his every desire fulfilled without regard for anyone else.

Anyone who doubts that a child possesses this inherent nature of sin need only observe untrained children in action. Imagine two children left in a room with a single toy of equal interest to each. Or, visualize a child left alone in a room with an open jar of candy. Finally, consider a child who has been left with the decision about his bedtime or anything else he may not wish to do (such as bathe, work, or study). These examples picture the reality of a child's drive for self-gratification.

Even when a child conducts himself with acceptable behavior, he may be acting out of self-interest to gain attention or future reward. An intelligent child or one who is strong-willed can deceive a parent into thinking that he is inherently good and only occasionally acts badly. Naturally, parents always want to see their child as they would like for him to be, not as he really is. You can avoid this deception when you realize that the nature of sin will motivate a child to do whatever bad, or even good, that he thinks will cause benefit to himself.

When parents recognize that the natural, normal tendency of their child is to satisfy his own sinful nature, they are ready to become successful parents. You cannot be successful in child training as long as you imagine that your child is an innocent, sweet cherub who is naturally good. The argument that "children will be children" is true. It is also true that they will remain that way if left to their own natures. For the child's own good, he must not be allowed to function under the control of his sinful nature.

Children Must Be Restrained By Their Parents

Proverbs 29:15 *"The rod and reproof give wisdom, but a child left to himself bringeth his mother shame."*

The word from the Hebrew translated "left to himself" is sometimes used of animals pasturing without fences or restraint. This word is also used in a general sense "to send off."[1] When contrasted with a child who is controlled by his parents, it pictures a child who is sent off into adulthood without being trained. The principle taught by this verse is that a child will grow up in conformity with his sinful nature if he is not restrained by his parents. In another verse God warns:

1 Samuel 3:13 *"For I have told him that I will judge his house forever for the iniquity which he knoweth, because his sons made themselves vile, and he restrained them not."*

In this verse, God is speaking about Eli, the priest who raised two evil sons. His sons are now adults, but Eli is being judged because as their parent he did not restrain their sinful nature. The Hebrew word here translated "restrained" means "to make weak or feeble."[2] In other words, Eli should have used his authority to cause his sons' sinful nature to have a feeble effect on them. Eli did not make his sons evil; *"[they] made themselves vile,"* but Eli did not prevent it. This verse indicates that the parent is responsible to control his child's evil tendencies.

A child left to himself, or unrestrained by his parents, is subject to the control of his sinful nature. He is born with neither the knowledge to know what is right and best for himself, nor the internal control to conquer his constant temptation to sin. The longer a child is allowed to grow up unrestrained, the more he becomes enslaved to the self-indulgence of his desires. It would be cruel not to help him control himself.

The primary role of the parent is to act as an external control over the child's nature. This helps to explain the reason for the almost limitless power of parental authority. Restraining the child's nature is not all there is to child training. However, until his nature is brought under control there can be little, if any, positive training. The parent must act as the child's external control until he can be taught internal controls. He is dependent on his parents to help control the sinful nature which seeks to enslave him.

Acknowledging the influence that your own sinful nature exerts on yourself will help you realize the importance of controlling your child's nature. As an adult, you can probably observe certain areas in your own life where the sinful nature still exercises its control. The normal desire to eat can be distorted by the nature of sin to produce gluttony — unfulfilled indulgence. Likewise, the normal desire for sex can be distorted to insatiable lust for pornography or immoral behavior toward the opposite sex. Even the subtle desire to be accepted by others may be distorted by the nature to the point where a person will compromise right principles because of approbation lust. You can probably see how stronger parental controls would have helped you. You now have the opportunity to help your own child become a mature adult by learning how to control his sinful nature while he is young.

AUTHOR NOTES TO THE 2ND EDITION

The following report was made after studying thousands of children in day care centers in Minnesota several years ago:

The Minnesota Crime Commission

"Every baby starts life as a little savage. He's completely selfish and self-centered. He wants what he wants when he wants it — his bottle, his mother's attention, his playmate's toy, his uncle's watch. Deny these and he seethes with aggressiveness which would be murderous if he were not so helpless. He is in fact, dirty. He has no morals, no knowledge, no skills. This means that all children, not just certain children, are born delinquent. If permitted to continue in the self-centered world of his infancy, given free reign to his impulsive actions to satisfy his wants, every child would grow up criminal — a thief, a killer, a rapist."

Teaching Self-Control

Parents can help their child to develop self-discipline early in life. When they teach a child not to interrupt (by action or noise), not to over eat, to stop what they are doing, to obey a command (put your toys away now, it's bath time); all with the proper attitude, they are teaching self-control. This is the same reason for **not** trying to child-proof a house instead of teaching a toddler the meaning of, NO! Control personalities would prefer to over-protect their child rather than train him. They attempt to manage his environment so that he can do no wrong or have anything bad happen to him. It is much better to teach a child to develop maturity so he can recognize and avoid dangers on his own. Tragically, some over-protective parents continue this obsessive control until the child is totally crippled from entering adulthood or breaks away from the stranglehold on his own.

The first commands that teach self-control are: No! Wait! Don't touch! On the other hand, psychological manipulation of "redirect" will not train the child. It only trains adults how to avoid the training opportunity (which appears to those who don't know better as avoiding unnecessary conflict). There is nothing wrong with redirecting an infant's attention, **prior** to his will and/or sin nature latching onto a non-permitted object. But afterwards it is too late. Then, he must have a training exercise in obedience and authority.

Parents must not feel wrong about being suspicious of their children's motives and actions. Until what age? Until you know a child has developed maturity, such as: personal responsibility and accountability for his own actions, self discipline, proper consideration for others (including you), self-confidence — not easily swayed by others. If your 19 year old doesn't meet this criteria for maturity, keep being suspicious. Obviously, parents must be suspicious of little children most of the time. I would never allow a three or four-year-old to be alone with an infant or a small animal until I had taught her how to behave and had watched her (satisfying suspicions) with them enough to know her heart. That is parenting. Once your children have proven their ability to make mature decisions you can begin to trust them.

By the time our children were in their teens, they were more mature than most adults I know. They could come and go as they pleased using one of the family cars (they still had to let us know where they were going, who they would be with, and when they would return. And, of course they paid for their own gasoline and auto insurance to be fiscally responsible.) We normally went to bed at 8:30 or 9:00 PM, but our three children often stayed up until 10 or 11 PM. It was a great joy for us and a delight to our children that we were able to trust them.

Psychology's idea that a person will act as you expect him to (in other words, you must give trust to receive trustworthiness) is **possibly** valid, but only if the person is capable of being trustworthy. To expect mature actions from an immature child is foolish. A child can only be expected to act according to his will and sin nature until trained. Don't worry or feel guilty about being like a warden or a policeman. Let your children know that when they act maturely, you will enjoy treating them accordingly. Trust is not a gift, it is a privilege that must be earned.

FOOTNOTES

[1] Hebrew, *shalach* "to send forth, to drive away"; here in the piel stem "be sent off" or "let loose" (unrestrained). This word is also used to describe a baby bird that is "cast forth" or "driven out" of the nest (Isaiah 16:2). (Foundation for Biblical Research, "Child Training.")

[2] Hebrew, *kahah* "faint, restrain"; here in the piel stem with negative proceeding "did not cause restraint." (Ibid.)

Chapter **8**

THE AGES OF A CHILD

Children progress through several more or less distinct stages of development on their way to becoming an adult. The Greek and Hebrew languages of the Bible utilize specific words to identify each of these different stages. We will use the terms infant, child, youth, and adult for these Biblical words (see Appendix C). Understanding the characteristics of each of these stages is important for knowing how to train children. (Please don't confuse these terms with psychology's stages of development.)

The term "infant" is used to describe the first stage of childhood. This period begins with total dependence on the parents, particularly on the mother. The infant is defenseless and must constantly be cared for physically. He demands that every need be fulfilled instantly. During this period he develops a sense of security through the care he receives. This care is evidenced by holding the baby, attending to his needs, stimulating his responses, and keeping him warm and free from the pain of hunger, wetness, pins, or any other discomfort.

The infant rapidly moves through this first stage as he develops strength. He begins to discover a sense of self-reliance in his increasing lack of dependency on others to fulfill his needs. He can no longer be considered an infant when is he able to express his independence by getting around on his own.

The term "child" is used to describe a little child in contrast to a youth in his teens. It is during this period that children will attempt to establish their own will as their only ruler. They can be expected to reject and fight against any restriction of their freedom. Their own desires will govern their actions as they seek to please only themselves.

When a child wants approval, he may do what others require of him for a time. When he wants attention, he may intentionally cause trouble to receive it. When he wants to express his own will, he will challenge the expression of any other person's will. Almost all parents have seen a child turn down a candy bar, or something else he likes, just to exert his own will and independence.

The child stage is when most of the behavior patterns are established for life. The patterns of respect of authority, obedience, respect for the rights of others, honesty, patience, self-control, study and work habits, concern for others, and personal contentment can all be developed during this period. Because of the formative nature of the child's mind during this stage, parents should establish and enforce all rules for acceptable and unacceptable conduct.

The child stage somewhat overlaps the infant stage. As soon as the infant begins to exert his will, he can also be considered a child. By the time the child reaches twelve or thirteen years of age he will have moved into the next area of development, youth.

The term "youth" is used to describe the period between twelve or thirteen and twenty years of age. During this period the individual personality develops. Personal interests and preferences emerge as the youth strives for his own identity. Masculinity or femininity comes into prominence as the youth sexually matures. His need to know the reasons behind the rules he has been required to obey now becomes extremely important.

A youth reaches out for more privileges, and at the same time his responsibilities constantly increase. He has the need to be accepted and recognized as an individual. He will seek for someone to whom he can look up to, with whom he can identify, and in whose leadership he can follow. It is a time in which the parent can be the maximum influence on his thinking.

Depending on how the parents handled the child stage, the youth will be prepared either to accept their teaching; or to reject their advice, way of life, or even them personally. The properly trained child will begin in his youth to operate on his own internal controls as he accepts increasing responsibilities and accountability for himself. A youth who was not caused to come under the control of his parents as a child will rebel more and more violently at any attempt by parents, school, or any other force to restrict his total freedom. The youth who has actually established his own control over the parents will increasingly exercise his dominion over them in order to satisfy his self-centered existence.

The term "adult" is used to describe a son or daughter twenty years old or older. Biblically, the adult male became fully accountable to God and the nation, including accountability for military draft and taxes, at twenty. The adult female still remained under the protection and leadership of her father until she was given in marriage.

No longer a youth, the adult has come to the end of the child training period. The youth who has been properly trained and is now in adulthood will continue to honor his parents, and his life will reflect their good training, thereby bringing them great joy. If the parents have also earned his respect for their character and wisdom, the young adult will continue to look to them for advice.

From the Biblical words used to describe the different stages of life, a chronological chart can be developed.

Figure 8.1 Stages of Biblical Child Development

The parents' recognition of their children's development stages, particularly those of "child" and "youth," will help them to understand the training functions of "control" and "teaching" described in the following sections.

From this section, therefore, we find that children are not totally innocent, blank tablets which are molded entirely by their environment. Instead, we see that they are actually creatures subject to a much more powerful force within themselves, and we can consequently establish certain principles concerning the child's make-up:

- Because of sin, mankind is now being reproduced in a corrupted state of God's original creation.

- Each child is born with an independent will of its own which seeks autonomy.

- Each child possesses the human nature of sin, which can control him and produce a totally self-centered person.

- It is the parents' responsibility to restrain the natural tendency of the child to be controlled by his sinful nature.

- Children are Biblically described as to their different stages of development. Each of these stages has specific characteristics.

Understanding the nature of a child should help parents realize the importance of their role of authority. It should also help them see their child's need for training — initially by their providing the needed external control, and ultimately by teaching him to control himself.

AUTHOR NOTES TO THE 2ND EDITION

Age of Adulthood

So many people have wanted to know why the legal age was twenty-years-old, here are the verses: Exodus 30:14; Numbers 1:3, 30; and 14:29. These verses state that a young man was counted as a part of the nation's census, was draftable for the military, and started paying taxes at 20.

Training As Related To Development Stages

While a child is in the "infant" stage, restrictions are necessary — NO! DON'T TOUCH! STOP! Not allowing the infant to have access to harmful foods, or dangerous situations (swimming pool, street, electrical sockets, ironing board, etc.) is proper child training. However, as the infant moves into the "child" stage, simple restraint should increasingly be accompanied with teaching — telling the child why you are restraining him. CAUTION: Parents are not required to justify their instructions before expecting obedience. All teaching should generally follow **after** a child's obedience, especially with a younger child (two through four). Finally, as the child moves into the "youth" stage, restrictions should only be needed concerning dangers which are beyond the youth's wisdom (like: not allowing wrong friendships, intimate situations with the opposite sex, or rejection of basic education). A youth should normally be expected to operate on the instructions received during his childhood, at least after a reminder or challenge is brought to his mind. This is the time for developing personal accountability — adult maturity. Much more follows about when and how to train effectively.

Three Negative Characteristics

Children seem to be born with one of three basic sin nature characteristics, or some combination of these three. In speeches to thousands of parents over the past several years, I have requested anyone to tell me if these characteristics didn't describe their own children. None have suggested that they didn't. Even though a child (or adult) may lie (deceive, manipulate), steal, cheat, disobey, or be cruel; I believe that all of these sins come from the three characteristics. In fact, most of them are used to cover up the big three, like a child cheating in school work to cover up his laziness, or to protect his pride.

The following descriptions should help you identify each of your children's predominate, negative characteristics. Suggestions are also given to help you assist your child in overcoming his major weakness. Note: These characteristics are not usually identifiable prior to about six to eight years old when a child is consistently challenged to do things he doesn't wish to do, such as physical work or study. A two year old is likely to appear that he has all three negative traits.

I. LAZINESS (SLOTHFUL)

A. Symptoms:

A child who operates below his ability on a consistent basis; doesn't complete assigned tasks (half finishes or fools around); excuses non-completion with forgetting; daydreams; cheats or lies to cover; blames you, the heat, the dog, anything, to avoid being pinned.

CAUTION: Not all children who exhibit these symptoms are lazy. Before you begin intensive training, you must check that the child does not have a hearing or eyesight problem, a poor diet or sleep schedule (its amazing how many parents today keep their children up past 8:30 or 9 P.M. and still expect quality performance), or is being required to perform work duties or to study school materials beyond his ability. For instance, if a child can only read on a third grade level, it's unreasonable to require him to function at the fifth grade level in his reading-dependent subjects.

B. Treatment:

If you determine your child has no excuse and is truly lazy, he must reap the consequences of his actions. A lazy person **hates** work. He must learn that laziness costs more work as a consequence. If your child dilly-dallied about cutting the grass, the treatment could be to add trimming the entire perimeter. If your child does sloppy, half completed school work to show his disinterest, he could be required to do it over in neat printing. Or, you could add more writing to the assignment as a consequence. Eventually, your child will catch on that laziness doesn't pay; or he will openly rebel against your authority. Then, you can apply the appropriate pressure to cure that problem (see chapters on rebellion and chastisement). Of course, you should also teach the child what God's Word says about laziness, **after** he accepts the responsibility of his action (the penalty).

II. PRIDEFULNESS

Definition: Self deception that one has concerning the importance of ones self. Pride thinks of self as being either better or more important than they really are, or as being less than they really are. (False humility is as much pride as is bravado.)

A. Symptoms:

Overtly — The over achiever who is obsessed with excellence (not out of personal interest in what they are doing or even for self-satisfaction; but to obtain praise from others). This child lusts for acceptance, compliments, and recognition from others. The perfectionist child usually has a high intellect with an obsessive drive to achieve. She will demand attention, especially when others (siblings, visitors, phone calls) or mother's work might interfere. Fathers, **beware**, this little girl can manipulate you at will. Jealousy, vanity, me first, me only, boasting, and a desire to control others, are manifestations of overt pride.

Covertly — The under achiever who gives up too easily, has average or lower intellect, will not compete, avoids calling attention to self (to avoid performance), decides he can't succeed before he tries, often looks like a lazy child, but is not. He is self-defeated by comparing himself to other children or siblings who are faster or appear smarter than he is. Whining, avoiding others, not joining into group games, and self-effacing are indications of the under-achiever.

B. Treatment:

Both the over achiever and the under achiever need teaching about God's plan, God's power, and God's acceptance of each of us; as well as teaching about the dangerous sin of pride.

NOTE: Psychology preaches the need for a positive self image as a cure for a poor view of ones self. The Bible teaches that a Christian's objective should be a Christ image instead. (To understand the difference, read *The Biblical View of Self-Esteem, Self-Love, Self-Image* by Jay E. Adams, Harvest House.

The Over Achiever — Praise should be withheld from the child who demands it. When such a child shows you a picture they have colored, you could comment on the nice colors or subject of the picture, but avoid compliments on her fine technique (don't support her drive for being a perfectionist). When she demands that you hang the picture in a prominent place, you could suggest she hang it on her own wall. **Never** allow this child to demand attention by interrupting adult conversations. Teach her courtesy and self-discipline. Compliment her on displaying good attitudes towards siblings and others, or for patience; not for physical issues such as her accomplishments or appearance. Try to compliment her when she doesn't expect it. Don't feed pridefulness. It is insatiable!

NOTE: An excellent therapy for self-centeredness is to require service for others. Volunteering at a rest home; or even making a sibling's bed or doing their wash can help change this attitude over time.

The Under Achiever — This child needs all of the praise and attention the over achiever demands, but for which he will never ask. Look for ways to recognize and reward this child's effort, not his results. Build him up with honest attention. His efforts should be privately praised for each small success. You could find his special interest area (model making, mechanical work, or whatever) and let him experience success there often. He needs to learn that he will be accepted for his attitude of diligence, willingness, and humility; not how his accomplishments compare with others. He needs to learn he is acceptable for just being himself.

III. WILLFULNESS

Definition: The compulsion to be autonomous (self-ruled) and the rejection of anyone else's attempt to dictate what, where, or when to do anything.

A. Symptoms:

Overtly — Willfulness is manifested in an arrogant, cocky attitude and a constant challenge to authority figures or rules. His objective is to make the cost of controlling him so high, you will tolerate his self-rule. The main sign is defiance!

Covertly — (Passive rebellion) — Willfulness is hidden by giving substitutes for obedience (you tell them to take out the trash and instead they bring you a flower), by operating just past the intent of the rules, and by manipulating parents to cause confusion and breakdown of authority. When confronted with her wrong doing, this child will be highly argumentative and will not accept any personal accountability. (Signs are: Argumentative, try's to blame you for her disobedience, blames others, pouts when caught.)

B. Treatment:

1. Give precise instructions (you can even write them down and post them or have the child read and sign them, if necessary). Warning of the consequences — this is like waving a flag before a bull. Look forward to the child testing your character — he will. (Conflict will occur as a natural part of correct child training.)

2. When the willful child disobeys, rebuke him (verbally judge him to be wrong) and if he does not immediately accept your rebuke, administer corporal punishment (see chapters on rebellion and chastisement).

The balance of this book will deal with how to train difficult children such as these — and your own.

Section THREE

TRAINING YOUR CHILDREN

Chapter 9

WHAT CHILD TRAINING MEANS

Before you can be effective in training your children, it is necessary to know exactly what training means. Training means "the process by which the one being trained is caused to show the results of the training."[1] Therefore, child training is the process used by parents that will cause a child to reach the objective for which he has been trained.

To train the growth of a plant means to cause it to grow along a predetermined path, like along a trellis. To train an athlete means to cause him to become fit for an athletic contest, specifically to be a winner. To train an animal is to cause it to accomplish a certain function like race, work, or perform a trick. To train a person in a certain skill is to cause him to become proficient in the use of that skill.

In each of these cases, training is not completed unless the subject actually attains the intended purpose of the training process. Training is not just the process of teaching only. If positive results are not obtained, training has not occurred. If the plant does not grow along the trellis, if the athlete does not compete well, if the animal cannot perform, or if the trainee cannot do the job, training has not been accomplished.

Parents do not train their child by just **telling** him what they expect of him. Unless the child actually arrives at the point of functioning on his own in conformity to what he has been taught, he has not been trained. Parents can have no comfort in saying, "I just don't understand why he turned out that way. I always told him what was right." Telling is not training.

Mere exposure to a good home environment is also not training. Being raised in a moral atmosphere is no guarantee that a child will "catch" the standards of his parents. Enough moral parents, including a significant number of ministers, have raised immoral or amoral children to prove this point. Parents who expect a child to follow their standards by the example they set, but do not train into him, will often be shocked when he acquires only their faults and rejects most of what is good in their lives.

Christian parents can deceive themselves into thinking that simply exposing their child to church or Christian school will eliminate the need for their personal training. Although a Bible-teaching church and a good Christian school can assist the parents, they are not replacements for parents training their own children. It is necessary that parents train their children in obedience and respect for authority **before** the church or school can be truly effective.

Raising a child is not training. Plants and animals are raised. To raise something means to grow it. To raise a child would only consist of feeding, clothing, and protecting him from destruction until he reaches physical maturity. While it is true today that most parents are only "raising" their children, raising does not constitute the training of the soul that God intends.

If you desire for your child to become obedient and willing to accept God's standards as his own, you will have to utilize the process that God has designed to obtain these results. Biblical child training produces a quality character much different than would have naturally developed had the child been left alone to grow up according to his own nature. God's Word commands parents specifically to so alter the nature of their children.

Parents Are to Train Their Children

Proverbs 22:6 *"Train up a child in the way he should go and, when he is old, he will not depart from it."*

The Hebrew word here translated "train" is translated dedicate in every other passage where it occurs. To dedicate means "to renew, inaugurate, or initiate."[2] Parents are commanded by God to initiate or start their child in a certain direction. He is not to be allowed to follow the path his sin nature would take him, but he is to be set on a new path. Dedication is not just a one-time initiation, but incorporates the entire training process. The result of this training is for this new way to become the child's own way of life. When this training transpires, the child will not leave the path even as he grows older and becomes an adult.

The ancient root of this Hebrew word for train means "to make narrow" and even "to strangle."[3] In other words, parents are to restrict the path their children may follow. The child described in this verse is in the "child" stage of development — under thirteen years old. Parents are not to wait for a child to choose his own way of life, but are to place him on the right path in early childhood. This directing does not mean dictating a child's career or personal preferences, but directing him in the way of life that agrees with God's standards.

Restraining a child's nature is not all there is to child training. However, until the nature is brought under control, there can be little, if any, positive training. Parents must act as the external control over a child while he is developing his own internal controls. The parents' role is not to remain as the child's control for the rest of his life, but gradually they are to work themselves out of this job as early as possible.

A child who has been trained to be obedient to his parents will respect their position of authority and will thus be prepared to accept their instructions. His parents can then teach him moral values and good manners as well as any academic instruction that matches his mental maturity. Parents of obedient children are in a position to teach whatever right, or even wrong, information they possess. Therefore, parents as teachers have an awesome responsibility for what they teach (James 3:1).

A danger exists: any teaching that cannot be substantiated by the facts is subject to rejection by a child as he seeks truth and reason during his youth. There is, therefore, a danger that not only unverifiable teaching, but also verifiable teaching may be rejected. This is one of the main reasons that youth tend to reject opinionated, religious teachings that are not based firmly on Biblical substantiation.

It is vital that the parent knows and teaches only what is right and true. Of course, the Bible is the ultimate source for the truth of all soul and spiritual information. So, parents who intend to teach their child the right way of life will teach him the standards that God has given to man.

Parents Are to Teach God's Word to Their Children

Deuteronomy 6:6 & 7 *"And these words, which I command thee this day, shall be in thine heart; And thou shalt teach them diligently unto thy children, and shalt*

> *talk of them when thou sittest in thine house, and*
> *when thou walkest by the way, and when thou liest*
> *down, and when thou risest up."*

Parents are commanded to teach their children all that God has revealed to man. The Hebrew word translated "teach" here means "to inculcate."[4] It means to train God's standards into the child intensively by the use of repetition. Notice that this teaching is to be on a consistent basis and at every opportunity. Training is a constant process until the results desired are achieved. Positive teaching will have to be repeated time and time again since it runs counter to the natural inclination of the child. These verses also show that parents need to know God's Word in order to teach their children properly. If you are going to teach your children the right way of life, you first must know what it is.

The word translated "children" in verse seven is not a word that refers to a specific age, but instead emphasizes the family relationship.[5] In other words, parents are responsible for teaching their own children. Our churches and Christian schools would do well to teach parents the importance of teaching their own children God's Word.

God uses another word for teaching in passages similar to the one just studied (Deuteronomy 4:10 and 11:19). The Hebrew word used in these passages means "to teach by intensive drill."[6] It is the same word that is used to describe the training of a soldier for war. The derivative of this word is the word for a goad, a stick sharp enough to penetrate an animal's hide, used for prodding cattle or oxen. The prodding this word suggests relates to child training. Parents may need to prod their child with a sharp rebuke occasionally to get the child's attention and to cause him to go the direction he must go.

In conclusion, child training is the process used by parents that will cause a child to reach the objective for which he has been trained. The process includes both restraining the child from following his natural inclination to sin and also teaching him the right way of life. The desired objective is for the child to learn God's Word, which can then direct him throughout his adult life.

What is the antithesis of proper child training? What are some of the pitfalls parents can encounter if they do not clearly train their child to reach God's objective? The next chapter deals with the problem of negative training.

AUTHOR NOTES TO THE 2ND EDITION

Comments On Proverbs: 22:6

Several interpretations of this passage have been suggested by Bible scholars in recent years. Some state that it is not an actual promise to parents, but merely a possibility that a child will turn out okay if parents do their best. I imagine this interpretation came about because we have observed the fact that good, moral, Christian parents have raised rotten kids on occasion. However, personal experience is not the basis for sound doctrine. Only Scripture may interpret itself, and we have many passages other than Proverb 22:6 that make it clear : good parenting produces good results (Proverbs 29:17; 31:28); while poor parenting produces poor results (Proverbs 17:21; 29:15b; I Samuel 3:13). Any attempt to alter this passage probably comes from a sincere desire to comfort those who have already raised a wayward adult.

Another interpretation of this passage is : "Train up a child in the way the bow is bent (or, in keeping with his individual gifts)." This interpretation is then further interpreted to mean that parents need to adjust their training of each child based on his age, temperament (personality and emotional make-up), and hereditary history. I'm afraid there is no Scriptural substantiation for this interpretation, but common sense does indicate that we should understand our children and their unique differences. Without a doubt, children need to be taught commensurate with their mental and emotional maturity (chronological age is an inaccurate gauge). However, **every** child has a sin nature that must be restricted; and **every** child has a need to be directed in The Way — God's standards and principles of life. Although each child will vary in how he manifests his sin nature (see author notes to Chapter 7); all children, at all ages, need to be trained by the same principles taught throughout this book — no matter what their temperament might be.

The most accurate translation that the Foundation for Biblical Research could determine for this very difficult verse was: "You dedicate a young child in accordance with his way (introduce or initiate him into the righteous way of life), and indeed (emphatic), when he becomes an adult, he will not turn aside from it." This verse is definitely a promise; parents are expected to direct their child in a particular path, not a path in conformity with his temperament or talents, but in a way of life pleasing to God — the purpose of Biblical child training.

Testimony

Ron and I were exact opposites (speaking of my son, Ron, when in his teens). Where I was athletic, a public speaker, a business leader, and probably too strong of a personality; Ron was non-athletic, quiet, a studious child with wide interests, but without clear objectives for his life. He later told his Mom and I that as a child his view of a "real" man was to be just like Dad. However, he knew he wasn't like his Dad at all. How, then, could he merit his Mother's love (since she loved Dad so much) or his father's respect and approval? We had not learned all of the things in this book at that time, especially about young adults , so we were sadly ignorant of the trauma our son was going through. We all suffered for this ignorance when at seventeen our son finally decided he didn't want to try to be like his Dad anymore. So, he left home and attempted to reject the standards he had been trained in (not just taught). His secular friends still called him Mr. Squeaky Clean, but he did make a number of decisions against his own conscience. Finally, at twenty-five, God broke his will while he was listening to a Don Francisco song on the car radio — PRAISE GOD!

When Ron came back to the way he had been trained, he was committed to God in a manner that was not possible for him before. One of the most meaningful comments he later made to us was: "I thought I was rebelling against you (Mom and Dad), but I was really rebelling against God." Ron has become one of the most mature Christian men I know. He is a highly principled, hard working, honest, and capable man. He is a computer programmer, a department manager, and the single parent of his son (whose mother deserted him as she had done to his father before). He is a strong man in his own right, however, we do joke that he is now more like me than either of us would have ever thought possible. He is a man, and I am exceedingly proud to call him my Son. Is Proverbs 22:6 a promise? It certainly has been for my wife and I!

FOOTNOTES

[1]   *Oxford English Dictionary, s.v.* "training."

[2]   Hebrew, *chanak* "train, dedicate, make narrow, be narrow." This word occurs only in Deuteronomy 20:5 (twice); 1 Kings 8:63; 2 Chronicles 7:5; Proverbs 22:6. Note that the building (place) or child (person) in each dedication has a purpose. Significantly, the dedication of God's House is analogous to the dedication of a child. The house is new at dedication; so a child must be dedicated (trained) from an early age. (Foundation for Biblical Research, "Child Training.")

[3]   See footnote #2.

[4]   Hebrew, *shanan* "to sharpen;" here meaning "to teach by repetition" or "to inculcate." (Ibid.)

[5]   Hebrew, *ben* "children." This word corresponds to the Greek word, *teknon* "children;" Biblical meaning "progeny" (see Appendix C).

[6]   Hebrew, *lamad* "exercise, learn;" here used in the piel stem meaning "to teach" (intensively). *Lamad is* used as a transitive verb for goading cattle (Hosea 10:11), and to train recruits in the military (1 Chronicles 5:18). (Ibid.)

Chapter 10

NEGATIVE TRAINING

As a parent, you are always training your child, even if you are not teaching him according to God's standards. Simply because you are in the position of rulership, your child will receive his direction from you — right or wrong. You set the standards for his acceptable conduct either by what you allow (training by default) or by what you unintentionally teach (overt negative training).

If a child is rude, inconsiderate, and selfish, he has been trained to be that way. If a child is lazy and sloppy or is disrespectful and a troublemaker, he has been trained that way. Parents do not intentionally train their children to reflect these negative characteristics; yet it is very easy to train a child in these undesirable behavior patterns because they reinforce his natural inclinations.

When parents simply do nothing, the child is trained to think that whatever he wants to do is all right. This inaction is negative training by default.

Negative Training by Default

Parents are training their child when they ignore his negative behavior traits. All parents do this to some extent. We all have blind spots, areas in our own life where we do not see our own faults. These areas tend to block us from training the same problems out of our children. A parent who has poor table manners is unlikely to allow himself to see and correct the atrocious mealtime behavior of his child. A parent who gossips and runs down others is unlikely to recognize and correct this trait. It is difficult to correct negative traits in our children that would condemn ourselves. Parents may teach the principles of right conduct, but if that teaching goes contrary to their own practice, they will not enforce those standards.

On the other hand, it is possible to be overly critical in the area of blind spots. This hypocritical approach also will be rejected by a child and result in negative training. You will be successful ultimately in training **only those** standards you yourself attempt to maintain in your own life.

Default training can also occur when parents do not enforce even those standards by which they live. This failure may be due to the parents' occupation with their own problems or duties, weariness of the child's need for constant correction, or just plain laziness. How often do you allow your child to get away with an action or attitude for which you would normally correct him? Training requires consistency, and it is comforting to realize that consistency pays. The more consistent you are, the sooner your child will become trained and the less frequently you will need to correct him.

Default training is often the result of leaving correction to someone else. A father does this when he leaves all the training to the mother, even when the need for correction is directly before him. A mother does this when she refuses to correct the child while the father is home in an attempt to force him into action. It is a great benefit to the child when both parents reinforce each other. In any event, neither parent should neglect a child's need to be trained consistently. If only one parent is willing to train the child, then he or she must do so.

Parents need to be careful not to depend on a teacher, baby-sitter, or particularly an older child to handle their own responsibility of training. An older child can be of great assistance in carrying a share of the work burdens around the house. However, that child should **never** be allowed to correct, or to be made responsible for the training of, a younger brother or sister. The delegation of parental responsibility to an older child can create confusion of roles, insubordination, as well as tension between children. Only the one to whom God has specifically delegated authority should ever exercise the power of that position. God holds **only** parents accountable for training children.

Overt Negative Training

Even more disastrous than negative training by default is overt negative training. This type of training occurs when parents actually train negative behavior patterns into their child. These negative characteristics then hinder the parents' ability to accomplish positive training. They will also affect the child's ability to receive instruction outside the home — at school, church, and work.

Overt negative training results from the way parents allow their child to react to their instructions. The following examples illustrate some of the situations parents should never allow when instructing their children:

1. A child can be trained that obedience is required only after instructions have been repeated a second

or third time: "Johnny, I want you to pick up your toys." Johnny quietly ignores the command and continues to play. (He wants to play, and he does not want to expend effort doing what has been commanded.) After a time interval, the parent realizes his instruction was not carried out: "Johnny, I told you to stop playing and pick up your toys. Do you hear me?" Johnny may or may not answer depending on which he has been trained to do. (Your child should be trained always to acknowledge your instructions so that you know he has heard and understood them. Responses such as, "Yes, sir" or "Yes, ma'am," **said with a right attitude,** will help to develop a proper respect in your child as well as tell you that he has heard your instructions.)

If Johnny learns to respond only to repeated instructions, he is being trained to wait until every instruction has been repeated at least once before obeying. The parent also is being trained by the child accordingly. If a child is able to get away with ignoring the first command, he will attempt to ignore even repeated commands. He has probably experienced the parents' forgetting between repeats and can thus look forward to possibly escaping the task altogether.

2. A child can be trained to obey only after instructions are accompanied by an implied threat (a raised voice) or an explicit threat of punishment. "Johnny, I told you to pick up your toys ten minutes ago," the parent may yell at the top of his voice after the child has already ignored the first command. Johnny learns that he needs to obey only when he is yelled at or threatened. Obedience means "to do what is told." It does not mean to respond only to threats.

3. A child can be trained to ignore instructions even if
    repeated or accompanied by threats. Being allowed
    to ignore instructions completely is actually train-
    ing in disobedience. This training occurs when
    there has been seldom, if any, enforcement by the
    parent issuing the instructions. Often a child will
    respond promptly to the instructions of one parent,
    but ignores those given by the other. This can hap-
    pen to any parent who does not enforce his own
    instructions, especially to the mother who passes
    all enforcement over to the father. It also happens
    when one parent treats a child with favoritism.
    Each parent must individually establish his own
    right to rule over a child.

When a parent threatens his child with "do it or
else," and the "or else" seldom follows, the child is
being trained to consider that the parent's word
has no value. A child trained this way will also
doubt the word of other authorities. He will think
that no one's word is any better than his parent's.
When he hears God's Word state *"and he that
believeth not the Son shall not see life, but the wrath
of God abideth on him."* (John 3:36b), will he not
also consider this to be just another empty threat?
The way a child first views God is through his parents. They are the authority that God has placed
over him to train him in obedience and respect. It
is vital for your child to learn to trust your word!

If follow-through is inconsistent, a child will make
a game out of disobeying. If there is even the least
chance that there will be no enforcement for not following instructions, he will play a game of Russian
Roulette. It is amazing what a child will try to get
away with to exert his will or to fulfill his desires.
Have you ever walked into the kitchen and caught

your child with his hand in the cookie jar and asked, "Johnny, are you taking any cookies?" only to have him respond with "No" while he continues to hold a little fistful?

4. A child can be trained to question or argue about every explanation. A child must initially learn to respond to the parents' instructions immediately and without explanation. This type of response may save his life, or at least prevent injury, as the parents can instantly direct him away from danger.

Parents do not owe their child an explanation for their instructions. He does not have to know why you want him to do it, let alone agree with you. You are his authority and thereby have the right to direct his activities. When a child is allowed to make parents justify their instructions, it undermines their authority and causes them to answer to the child instead of the child to them. Until a child learns unquestioning obedience, it is better not to justify your instructions in advance. If you think it is necessary to explain your reasons, do so only **after** he has obeyed.

A clever child who is allowed to question his parents' instructions can confuse the issue and thereby avoid obedience. He may even turn your own words back on you: "But you said. . ." While it is true that you will make some mistakes with the use of your authority, it is not your child's responsibility or privilege to correct you.

When a child is allowed to back talk and argue, he makes his parents pay a penalty for interfering in his life. If he makes the price high enough in unpleasantness, his parents may get off his back. Many parents who have trained their children to argue have done just that. They have let the child go his own way because they are tired of the hassle that they allowed in the first place.

5. A child can train his parents to wait until he decides **when** to obey. This behavior is not obedience, but a subtle form of rebellion which is most often practiced by little girls (and a lot of old girls who learned its success). Where a boy is more likely to rebel in an overt manner, a girl will often express her will by passive rebellion.

When you tell your child to do something and he responds by saying, "Just a minute," you are being trained to wait for his timing. The child has just said, "I will do your will when it becomes my will." Mother tells her daughter to go wash the dishes and she responds with, "Okay, Mommy," and then proceeds to wait thirty minutes. She may eventually go do her duty, or she may wait until Mother asks again, whereupon she says, "I was just on my way," as sweetly as possible. She, not the mother, has been in control of the situation as she has deliberately delayed in following the instruction.

The "camel's head in the tent" is a common example of rebellion by degree. This is when the child negotiates his own deal. For example: a parent puts the child down for bed and goes downstairs. Pretty soon the child tip toes downstairs where he is told to go back to bed. Instead, he smiles sweetly and moves more into the room for a hug. The weak parent then tells the child he may stay if he sits down and remains quiet. The camel gets into the tent by inches; first his head, then his shoulders, and before you know it his whole body has been allowed into the tent. Don't bend your rules and allow passive rebellion to rule your tent!

Passive rebellion also occurs when a child is able to cause his parents to submit to certain terms before obeying. These terms are usually a form of bribery, like when mother has to say: "If you pick up your toys, I will give you a nice surprise." More often, the condition for obedience is causing the parent to help in accomplishing the instruction: "Let Mommy help you pick up your toys." That same mommy will be working her child's homework when he later refuses to follow the teacher's instructions. Parents should never do that for which the child is held accountable. Parents must make their instructions clear, which may involve a demonstration of what is to be done, but the child must assume the responsibility to follow instructions on his own.

6. A child can be trained to give an excuse for his disobedience or wrongdoing. An excuse is seldom the true reason for an action; instead, it is an attempt to justify, to make right, a wrong. It is a law of human nature that if you ask for an excuse, you will get one. In fact, you are likely to receive one whether you ask for it or not. Excuses are attempts to share, or avoid altogether, the responsibility for wrongdoing.

When parents train a child to give excuses, they are also training him not to accept full responsibility for his own actions. He will grow up seeking others to blame for his failures instead of facing the true problem. Acceptance of full responsibility for one's own thoughts, words, and deeds is one of the cornerstones of maturity. Without this acceptance, the reality of personal shortcomings or wrongdoing is avoided, thereby making the need for personal change and improvement unnecessary.

Parents who ask their child why he disobeyed or did something wrong may be attempting to understand the reason. However, the reason why is not nearly as important as the fact of the deed. The administration of justice should not be based on the why of guilt, but the fact of guilt.

Only after the child's guilt has been firmly established as fact should parents attempt to analyze the reason. The reason may be important for future training or for more parental control of the circumstances (such as a child not being allowed to play with someone who is a negative influence on him). The **reason why** does not alter the **fact** of guilt. A child must be taught that outside circumstances are no justification for his own wrongdoing.

Often, more than one child has been wrong when another is caught. A brother, sister, or another child may have instigated a situation that led to the wrong of which the child in question is guilty. Two wrongs do not make a right. Each child must stand responsible for his own actions, even when others may also be guilty. The guilt of others must not distract parents from the issue of their child's wrongdoing. Appropriate action can be taken later concerning others who may have been involved, but their involvement must not be an excuse or hinder dealing at the time with the one caught.

A typical situation might occur after the rule has been set down that your children are not allowed to call each other names. You overhear one of your children verbally attack his sister, calling her a "big, fat pig." You confront the guilty child with his deed: "What did you say?" (not: "Why did you say that?"). The child will probably avoid your question and instead begin to offer an excuse that justifies his breaking the rule. Although it may be true his sister made a face at him or called him a toad, the fact of his guilt does not change. After you properly enforce your instructions with the brother, determine the possible provocation of the sister, and then use this occasion as a training experience for her as well.

One of the reasons parents ask for an excuse is because they inwardly want the child to have one. They hope there is sufficient justification to prevent any need for an unpleasant confrontation. It is natural to want to avoid confrontation (unless your sinful nature actually enjoys conflict). However, conflict is a necessity in training children.

The parents' pride also interferes with their desire to know the truth. A child's disobedience or wrongdoing can reflect on his parents. When parents look for excuses for their child's misbehavior, they may be trying to protect their own pride. If a child can excuse his actions, the parents can deceive themselves into not accepting any responsibility for the child's poor training.

It would be natural for a parent to desire his child not be at fault when that child has failed a test at school. It would be easier to accept that it was really the teacher's fault. Parents can hope it was not their own child's fault when he broke a neighbor's picture window. Instead, the other boys who were playing with him could have been guilty. Everyone would like to have a patsy to blame for their own faults. Never allow your child to use one, and you can help train him to be a responsible individual.

Instead of wishfully hoping that your child will always do the right thing, remember that his nature is to sin. Realistically expect your child to act in conformance with his nature until he has been well trained. Be fair with him, but look on every disobedience or wrongdoing as an opportunity to train him to conform to God's standards. Having this viewpoint will keep you from being deceived and will help you face the necessity of the training task.

In conclusion, negative training results from parents' tolerance of their child's negative behavior and from how they inadvertently train him to respond to their instructions. A child who is not trained to follow instructions promptly and correctly the first time has been allowed to exert his own will over that of his authority. Parents who train in this manner will be erratic in their enforcement. Sometimes they will allow their instructions to go totally unheeded, thus giving little value to their word. At other times, they will crack down inconsistently after the first, second, or third declaration, thus being unfair with their power. This teaches your child that authorities are unjust.

The solution is simple. The only fair and correct way to train your child is to expect his obedience in consistently and promptly following your instructions the first time you give them. This is not only best for the child, but it is much easier on the parent since it prevents frustration, unfair enforcement, and wear and tear on the vocal chords. It also prevents the need to be constantly checking on the child to see if your instructions have been carried out. If you really intend for your child to become obedient to your will, he must be trained to follow your instructions without your repetition or threats and without his back talk or excuses.

It will seem at times (especially in the beginning) that all you do is instruct, warn, punish, or say "no." Do not despair. Anything of value requires a cost. When you see your child begin to respond to your training with respect and obedience, all your efforts will have been more than worth it. When your child happily follows your every instruction, you can be properly proud of the reflection he has become. Confrontations will decrease, and you will begin to have an improved relationship with your child. Remember, great joy for the parent and prosperity for the child are God's promises for a job well done. You have benefited both yourself and your child when you determine to train him properly and consistently.

Knowing how not to train your children is important, but even more important is knowing how to train them properly. The two facets of positive child training, controlling and teaching, will be developed in the next chapter.

AUTHOR NOTES TO THE 2ND EDITION

Negative Character Training

Parents can also negatively affect their child's soul by ridiculing him or her physically, such as:

"You're too small to ever be any good in sports."

"You're too plain to perform in public."

"Your nose, ears, hips, are too big."

Or, belittling their character, like;

"You're such a bad boy, you'll probably be a criminal when you grow up."

"You don't even try, you'll probably never amount to anything."

"I just don't know what's wrong with you!"

Children's souls can be distorted for life from this kind of negative training. It is extremely harmful whether they give in and feel rejected, or overcompensate and become a clown or a bully in an attempt to gain acceptance. DON'T DO THIS TO YOUR CHILDREN!

Sometime in the late 1960's, a report was issued by the Cheif of Police at Houston, Texas entitled:

Twelve Rules for Raising Delinquent Children

1. Begin with infancy to give the child everything he wants. In this way he will grow up to believe the world owes him a living.

2. When he picks up bad words, laugh at him. This will make him think he's cute. It will also encourage him to pick up "cuter" phrases that will blow off the top of your head later.

3. Never give him any spiritual training. Wait till he is 21 and then let him "decide for himself."

4. Avoid use of the word "wrong." It may develop a guilt complex. This will condition him to believe later, when he is arrested for stealing a car, that society is against him and he is being persecuted.

5. Pick up everything he leaves lying around—books, shoes, and clothing. Do everything for him so he will be experienced in throwing all responsibility on to others.

6. Let him read any printed matter he can get his hands on. Be careful that the silverware and drinking glasses are sterilized, but let his mind feast on garbage.

7. Quarrel frequently in the presence of your children. In this way they will not be too shocked when the home is broken up later.

8. Give a child all the spending money he wants. Never let him earn his own. Why should he have things as tough as YOU had them?

9. Satisfy his every craving for food, drink, and comfort. See that every sensual desire is gratified. Denial may lead to harmful frustration.

10. Take his part against neighbors, teachers, and policeman. They are all prejudiced against your child.

11. When he gets into real trouble, apologize for yourself by saying "I never could do anything with him."

12. Prepare for a life of grief. You will be apt to have it.

NOTE: These twelve rules were originally created by Dr. Paul Cates and published in *Strictly for Parents*, a newsletter and radio show on WMBI in Chicago, Ill. about 1961.

LIKE FATHER/LIKE SON

Chapter 11

THE TWO FACETS OF CHILD TRAINING

The two facets of child training, **controlling** and **teaching,** basically parallel the specific stages of a child's development. The control aspect of training corresponds to the "child" stage (to age thirteen), while the teaching aspect corresponds to the "youth" stage (the teen years). A child must be told **what** to do; a youth needs to be taught **why** to do it.

While children are in the child stage, they should be expected to follow the commands of their parents to the letter. This period of development is characterized by the child's immaturity and need for constant restraint. It is the time for maximum, external control by the parents; a time of law, when the child is trained about what to do, or not to do. Sufficiently intense parental pressure will require the child to comply with and to learn to obey these laws.

By the time a child reaches thirteen years of age, he should be obedient to, and respectful of, his parents' right to rule. He should exhibit manners that demonstrate an attitude of respect. His self-discipline should be highly developed; that is, he should possess a great deal of internal control over his own desires. Confrontations and conflicts should be all but over for the parents who have properly controlled their children throughout the child stage.

During the time children are in the "youth" stage, they still should be expected to obey their parents. However, obedience should now begin to result from willing submission rather than from forced compliance. This period of development is the time when children are to be taught the reasons behind the laws for which they have been held accountable. These reasons constitute why he should or should not do something.

A youth should begin to experience the personal benefit of self-control over the destructive desires of his own nature. For example, a young girl who is able to control her desire for sweets and junk food can avoid obesity and poor skin. Her self-control produces a stronger will power and a better physical appearance. The young man who is able to control his desire to loaf and be entertained constantly can instead apply himself to his education and the development of skills toward a future career. His self-control can thereby contribute to his self-confidence as he becomes able to satisfy the legitimate masculine ego in an acceptable manner.

The two facets of child training can be represented graphically as follows:

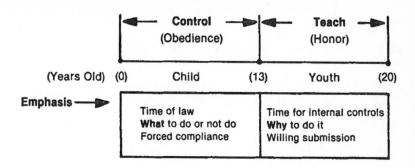

Figure 11.1 The Facets of Child Training

Parents need to emphasize each facet of child training during the proper stage to obtain the maximum results. When parents exercise control over a child until he becomes obedient, they then can be successful in instructing him as a youth. Their success is possible because their child will respect their position of authority and their right to teach him. No one will accept instruction from one for whom he has no respect.

Parents who attempt to reverse this procedure will experience great difficulties. A child who has been taught but not controlled will become less and less teachable. When he is a youth, he is likely to rebel at any attempt to control him. Finally, he can become impossible to control. Attempting to reason with a young child while being permissive toward his disobedience guarantees losing control.

Another way parents risk failure in child training is by extending the control aspect throughout the youth stage while omitting the needed teaching. When a youth is not taught by his parents, he is likely to forsake their standards as he grows older and begins to search for reasons on his own. Without teaching why he should follow the standards set down by the parents, the youth has no way to internalize those standards as his own. It will be many painful years into adulthood before an untaught youth learns on his own by means of experience. Experience may be the best teacher, but it is not the only way to learn. Parents who properly train their children, first by controlling and then by teaching them, can help their children bypass many painful experiences of life.

The emphasis of the two facets of child training definitely match the "child" and "youth" stages of human development. However, there is a certain overlap of both controlling and teaching. A youth who is not obedient must still be controlled, while an obedient child can be taught many standards even when he is quite young. The principle to follow is: **A child is to be controlled as a child as long as he chooses to act like a child, and a child should be taught to the extent he demonstrates obedience and respect.**

The different sexes and even individual children vary in their need for being controlled and their willingness for being taught. Generally, most boys and strong-willed girls will require more intense controls for a longer period than most girls and more passive boys. Children also will undergo cycles consisting of periods when they are more receptive to teaching and other cycles when they require strict controlling. The wise parent will recognize these differences in their children and modify their emphasis accordingly.

Therefore, a more accurate graph of the two facets of child training can be represented:

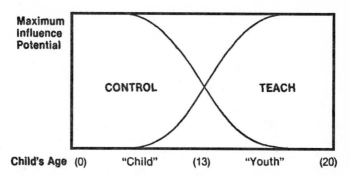

Figure 11.2 Teaching and Controlling Overlap

This graph reflects the overlap of the controlling and teaching phases during childhood. Parents have the natural ability to exert maximum control over a child when he is young. This ability is due to the child's lack of strength, mobility, and knowledge. Parents increasingly lose their ability to exercise control over a child as he becomes older, stronger, and less dependent. Conversely, a young child has a limited ability to comprehend the reasons for his parents' instructions. However, parents can have the maximum influence in teaching a properly trained youth as he increases in knowledge, experience, and the ability to reason.

The time for reason in childhood is after the rules have been understood and repeatedly followed. For example, one of the failures of the "new math" approach to education is due to the introduction of reason before the rules themselves have been mastered by the child. When parents give a child all the reasons for their instructions, he will tend to become confused and unable to remember what to do.

Parents have a God-given time in which to train their children for life. When the two aspects of controlling and teaching are emphasized in the proper order and wisely administered to the child, parents can produce a well-trained young adult. Their success will benefit the child and themselves; more importantly, it will glorify God.

The next section will deal with the mechanics of controlling a child. The control facet is crucial to successful child training. It is also the area most parents fail in handling properly. The majority of parents will do anything to avoid controlling their children, but some will actually overcontrol them. This section will show you how to balance the control of your children.

AUTHOR NOTES TO THE 2ND EDITION

When Do Controls Begin?

From the very first day of the baby's life, either the baby is going to be allowed to determine his own arbitrary schedule; or his parents will decide when he should eat, sleep, and play in a logical, orderly fashion. Since parents have the responsibility to first control and then to train their children; obviously, a parent-directed philosophy of baby care is correct. Of course, this is the exact opposite of the child-centered philosophy that has started so many children in recent generations on their self-centered journey through life. If you would like to learn about a philosophy of baby training that will produce a secure and happy child, while providing a tranquil and orderly home for everyone else, I recommend that your order and study:

- My First 300 Babies, by Gladys Hendrix
    Windsor Publications
    818-358-7557

For difficult potty training solutions, try:

- Toilet Training In Less Than a Day,
    by Ph.D's Azrin & Foxx
        Pockett Books
        1230 Avenue of the Americas
        New York, New York 10020

Transitions

How do you know when to take controls off and just rely on teaching? Let's take the example of potty training. It would be foolish to depend on teaching a little ten-month-old, "Okay Billy, I'm tired of washing diapers so, put on these new training pants and start using this nice blue potty I've bought for you. I'm going to show (teach) you just how to use it, and then expect you to go to the bathroom on your own for now on."

Obviously, removing the controls (diapers), attempting to teach, and holding the child accountable are all being done too early. Instead, the diapers should stay on while the teaching is being done. The child is given frequent opportunities to perform while you are personally controlling the environment. The training pants (a symbol of passing the test and of growing up) are rewarded only for his success. And, accountability is required only after he has demonstrated he has the knowledge and self-discipline to interrupt what he is doing and conduct his business on his own (of course, you are quietly watching for any final instructions he might need).

NOW, you've got it! Everything from making a bed to driving the car has the same elements: You control completely; you teach and let the children try under your watchful eye; and, after, they have fully demonstrated their understanding and maturity, you let them go on their own. If you are wise, you will continue to checkup occasionally on the really serious areas such as: driving a car, choice of friends, entertainment amount and type, quality of work, etc.. Remember, your objective is to work yourself out of the parenting business. This is accomplished when you have trained your children to be self-reliant, responsible, and considerate adults. This can be accomplished by age fifteen or sixteen in most children.

Principle: A child can be taught any time he respects your right to teach him; a child must be kept under control in any area he has not demonstrated that he is responsible.

We are not trying to rear children who are independent (autonomous, fighters for their own rights, observers of few boundaries, self-centered, and insecure — defensive). Our objective is to train up children who are self-reliant (confident within reasonable boundaries, secure, personally responsible for all their own actions, and who accept accountability for their own actions — including any consequences). Street urchins (and plenty of politicians and business people today) are independent. They arrogantly think they don't need anyone since they are survivors by their own cunning, physical strength, wealth, or ruthlessness. What the world needs now is not more characters, but more adults **with** moral character.

Section **FOUR**

CONTROLLING
YOUR CHILDREN

Chapter 12

WHAT CONTROL MEANS

The control aspect of child training is crucial to being a successful parent. The older a child becomes without coming under control, the less chance his parents will have of ever training him. Parents can easily control a little child, but to control a thirteen-year-old youth who has never had to obey, they must exert intense force. This chapter will define what is meant by control and will show how control is, in reality, the expression of parental love.

The Definition of Control

For you to gain and maintain control of your child successfully and correctly, you need to understand fully what control means. A standard definition of control contains such modifiers as "regulate," "hold back; restrain or curb," "verify, as an experiment by comparison with a standard." [1] Control is the force, or pressure, by which you exercise your right of parental rulership — the right to set the standards for, to direct the actions of, and to administer justice to your children. As a parent, you have the legitimate right to exert pressure on your children.

Control is divided into three functions. The first is the power to direct. To control a child means to use the force necessary to cause him to follow your directions. The second function of control is the power to restrain. To control a child means to use pressure to hold him back from what he would do if left to his own will and desires. The third function of control is the pressure that results from the rules (standards) given to the child and by which he is tested and judged. Therefore, we can define child control as the use of power, force, or pressure sufficient to cause a child to follow parental directions: to restrain him from doing that which his parents do not want him to do; and to test him against established standards.

Sometimes pressure is to be applied before the child acts, and other times it is to be applied after his action. When parents give rules to their children and warn them of the consequences of disobedience, those parents are using the advance pressure of direction and restriction. When a child disobeys his parents, their discipline is the "rear" force that is necessary after an action to establish their right to rule.

Children are born without controls. (Remember their need for diapers?) Children must have external controls (diapers) until their internal controls can be developed (toilet training). Similarly, they have the need for external restrictions and the development of internal controls in every other area of their lives. Children need to have controls over what and when they eat, when to sleep, what clothing to wear, how to act, and what is allowed to influence them.

When parents fail to control and then train their children in any area of life, they are doing something similar to not using diapers and never toilet training. You can visualize what lack of controls would mean in this illustration. No one would want to face the consequences of an undiapered baby or change and clean diapers any longer than necessary. Externally controlling children and then teaching them to control themselves is to the advantage of both parents and their children. Training children is always easier than facing the mess that results from a lack of controls.

Controls are like boundaries; they fence out that which is dangerous from an area that is thereby protected. Such an area becomes safe, secure, and peaceful. In other words, there is a quality of freedom within restraints. A toddler left in a playpen is free to play without endangering himself or destroying the rest of the house. Likewise, a child who is restricted from eating the wrong foods and required to go to bed at the proper time is able to enjoy good health and a restful day's activity.

The child who has been restrained from always getting his own way, arguing, throwing temper tantrums, or disobeying is also set free. He is free to enjoy a peaceful co-existence with his family and to develop his individual personality. When a child's outside influences (playmates, school, church, and entertainment) are controlled, he is free to learn the standards for acceptable conduct from his parents without any contradictory information to confuse him.

Children desperately need these boundaries. They are insecure and unhappy without firm guidelines and directions that provide order to their lives and protection from the unknown. Like an adult who wants to know exactly what is expected of him on a new job, a child faces new situations daily and needs his parents' help in setting the boundaries for his acceptable conduct. God's Word declares parental control to be essential:

Proverbs 29:15 *"The rod and reproof give wisdom, but a child left to himself bringeth his mother to shame."*

I Samuel 3:13 *"For I have told him that I will judge his house forever for the iniquity which he knoweth, because his sons made themselves vile, and he restrained them not."*

Control Equals Love

Controlling a child is an expression of parental love — true concern for the benefit of the child. True love will require a personal sacrifice on the part of the parents. They must be willing to take the time to monitor closely the child's behavior. They also must be willing to face the inevitable conflict that occurs when the child must be confronted with his disobedience. The sacrifice involved in controlling a child also includes the instant handling of unplanned interruptions into the parents' life. These interruptions often interfere with what the parents want or need to do. Therefore, loving parents must be more concerned with doing what will best benefit the child rather than what they would like to do to benefit themselves.

Parents have to overcome some natural hindrances to applying force before they can effectively control their children. Anyone in a position of authority is reluctant to apply force to a subordinate for several reasons. One reason is the knowledge that no one can always be right, and another is that parents themselves may be guilty of rebellion against God or His Word.

You can overcome the hindrance of your lack of perfection by realizing that even though imperfect, you have been delegated the responsibility of training your children by God. He knew that you would not be perfect and that not every decision you would make would be right or fair. God's plan is not dependent on your being perfect. You are only responsible to learn God's Word about child training and then apply that knowledge in your life.

The only way to overcome your possible hindrance of rebellion against God is to accept Him and His way as the authority over your life. Your submission to God will require the voluntary setting aside of your own opinions and a commitment to do things His way. It is natural for man to worship his own opinion, and this pride can prevent effective control of children.

Another hindrance to applying force is the parents' fear of rejection by the child and the loss of his love. A child has limited capacity to love anyone outside of himself. True love is the concern for, and the expression of, that concern in doing that which best benefits the object of the love. When a child says "I love you," or "I hate you," he normally is expressing what someone has done for his enjoyment or against him. His "love" is not an expression of desire for the benefit of another.

A child loves himself and will express this love toward anything that pleases him. When he says, "I love candy," what he means is he loves himself and that candy pleases him. A child may tell his parents he hates them when they forbid him to eat candy. What he means is that he loves to give himself candy, their restriction has prevented him from pleasing himself, and he hates not to please himself.

The concept that love results from the satisfying of personal desire is a deception. If parents allow themselves to be deluded by this deception, they will produce self-centered young adults. Parents who provide strict controls over their children's insatiable and self-centered natures are the parents who will eventually receive true appreciation and love from their children. Conversely, parents who give their children everything they want eventually receive the rejection and hatred they sought to avoid by trying to buy love.

Counselors who work with runaway youth have isolated a consistent attitude in many of these children. They have found that these youths usually believe their parents did not love them because the parents would neither restrain nor direct them. They felt rejected because their parents did not care enough about them to protect them from themselves. These parents rejected their parental responsibility, and thereby the youths felt rejected. Delinquent parents produce delinquent youth.

A child inherently equates parental pressure to parental love. His soul has been so designed by God to identify this pressure as being an expression of love and even as verification of the family relationship. Children know they are loved and accepted by parents who care enough to use the necessary pressure to control them. The following article illustrates this point:

> Dear Ann Landers: Every now and then some teen-ager complains about his folks treating him as if he were still in rompers. He resents being asked, "Where are you going?" "Who with?" "When will you be back?"
>
> Well, my folks never ask me any of those questions. I am free to come and go as I please, and I don't like it much. I have the feeling if they really cared about me they would make some rules. But when rules are made, somebody has to enforce them — and that means work. It's easier to let kids run wild.
>
> How I wish my mother would say, "No, you can't go ice-skating with that clod." But she never would. She always says, "It's up to you." I feel frightened and alone because I have too many decisions to make.
>
> I hope those kids whose parents ask a lot of questions and do a lot of bossing know how lucky they are. It

means somebody loves them. — On My Own In Bridgeport, Conn.[2]

Here is a young person who recognizes the need for controls; and that the lack of controls by parents is an indication of no love and concern.

Can it ever be too late to gain control over a youth? Yes. If a child chooses to leave home after he reaches "legal" age, or cannot be kept at home when younger, the parents have lost their chance. They can only wait for the natural discipline of the world to work on such a rebel and pray for God's heavy, but loving, hand to bring him under control. However, as long as a youth lives with his parents and will accept the force needed to bring him under control, there is still hope. If you are facing an apparently hopeless situation with an uncontrolled teenager, Appendix B, "Hope for the Failing Parent," may be of assistance.

Most of you still have time to bring your children under control. However, the sooner you begin, the easier will be the task. The principle is similar to that of controlling any substance that produces pressure. It is infinitely easier to control pressure as it builds than to try to cap a "full head of steam." If you are just beginning to exercise control over a previously uncontrolled youth, brace yourself for some intense conflict (pressure). Never lose sight of the importance of winning this conflict. The cost to your child for not bringing him under control is more than you would want to pay.

The next chapter will explain how parents can establish control over their children at an early age and not need to fight for that control as their children grow older.

AUTHOR NOTES TO THE 2ND EDITION

As our nation's people move away from God's Word as their manual for living, more and more parents choose one of two extremes in child training: lenient (permissive); or strict (intolerant or over-protective). Of course, there are always a few parents who follow the Word of God correctly, or who luck onto some of the important principles by reasoning or observation.

There are many more "lenients" than "stricts" in parenting today, so they harm more children than do the "stricts." "Lenients" produce thousands of self-centered, egotistical adults each year who each have an insatiable desire for self-gratification (the "me" and "x" generation). On the other end of the imbalance, the "stricts" produce fewer in numbers, but the most in seriously-damaged souls. Among their contributions are uptight perfectionists and compulsive/obsessive personalities. It is these adults that psychologists and psychiatrists often counsel and therefore determine that any kind of controls are evil, especially if corporal punishment and/or the Bible has been mentioned. The proper control stage of child training is necessarily strict, but it is always done for the child's benefit and it diminishes as the child becomes more mature. The problem is that "stricts" won't ever let go.

Let's examine the motivation and tactics of these two off-balanced extremes, to see how to avoid them in our child training.

Too Little Control

Permissive parents usually cater to their child's every whim (they may be trying to compensate for their own parents' strict parenting). They pretend that the child doesn't have a sin nature. When their child misbehaves, they excuse him by saying, "He's just a baby and doesn't know better." Or, "Children will just be children." They will go to great extent to avoid any conflict that might train the child. Mother will blow up a swimming pool to place under her toddler's high chair. She would rather clean up after her son, than train him to eat properly. This is the same parent who puts the Christmas tree in a play pen (so the child can't reach it) rather than train the child it is not to be touched.

The children of permissive parents normally grow up to be unruly, rude, insensitive to others, slaves to their own sin natures, and self-centered. As adults these sons and daughters frequently fail to assume personal responsibility or accept accountability for their own actions. Sons often expect the world to cater to their whims just as Mom and Dad did. They have trouble holding jobs and many have trouble with the law. Daughters usually grow up spoiled, vain, and self-centered. They make terrible wives and mothers themselves. Is there no hope for these untrained children? By God's grace, some of these young adults begin to grow up once they have experienced the harsh realities of life. The school of hard knocks tend to either harden or break; but it is a harsh teacher. It is far better to be trained by a loving parent.

Often, permissive parents will use manipulation to get their way without using their authority. Manipulative parents often coax, plead, and attempt to persuade their child by reason to do what they wish. They may threaten punishment for disobedience, but they usually try to avoid following through with their threats. These parents make authority look like a joke. By ignoring their child's disobedience and sin nature traits they encourage his poor behavior. A mother may say to her two-year-old, "Sweetie, if you touch the pretty vase it might break and hurt you." This mother foolishly (or naively) presumes her many words will persuade her child, but they actually make no sense to a two-year-old. When he reaches for the vase again, mother will then say, "**Please** honey, Mommy wants to leave the vase there. You don't want Mommy to have to move the vase do you?" And so on, and so on until the vase is finally broken. At this point the non-authoritative mother will sometimes punish her child in anger. This lesson may teach the child that he will be severely punished for broken vases, but it will never teach him to obey his mother's instructions. The poor child never heard mother just say, "no!"

Parents who will not insist that their instructions are to be obeyed the first time they state them, make their words appear like just a game. The name of the game is "Battle of the Wits" and the contestants are the children against the parents. The winner of the game is he who is the smartest and more cunningly convincing. Since most children are far more cunning than their non-authoritative parents, they are usually the winners. However, when these children win, they actually loose. Children need dependable boundaries so they know where they stand. When there are no definitive rules the children are uncertain as to what is right and what is wrong. Because non-authoritative parents provide their children with an uncertain world, some of them become frightened, whiney, and nervous. Smarter children learn how to out-manipulate, out-persuade, and out-con their parents. These become the teenagers whose mothers say, "I can't do anything with him, he has never listened to me!"

Many parents don't realize what it takes to follow through with controlling a child. Let's say you tell your five-year-old daughter that you want her to go upstairs and brush her teeth. You have shown her how to brush several times and have even stood by while she demonstrated her ability to do the job, as well as you could expect of a five-year-old. Most parents will stop their training at this point and naively expect their daughter to brush her teeth, conscientiously improving her performance each year thereafter.

This would be fine if children were robots that merely needed programming — but they are not. The wise parent knows "the child" and her child. She knows "the child" has a will of its own and a sin nature that tempts it to sin. She may know that her child has a tendency for playfulness and willfulness. Therefore the parent's control responsibility is not over until her child has consistently demonstrated self-control and willing submissiveness — i.e. conducts herself responsibly and maturely, at least in this area. **Control means to test and verify!**

But, what about trust, you say? Won't my little girl think that I don't trust her if I check up? Children must be trained to control their sin nature and their own will before they can become trustworthy. Trust is not to be given away, it must be earned step by step. *"Well done, good and faithful servant; thou hast been faithful over a few things, I will make thee ruler over many things"*

(Matthew 25:23). NOTICE: First comes the test for faithfulness as the basis for trust.

Therefore, parents need to be suspicious that their children are likely to succumb to their own will and/or sin nature until properly trained — especially during the entire "child" stage. The procedure for success is: to direct; restrain, and **test** that the directions have been followed and the restraints have been observed. The exercise could go something like this: "Mary, please go upstairs and brush you teeth by yourself (Direction). I don't want you to play around, but to do a good job like I have taught you (Restrict). I'll be up soon to see how you're doing (Check-up)." Once the follow through is complete, true training by control has occurred. Either the little girl is found trustworthy, or deficient, and corrective action is taken. Additional checks may be necessary depending on the immaturity level of the child.

Too Much Control

"Strict" parents may have become that way because of the inability to control temptations in their teen years, or because of their lack of personal success during adulthood. They are intolerant and over-protective of their children because they don't want them to fail like they did. Also, parents who experienced deprivation in their childhood are sometimes over-protective because they don't want their children to suffer as they did. Adults who grew up between 1925 and 1945 experienced the Great Depression and a World War. It's hard to grasp what they went through; but this period of history produced men and women of exceptional moral character — honest, hard working, competent, and covenant keepers (from hand-shake commitments to marriage vows). Sadly, many of these adults protected their own children from experiencing any type of pressure that might produce the same good character in them. (Those untrained children produced a second generation of untrained children who are now producing a third generation.)

Parents who overcome their own deprivation often spoil the next generation with over-indulgence of things and protection from reality. Humans have to learn some things through failure.

When man has overcome a dehibilitating situation (lack of education, a depression, bankruptcy, or a personal handicap, he tends to become proud and think he can overcome anything by his own power.

One area that Virginia and I over-protected our children was concerning the trials and pressures that came into our life. When we were down to our last dollar and sold our lawn mower to buy food we never told the kids (don't want to worry them you know — or maybe we were too proud to let them know how desperate we were). We prayed for God's help, He did, and we gave Him the glory. We only told the kids that He had brought a buyer for the lawn mower. But, they never knew how deep was our need; they didn't have the opportunity to pray and see God's answer for themselves. We had unknowlingly cheated them out of a Spiritual lesson.

Our children never knew of my committment to serve God with my whole life, never knew what financial gain we gave up along the way, and never experienced the peace and security He provided through every trial He took us through. God's abundance was always so gracious, our children probably gave the credit to me. All because we over-protected our children.

Most mothers are naturally over-protective parents. This is due to several reasons:

1) Women are natural caretakers — they protect, comfort, encourage, nurse, feed, and clean their little ones. They have to be taught when to modify, or to withhold, this "natural love" for their children's best interest (Titus 2:4).

2) Woman was cursed in the garden with the strong desire to control her husband, **but** he is to rule over her (Genesis 3:16). I believe the frustration some women experience with being subordinate to their husbands, is redirected to over controlling their children — especially little boys.

3) Women are naturally detail-conscious and, therefore, tend to see every little infraction or potential danger to their children's lives as if through a microscope. A hus-

band acting in the responsible role as father is essential to balance the natural tendencies of the mother.

Example

An over-protective mother may simply wish to protect her children from the dangers of this world, but she goes to far. She almost always gives her children the impression that they will be hurt or embarrassed severely if they try to do anything without her help. She worries over things that have not happened, hovers over her children in order to prevent them from making mistakes, and smothers them with her excessive doting. When the children do attempt to do something on their own, she may also point out how it could have been done better. Thus, they are driven toward giving up, or toward debilitating perfectionism. This mother "protects" her son by refusing to let him play in sports activities and she discourages her daughter from learning to cook, because she might mess it up or get burned. The children of an over-protective mother will often become rebellious in their adolescent years as they desire to function on their own. "Mother, I would rather do it myself."

Some children of an over-protective mother will grow up to be rebellious, but others become perfectionists who fear failure so much that they refuse to try anything new. Such children are often unable to think for themselves, are very passive, and have little individual initiative. Their joy in life is severely stunted. Even as adults they will wait to be told what to do or will expect others to take care of them. Many of them continue to live at home into their adulthood, not able to leave the nurturing of Mommy. Over-protectiveness is particularly harmful to sons because it inhibits their manhood and tends to cause them to become effeminate. Adult sons who have been over-protected tend to marry women who will take over where Mommy left off, or they may even become homosexuals. They normally have little respect for women in general, and yet fear them as well. Biblical child training principles can be self-applied by any adult who identifies himself with this type of upbringing.

FOOTNOTES

[1]   *Oxford English Dictionary, s.v. "control."*

[2]   *Austin* (Texas) *American Statesman,* May 4, 1980.

Chapter **13**

WHERE DO I BEGIN?

This chapter will answer the question of when and how to establish and then to maintain parental control. The optimum time to begin, of course, is when a child is still an infant.

It is important for parents to cause their child to respond to their word as young as possible. The child's response should be immediate upon the parents' command. One of the reasons for establishing parental control is to be able to protect a child from imminent danger. A young child can get himself in trouble in a split second. He can dash into the street, reach out for a hot stove, or climb onto a chair before his mother can physically catch him.

Requiring a little child to respond **instantly** to the parent's command of "no" could prevent his injury, or even his death. It should not be necessary for a child to burn his hand badly or receive other injuries to learn the lessons of life. An infant can be taught to respond to his parent's firm command of "no" at a very young age.

A wriggling six-month-old baby who intentionally refuses

to be diapered can be taught the meaning of "no" in one or two simple lessons. When he tries to crawl away during a changing, he can be told "no," pulled back, and held in place for a moment. The next time he tries to crawl away, he should be told "no" once firmly and lightly tapped once or twice on the upper leg with a small switch. The shocked look and tears will indicate you got his attention and that the command "no" has taken on a real meaning. An angry cry and continued squirming may indicate a strong-willed child who will require more pressure in both intensity and frequency. After the child has been diapered, he should be held and comforted. This process should be repeated as often as necessary until he responds to the command alone. Of course, you could turn this into a fun playtime for you — chasing the baby, pulling him back, and laughing with his sweet giggle — but then he wouldn't learn his first lesson in self-discipline. Also, he won't understand the times you won't play because you don't have time or because he's a real mess.

A child needs to learn that his disobedience results in receiving his parents' disapproval. The parents' controlled use of pain is not cruel and will not cause the child to fear his parents personally. He will only learn to respect their word and the authority they possess. The child soon learns that the choice is his. If he chooses willfully to ignore the commands, he chooses to receive pain. The minor discomfort a child must experience in order to learn to obey his parents' command will save him much pain in the future.

Parents should not hesitate to establish a healthy respect for their authority as soon as the child is capable of doing what is expected of him. The commands "stop" and "come" can be added to a child's vocabulary of obedience words even before he can speak. These words become an external control by which parents can protect the child from danger. The child who learns to respect his parents' word while young can be directed away from unseen dangers throughout his later childhood.

When a young child learns to obey the commands of "no," "stop," and "come," he can easily be taught the boundaries of his exploration. He can be taught not to touch such potential dangers as electrical cords, wall sockets, hot items, or fence gates. It is not necessary that he understands why these things are dangerous at this point, only that it is painful to disobey his parents. Imagine trying to explain to a two-year-old why he should not stick a hair pin in an electrical socket. Parents could never explain all of life's dangers to their children; therefore, children must learn to accept warnings without question.

Of course, a child should never be exposed to potential danger without dependable supervision being present. For example, an infant requires almost constant supervision and external controls to protect him. On the other hand, a young child can be left unsupervised in an area where he understands the dangers present and has proven that he will avoid them. Very simply, the parent must never allow a child to be tested beyond his ability to comprehend exactly what is "off limits," or beyond his willingness to observe his parents' restrictions.

You would not put a pair of scissors in a child's playpen and expect him not to play with them. Likewise, do not subject your children at any age to tests for which the consequence of failure is too severe for the lesson learned. Even parents of a teenager must continue to provide controls for things that are beyond their ability to explain to the child. A teenager can no more understand the consequences of his association with the wrong peer group than the toddler can understand why he should not play with the scissors. Do not hesitate to act as an external control whenever the pain to your child, or to others he might affect, is beyond his comprehension.

Learning obedience is not only for a child's protection. It is also the basis for controlling him while he is being taught to conform to his parents' standards. A child needs to learn at the very beginning that it is not his will or wants that will dictate policy in the home, but the will of his parents.

Parents are infinitely more qualified to know what is best for even the most intelligent child. Experience has taught them much about life. They will always be ahead of their child in experience. This experience and their position of parental authority provide the qualifications for them to set policy. Parents who consider themselves under-educated or not intelligent should never allow this thinking to prevent them from controlling their child. Parents know better than a child what he truly needs.

Never deal with your child on the basis of his "wants," but on the basis of what he "needs." Teach your child early in life that you will always respond to what he needs, but that much of what he wants probably will be denied. Never give in to a child who is begging for something he wants. Play down his wants by asking him instead what he needs and by teaching him how to make his legitimate needs properly known. This teaching will help him develop the self-control that can lead to self-discipline.

When a child consistently and instantly obeys his parents on command, he has learned the most important standard. In other words, he has learned that his parents are in charge and that their word is law. This fact of life can be taught to children early in life, but it will be challenged time and time again. Every time parents attempt to direct their child against his will or restrict him from what he wants, they should be prepared to re-establish their right to rule.

Again, establishing parental control should begin when a child is quite young. But, what do you do with a child who is already several years old, perhaps even in adolescence? The principle is still the same. Children must be brought under control before teaching can begin. A child must respect the word of his parents before he can be taught; and before he will respect their word, he must first obey their word. Therefore, the first stage for even the older child is to be required to obey his parents' commands — instantly and without back talk.

Every child has a will of his own and strong desires, both of which are driven by his inherent nature of sin. To bring a child under control and then maintain control, parents need to be aware that there will be conflict. This conflict will normally exist throughout most of the "child" stage. The next chapter explains how to evaluate this conflict.

Chapter 14

EVALUATING THE CONFLICT

Attempting to control your child (to direct or restrict his activities) will inevitably create conflict. Most normal people do not enjoy conflict and would prefer to avoid it at almost any cost. As a parent, you must overcome this natural tendency for the sake of your child. This can be accomplished only when you firmly establish that the objective of training your children is more important than avoiding undesirable conflicts. Facing conflict is simply a part of the cost you must pay in order to succeed in reaching the goal.

Parents must face the fact that conflict will exist in child training partly because there is more than one will involved. Marriage has certain conflicts because there are two wills. Business partnerships have conflicts. The board of directors of most corporations consists of an odd number of members. This odd number is a provision to ensure that issues can be decided even when almost 50% maybe against them. When there is more than one person involved, there is always the potential for conflict.

The second major cause of conflict is the child's strong desire and constant temptation to try to satisfy what he wants (discussed in Chapter 8, "The Child's Nature"). The child's natural inclination toward self-centeredness will be in opposition to many parental controls. He can be expected to lust for sweets and junk food while rejecting foods that are good for him. He will strongly desire to be the center of attention. He can be expected to consider his own play and entertainment more important than anything his parents might want him to do, such as sleep, dress, eat, take a bath, or go to the bathroom. When parents interfere with their child's selfish and perpetual pursuit of happiness, conflict will be the result. The point of conflict can be depicted as follows:

Figure 14.1 Child-Parent Conflict

Parenting, like any position of leadership, has a goal to reach. The conflict of wills that results when anyone in leadership attempts to direct or restrict the activities of others is equivalent to the obstacles that must be conquered in any other human endeavor. Nothing of value can be attained without facing and resolving those problems that hinder progress.

Likewise, an athlete must conquer any obstacle to his self-discipline in order to become a winner. He must restrict his diet, push himself physically to build and condition his muscles, and overcome any mental obstacles that might prevent his winning. Parents should view the conflict that will result when they establish and maintain control over their children as their major obstacle in child training.

Recognizing conflict as a type of problem allows us to solve it like any other problem. There are three basic steps to problem solving. The first step is to identify the problem. This means to separate the problem from its symptoms and to isolate it from any other problems. The second step is to evaluate the problem and to determine its importance, the method and cost of its solution, or whether the goal can be reached by by-passing the obstacle altogether. The third and final step is to take the action necessary to solve the problem.

It is easy to identify conflict as being a problem. You give your child an instruction, he argues and applies pressure, and you end up with a headache. Or, you repeatedly warn your child to stop doing something that annoys you until, out of frustration, you lose control and wrongly hit him in anger. Finally, you may tire of the headaches, frustration, and emotional hangover that result from repeated conflicts with your children. Therefore, you give up on training your child and just let him have his own way.

Evaluation of the problem is more complex than identification of the problem. Why is it true that if children intrinsically desire to be controlled, they fight so hard against those controls? The answer to this question can be found in ourselves. Adults fight against any external attempt (diet, good advice, conscience, etc.) to restrict their wants, but after they indulge they wish someone would have stopped them.

This dichotomy between the desiring of autonomy during temptation and the longing for controls after it is too late is simply a fact of human nature. The old parental adage, "I know you don't understand now why it is good for you, but when you grow up you will thank me," states the correct parental position. It is difficult enough for adults to exercise self-control. Adults have already experienced harmful results from doing what was not good for them, and yet they still have difficulty in preventing future recurrences of the error. It is ridiculous to expect children to control themselves to avoid future consequences they have never experienced. Expecting a child to brush his teeth well because of the threat of tooth decay is unrealistic. Parents **must** control the child so that he will do what they know is right for him in the long run.

In further evaluating the problem of conflict, we can see why conflict is inevitable when any true child training takes place. First of all, the child has a will of his own. He has the power to choose a course of action independent of any outside influence. In demonstrating this independence, children can ignore such obstacles as furniture and people in their rush to get where they want to go. Children may try to get their way by throwing temper tantrums so severe that they black out from holding their breath. Children will often exert their independence in the face of certain danger such as by defying a promised whipping by immediately disobeying.

For parents to be successful in training their child, they must direct him according to their will. Often their directions will not be the way the child wants to go. The result of this difference of will is conflict. Parents would be naive to expect their children to receive their instructions with joy in their hearts and smiles on their faces. Child training just does not happen this way. Instead, parents need to expect conflict and learn how it can be conquered.

The Result of Winning the Conflict

Now that we have analyzed the nature of the child-parent conflict, we need to recognize that conflict is unavoidable if we are to reach our goal of training children. This obstacle cannot be by-passed, in fact, conflict itself is an integral part of the training process.

Child training is not just a matter of winning battles; it is actually altering the nature of children. This alteration results from consistently directing children in paths different from the ones they would have chosen on the basis of their own wants. Therefore, the points of conflict represent the points of change. Parents actually should welcome these confrontations as opportunities to effect the necessary changes. The sooner these confrontations occur and the more intense they are, the sooner a child can be brought under control. From then on, training can be completed in a much more peaceful atmosphere.

The turning point when a child actually chooses to accept the rulership of his parents is his year of decision. It sometimes is preceded by the most traumatic year yet experienced in the training of that child. Therefore, do not lose heart and back off from the pressure when conflicts intensify for a period of time. The last battle in a war is often the most intense. This final challenge to your rulership is a test by the child to determine your worthiness to lead him. He needs to sense that you love him enough to trust you with his life.

As soon as a child knows his parents are in control, he becomes secure. It is no longer necessary for him to push against the restraints to determine if they are strong enough to hold. It becomes obvious to him that his parents love him enough to protect and give him the best. Even though he will still occasionally test his parents for confirmation, the conflicts generally will be over.

The preceding analysis of conflict as a problem in child training should help you understand its nature. It also should enable you to realize that conflict is not an obstacle that can be avoided since it is actually a part of the training process. As such, it is a problem that is not only important, but one that must be solved regardless of the cost to you.

What then is the correct method for solving the problem of conflict? The rest of this section will deal with the solution for conflict as defined in God's Word. God's method is not only the correct method, but also the **only** method by which parents can successfully solve the problem of conflict. Once parents fully understand the mechanics for overcoming conflict, they only need to commit themselves to use them consistently in order to become successful in controlling their children.

AUTHOR NOTES TO THE 2ND EDITION

WELCOME CONFLICT AS TRAINING OPPORTUNITIES.

1. Look forward to your excitable four-year-old bursting into the room talking and interrupting your conversation. (It could be with your insurance agent, your mate, or even a sibling.)

   a. Unless the house is on fire or the baby has crawled into the street, this is training time.

   b. Excuse yourself, firmly take your child, and head for a quiet room.

   c. Teach the child what it means to consider others more important than yourself and about humility. Also teach him about self-discipline and the proper way to enter an occupied room.

   d. Return to the main room and allow your son to apologize to your guest (in keeping with his maturity).

e. Let him sit down or leave the room for awhile until
    you are ready to acknowledge him and let him tell
    you what he wanted. Of course, he is learning self-
    discipline and humility through this wait.

Some mothers will wince at not giving their baby
instant attention and even for what they consider sham-
ing him in front of company; but fulfilling a child's self-
centered desires and helping him avoid accountability
will not create a quality character in him. Remember
that he chose the stage for his shameful interruption.

You might say, "But what if he is hyperactive and can't
help himself?" Hyperactive is a psychological classifica-
tion of students that qualifies a school district to receive
additional funds from the Federal Government.
Hyperactivity is not a disease caused by some new virus.
In most cases, it is a condition of the soul brought on by
allowing children to live the first six to eight, self-centered years of their life without parental controls, and
without being required to develop **any** self-discipline.
Some of this condition can also be duplicated in children
who exist on a diet of sugar-rich foods and caffeine-
loaded drinks.

We have had an epidemic of children diagnosed hyper-
active because our country's children live on junk food,
aren't trained in self-control, have no fear of authority,
and whose schools benefit from the tag. Aside from a few
(perhaps 1%) of all students who have a physiological
predisposition to fidgeting and nervousness, hyperactivity is a label that helps teachers and parents not to take
responsibility to control the tyrants they have raised. It
is sad that these children will have to wear this label
and attend dumbed-down classes for years through no
fault of their own.

Testimony

"I have a degree in social work and my husband is a
physician, but we didn't know how to deal with our prob-

lem son until we read your book. He was totally withdrawn from the time of his adoption at 2 1/2 months — no eye contact until months later, rarely smiled, and didn't even cry when we left him in someone else's care. At 11 months he began acting hyperactive — banging, climbing, and getting into things. His aggression to others was alarming — constantly hitting, biting, and spitting.

I spanked him with my hand, but also loaded him with love. The more I excused his behavior, tried to be loving and accepting, the worse he got! The societal answer would have been Ritalin, attention deficit disorder labels, and special classes. But, Biblical discipline has turned the tide, redirecting his life toward well-adjustment. Thank you!"

Ginger Garbacz

NOTE: "A child put on drug therapy (i.e., Ritalin, Dexedrine, etc.) will outgrow the sedating effects around the age of 12 or 13. Now you have a child who is older and more difficult to deal with."

William W. Halcomb, D.O.
Texas

Ritalin Pharmaceutical Product Description

Actions: "A mild central nervous system stimulant. The mode of action in man is not completely understood, but Ritalin presumably activates the brain stem arousal system and cortex to produce its stimulant effect.

There is neither specific evidence which clearly establishes the mechanism whereby Ritalin produces its mental and behavioral effects in children, nor conclusive evidence regarding how these effects relate to the condition of the central nervous system."

Warnings: Too many to list here.

CIBA Pharmaceutical Company
Summit, New Jersey 07901

2. Look forward to the twins getting into a verbal donny-brook in the other room while you are cooking a three-burner dinner. It would be easy to ignore them, if they just don't yell your name. Maybe they will quit if you yell real mad-like to stop. Don't — you will be avoiding a training opportunity.

   a. Turn off the fires, the meal won't be ruined and even if it is, your children's life-long character is much more important than one meal.

   b. Go and deal with the twins according to your pre-set standards, like: thou shalt not fight or even argue loudly with each other or you **both** will be punished. This way you will have two helpers to prevent the next altercation. (We are too smart to worry about who started it. It takes two to tango, so they know if they are both heard or seen fighting, they both will be judged guilty.) Punishment can be separation for a period of time for the first offense. However, it will probably require chastisement before it becomes worth it to them to exercise self-control over their emotions. Fighting and quarreling comes from the uncontrolled sin nature (James 4:1-3). Don't allow it!

3. Look forward to your little Miss Chatty Cathy talking in church after being carefully coached not to, and even warned of the consequences. (Do you remember when whole families used to sit together for the main church service? Not only did the children learn self-discipline, I think they learned that worship was important to Mom and even to Dad.)

   a. Forget your pride, your child's training is more important; after being trained, she will make you legitimately proud of her.

   b. Quietly remove her from the sanctuary to the rest room, an unused room, outside, or to the car. She should be taught about her selfishness (bothering others), rudeness (to the pastor), and lack of self-control. Chastisement, or warning of chastisement, should be followed by returning to the church service after she has regained composure. Missing part of a service on one or two Sundays is nothing compared to training your daughter in maturity.

4. Look forward to the time when your reckless and somewhat clumsy son spills his tray of food at a fast service place **because he was rushing to beat his sister to the choice seat.** You could yell at the child and insult him for his carelessness — thereby making a fool out of yourself for exposing your hurt pride and embarrassment; and belittling your son just like the Bible says not to do (Colossians 3:21 & Eph. 6:42). WRONG!

    a. Your son dropped the tray, not you. Your don't need to raise your voice or heighten his embarrassment any more. Simply and quietly give him the instructions to pick up and throw away everything that he dropped, and ask the manager for a mop to clean up any mess. Make sure he does as much of the work as possible to learn the consequences of his recklessness. Simply refuse the busboy's offer to clean it up for you, if offered.

    b. Don't acknowledge any excuses from your son about how he thinks he tripped. Tell him that you will discuss it later.

    c. He either buys his own meal, misses his meal, or receives Dad's grace in re-buying the meal, depending on his accountability (i.e. is this the first time, or has he ignored less painful warnings in the past?).

    d. Don't let Mom help him. Her compassion will probably want to excuse him because of his suffering.

    e. Afterward, privately tell him why he spilled the tray.

You wouldn't think of deliberately setting a child up for an embarrassing situation like this, but such naturally occurring training experiences can impact a young child positively for **life**, especially if he is a little insensitive to normal correction.

Chapter 15

REBELLION

We have analyzed the conflict that occurs when parents attempt to control their children. This conflict is the result of a child's rebellion. Rebellion, formally defined, is "(the act of) open or determined defiance of, or resistance to, any authority or controlling power."[1] Parents must learn to recognize the ways children express their rebellion and how to handle rebellion when it occurs.

Rebellion is the willful rejection of authority expressed either actively or passively. In other words, a child is obviously in rebellion when he says "no" to your instructions, hits you, or acts in direct disobedience. But, he is also in rebellion when he continuously chooses to ignore or "forget" your instructions. When a child consistently "forgets," he actually is choosing not to remember. Your word simply is not important enough to keep in his mind.

One example of active rebellion is when your child will not listen to, or accept, your instructions. The typical expression of such rebellion is when he "throws a fit," responds with "no" or "I won't," or defiantly walks away while you are still talking. None of these overt demonstrations of disrespect should ever be tolerated. Your child should be required to listen quietly to your instructions without back talk or complaint. When he continues to play (or otherwise focuses his attention away from you), chatters, or ignores you when you are giving him instructions, he is also expressing rebellion. Your child should be required to pay strict attention to you by looking you in the eyes and verbally acknowledging his acceptance of your instructions with an attitude of respect. If you demand respect to be shown by his saying "Yes, ma'am" or "Yes, sir," you will gradually make respect a part of his manner.

Another example of active rebellion is when your child will not accept your correction. He may refuse to accept your reproof for some action or attitude of his by stubbornly avoiding the acceptance of his guilt, He might argue with you, charging that it was really not his fault; it was someone else's fault, even your own, that caused him to do whatever it was for which he was accused. Some children will "clam up" instead of arguing. Their unwillingness to admit their wrongdoing and to thereby agree with your reproof is a silent act of active rebellion.

Passive rebellion is practiced by children when they meet the external requirements for obedience, but internally are resentful. It has sometimes been described as sitting down on the outside while standing up on the inside. This type of rebellion begins in the child's hidden mental attitude, but eventually will surface in his facial expressions of disrespect, disgust, or anger.

Passive rebellion can be expressed by a child who politely listens to your instructions, but who consistently fails to follow them without reminders, threats, or pressure. Girls are most prone to this type of rebellion. They nod their heads sweetly and say, "Yes, Mommy." When they are later caught not following the instructions, they declare that they were just about to do it, or that they forgot. The most subtle form of passive rebellion is to wait to obey until just before getting into trouble. A child considers that it is a victory of his own will over the will of his parents when he does not obey until he himself decides to do so.

Another subtle form of passive rebellion is to do **what** is required, but not in the **way** it should have been done. A child should be trained that obedience is not just following instructions; obedience includes following instructions in the right way. Often children will assert their own will when carrying out instructions by doing it their own way. They only partially follow the instructions and then improvise by adding something or doing it however they want. Obedience is not the place for creativity. It is the place for strict compliance (1 Samuel 15:22, 23).

Some children would not dare to disobey openly or even talk back to their parents. Instead they seethe on the inside. This type of internal rebellion will often reveal itself in facial expressions. Such children will act melancholy and have the disposition of a lemon. They will withdraw, sulk, pout, and in general make everyone around them miserable for not having their own way. This type of rebellion must be drawn out into the open so that it can be overcome. If it is not, it is likely to explode in the teenage years. Parents must be aware of the potential danger in a quiet but sullen child!

Basically the principle is that a child is in rebellion any time he **knowingly and willingly** places his will above the stated will of his parents. When a child deliberately refuses to accept his parents' right to rule, he is choosing to be rebellious.

Rebellion is the Overthrow of Authority

The conflict of rebellion will occur naturally in the process of child training. On the one hand, parents must direct and control their children in order to train them. They not only have this right; they are responsible to use it (as discussed in Chapters 5 and 6, "Parental Authority" and "Parental Responsibility"). On the other hand, children possess a will of their own plus the powerful temptations of their sinful nature.

Parents are not responsible for the conflict, the child is. Children are to be obedient to the parents *"in all things."* When parents are simply exercising their God-given right of rulership and conflict results, it is the child who has chosen to revolt. He has chosen to challenge the parents' right to rule him and thus has become his own authority. He has rejected their external control and has come completely under the control of his own sinful nature. Rebellion could be pictured as:

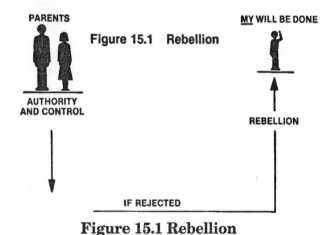

Figure 15.1 Rebellion

Figure 15.1 depicts the fact that the child no longer is under authority, but has placed himself on an equal level with his parents. When this occurs it is similar to Satan's rebellion when he said, *"I will be like the most High"* (Isaiah 14:14). The phrase "Most High" is the title of God's ultimate authority — His absolute right to rule. Satan has said in effect, "No longer do you have the right to rule me. I will become like you. I will place myself on your level. No longer do I have to take your commands. No longer do I have to follow and be obedient to you." Rebellion is a conflict of two opposing wills. It is the expression of the will of the one under authority against the will of the one in authority. Every child has a will of his own. He chooses when and whom to obey. At whatever point a child chooses to rebel, his parents must utilize sufficient force to put down the revolt immediately. God's Word equates the sin of rebellion with witchcraft, indicating that Satan has a part in all rebellion.

1 Samuel 15:23a "For rebellion is as the sin of witchcraft,"

Child rebellion is the willful attempt by a child to overthrow parental authority. If rebellion is not put down, revolution will occur. Revolution is the **complete** overthrow of authority. When a child places himself on an equal position with the parents and is allowed to remain there, revolution has come to pass.

From this position, some children actually take over the rulership of their parents. They control the family, demanding to be the center of attention, and they may even dictate what the parents can or cannot do. When a child can throw temper tantrums to get his own way or is able to tell his parents to shut up, for example, complete overthrow of parental authority has occurred. Revolution destroys the orderly arrangement ordained by God and will result in chaos and cursing for both parents and child.

The Wrong Way to Deal with Rebellion

After a child has successfully overthrown his parents' authority, they can only negotiate with him or attempt to manipulate him in order to get him to do anything other than what he wants to do. Households where such a revolution has taken place are chaos. The children in that home control their own bedtime, diet, dress, entertainment, and almost every other issue. The parents have been reduced to counselors whose advice can simply be refused. Since these parents have lost the authority over their children, they may try to appeal to the undeveloped reasoning abilities of the children in an attempt to direct them. Such parents try unsuccessfully to convince their children to do the right thing or to do what in their opinion would be best for them. Of course, a rebellious child will consistently choose only to do what pleases himself.

When the reasoning approach fails, these parents have only one recourse left. They must now attempt to manipulate their children by means of bribes, threats, or deceit. They offer to give them something they want in return for obedience. Or they threaten them with the loss of something they want unless they cooperate. Bribery is the feeding of one sin nature desire in an attempt to control another, for example, offering candy, or any other treat, to a child if he will do what he should do or stop doing what he should not do. Bribery will never help a child to develop the internal controls he needs for life. Only exercise in controlling his will develops self-discipline.

Many parents who have lost their right to rule resort to manipulating the child indirectly. This manipulation is accomplished by playing on the child's emotions, by using mental deception, or by using the weakness of the child's own sinful nature. Such techniques include withholding any demonstration of love or approval in an attempt to make the child "feel" guilty, tricking the child by use of the parents' superior intellect, or playing on the child's jealousy, pride, anger, or other evil drive. Redirecting the child's interest from an unacceptable activity to an acceptable activity is also a form of manipulation. It is a legitimate technique to use when no conflict exists, but redirection will not train a child in self-control and should never be used with one who is being rebellious.

It is no wonder that children who have been raised in this type of environment have no respect for their parents. They were denied external control when it was needed and were not trained to develop the self-control without which they now suffer. No one can respect or honor any person in leadership who abdicates his right to rule and resorts instead to manipulation to get his way.

Leadership requires a direct, open approach — one that clearly defines the rules to be followed and decisively eliminates all rebellion. Child rebellion must not be tolerated by parental authorities. God has provided parents with the right and the power to maintain their position of authority. God's Word defines the only solution to the problem of rebellion, as will be discussed in detail in the following chapters. A summary of the principles of control and rebellion will prepare for such a discussion.

Summary

- Parents have been given their responsibility by God, and are accountable to Him, to train their children according to His standards.

- Children are commanded by God to obey their parents *"in all things."*

- Parents have the authority (right to rule) over their children. This means they have the right to make the rules and to command their children to follow them. It also means they have the power to administer justice, to punish for disobedience or to reward for conformity to their commands.

• However, children have a will of their own. They want to rule themselves according to their own desires.

• Children also possess the internal nature of sin. This nature relentlessly tempts them to feed the desires of their flesh — the lust for attention, power, and self-gratification.

• The parents' responsibility to direct and control their child is in direct opposition to the will and nature of the child. As a result, conflict will occur. When parents attempt to direct their child's activities, it often conflicts with what he wills. When they restrict his desires, it conflicts with what his sinful nature wants.

• When a child rejects his parents' authority (the right to rule him) he has created the conflict called rebellion.

• Rebellion is the act of open resistance to authority or opposition to its controls. In children, it is their rejection of the parents' right to rule them.

• Children actively express their rebellion by willful defiance: not listening, arguing, talking back, refusing to answer, walking or running away, hitting, throwing temper tantrums, refusing verbally, or disobeying directly.

• Children passively express their rebellion by consistently forgetting instructions, waiting until they are ready to obey, not obeying in the right way, or obeying externally while seething internally.

- Parents cannot solve the problem of a child's rebellion by reason, bribes, redirecting his attention, playing on his emotions or sinful nature, intimidation, deception, or manipulating him in any way.

- Parents can neither avoid the problem of a child's rebellion nor attempt to negotiate with it. Rebellion must be conquered.

- Conquering rebellion means to re-establish parental authority. Parents must be willing to apply enough force to cause the rebellious child to choose to do the parent's will instead of continuing to choose to rebel.

The force defined in God's Word that is to be used by parents to control children when they rebel is "chastisement." This force will be explained in the following chapters that cover one of the most important concepts in this book. The proper use of chastisement will make the difference between success and failure in training children.

AUTHOR NOTES TO THE 2ND EDITION

Examples of Rebellion

1. My son enjoyed trash at an early age. He dearly loved to get cans and papers out of the kitchen trash container beginning at two-years-old. His mother had repeatedly warned him, told him no, and lightly slapped his little hand to prevent this unsanitary and potentially dangerous game. We could have placed the container on the kitchen cabinet as a decoration and simply avoided the problem. However, even as unbelievers, we knew better than that. We knew it was our home and Ron needed to adjust to us, not us to him. Also, we knew he was supposed to obey us — period.

One day, my wife saw our son from across the room, gaily pulling his precious treasures out of the forbidden trash container. She immediately said, NO!, in a loud voice, and started to walk toward him, Ron glanced at her and began crying as he continued to pull things from the can at a frantic pace. The closer she got to him, the more he cried and the faster he pulled out his treasures. He was crying because he knew he was going to be stopped and that a spanking was coming, but he kept on because of pure will power. Even when she reached him, he held on with all his strength and his little hands had to be physically pried from the trash can. Now, THAT'S a strong-willed child! I hope your children's rebellion is so easy to discern.

2. Our youngest daughter was always a sweet, obedient little girl. She was my little cuddle partner and I probably spoiled her a little bit. I don't remember needing to spank her except as a normal two or three-year-old. She was very intelligent, plus extremely observant. She saw what got her brother and sister in trouble, and just didn't do those things. However, she was also moody, temperamental, overly sensitive, and self-centered.

By the time she was twelve-years-old, she could no longer hide her sin nature traits of pride and willfulness. She had a lust for all kinds of sweets and was already about twenty pounds over weight. We forbid her to eat sweets, but we found her stealing them during the night. Her formerly sweet disposition changed to sour and implacable — unable to get along with anyone in the family. Much to my shame, I began to embarrass her by calling her "The Lemon." Like most parents I wanted the immature child to take hold of herself (like the mature adult she wasn't) and change her own behavior so I wouldn't have to parent her. How unfair of me!

Finally, it dawned on me that I was violating Scripture by exasperating my daughter and by not giving her clear leadership (direction). I apologized to her and told her I would do my job of being Father from now on. I then told her that she was to change her attitude and begin to treat others with respect and dignity. I warned her that I would spank her soundly, if she continued acting as a self-centered prima donna, intent on making others as miserable as she pretended to be. A couple of days later she moped around the house, spoke nastily to her brother and sister, and sneered at her mother when she was warned that her attitude was breaking my command.

She spent most of the day in her room feeling sorry for herself (you know, the nobody understands me bit). I received the report when I returned home from work that she had treated everybody miserably that day. Mother and I proceeded up the stairs to her room. I told her that I was here to help her develop internal controls by giving her a tangible reason to straighten up her attitude. I said I was sorry this step was necessary, but that I wouldn't let her down anymore, and if this treatment didn't work, we could repeat it again every day until she chose to control herself. I then spanked her about three fairly hard licks. The humility of being treated like a child was worse than the slight physical pain. But, the whole treatment was a life-changing event. I hate to think what a moody, self-centered person she would have become without our willingness to win the conflict that day. The change in our daughter was dramatic. From that day on she began to act like a little lady — polite to others, offering to help her mother without being asked, and very respectful and loving to me. She had to be warned a couple times when she began to slip, but she never needed chastisement again.

Not long after, our daughter began to eat a balanced diet, control her lust for sweets, and lost the twenty pounds she was overweight. She grew to be a **beautiful** girl on the outside, but we often commented that she was even **more beautiful** on the inside. She had truly become to us what her name implied — Gift from God. Today, our lovely daughter is a delight to us, to others, and to her husband of 14 years. We are very proud of our Gift from God.

FOOTNOTES

[1] *Oxford English Dictionary, s.v. "rebellion."*

Chapter 16

CHASTISEMENT

As a parent, you occupy a position of human authority that is ordained by God. It is sometimes necessary for authorities to utilize force in the proper exercise of their responsibilities. Governments must use force to protect their citizens from both internal rebellion and external threat. The authorized use of punishment for internal crime and the legitimate function of defensive warfare are forces available to government. Parents must also utilize force in the proper exercise of their authority.

The forces available to parental authorities are chastisement for their children's rebellion; and punishment for their disobedience. Punishment will be fully explained in a later chapter. Basically, punishment is the administration of just consequences for the breaking of an established standard. It should never be confused with chastisement, although such confusion commonly exists.

Chastise means "to inflict punishment or suffering upon, with a view to amendment; also simply, to punish, to inflict punishment (esp. corporal punishment) on."[1] We often use the word "discipline" in today's language when we refer to this action. However, discipline can refer to many facets of training other than chastisement. Discipline has a wide range of meanings such as: to instruct, educate, or train; to train in military exercises, drill; to chastise, punish; to deal with in an orderly manner. As a noun, "discipline" also includes the following meanings "instruction imparted to disciples, education, schooling; a branch of instruction or education; instruction having its aim to form the pupil to proper conduct and action, the training of scholars or subordinates to proper or orderly action by instructing and exercising them in the same, mental and moral training; training or skill in military affairs; a trained condition; the order maintained and observed among pupils, or other persons under control or command; a system of rules for conduct; correction, chastisement."[2]

Therefore, the word "discipline" is a more general term, which could well describe the entire process of child training, whereas the word "chastisement" is specifically limited to the infliction of pain for correction or restraint.

The meaning of the English word "chastise" comes the closest to God's meaning for both the Hebrew and the Greek words used in the Biblical passages quoted in this chapter.[3] Chastisement (or corporal punishment) is the legitimate physical force parents are to use in correcting or restraining a child's rebellion. We are only discussing chastisement in relationship to a child who is in rebellion as defined in the previous chapter. **Chastisement should not be used for all disobedience**. (The way to handle disobedience that is not a result of rebellion will be explained in Part Five, "Teaching Your Children.")

It is difficult for parents in our generation to accept the need for the use of physical pain on our children. In recent years parents have been bombarded with misinformation about the proper role of authority. Parents have come to feel guilty about even the legitimate use of force. Many parents are ready to accept the anti-Biblical concepts that underage children have rights of their own and that chastisement is cruel and unusual treatment.

It should be apparent to anyone who will honestly evaluate the facts, that most children who have been raised without the proper use of chastisement are poorly trained. In general they lack self-discipline, are self-centered, and disrespect all forms of authority. Many of today's young adults have a vacuum in the place of moral standards. Obviously, parents have been doing something wrong.

Throughout recorded history, chastisement has been the normal method to control rebellion in children. Even in cultures that have not been based on the Bible, chastisement has often been the standard. Only when a civilization becomes proud in its own wisdom does it become too sophisticated to utilize God's rules for the proper administration of authority. Such a civilization questions and then denies the existence of any absolute standards. That civilization becomes decadent and ultimately is destroyed by a stronger civilization that does follow absolute standards.

In the author's opinion, most of Western Civilization is in the decadent stage at the present time. Only a return to God's absolute standards will prevent its imminent destruction. Because of the current worship of human reason and anti-authoritarian philosophy, parents are in need of a clear presentation of God's absolutes concerning their role.

Parents have become disoriented to the truth of what actually is normal. God considers chastisement so natural to parents that He uses it for an illustration of the way He would deal with a rebellious child. Obviously, God would not use this example if it were not His standard:

2 Samuel 7:14 *"I will be his father, and he shall be my son. If he commit iniquity, I will chasten him with the rod of men, and with the stripes of the children of men;"*

Significantly, the rod[4] is used for chastisement. The rod is the ideal instrument to be applied to a rebellious child (discussed later). There is no mention in the Bible of utilizing any other instrument or the bare hand to whip a child. This verse indicates that the normal relationship between parent and child includes chastisement and chastisement by a specific means.

Parents Who Love Will Chastise

Chastisement is actually an expression of parental love as shown by such verses as:

Hebrews 12:6 *"For whom the Lord loveth he chasteneth, and scourgeth every son whom he receiveth."*

God, our Father, cares enough for us to chasten us when we are rebellious. The word translated "scourgeth" means "to whip or lash with a whip or small flexible rods."[5] This verse is hardly a recommendation for the lenient methods that man in his arrogance has attempted to substitute for God's way. When man rejects God's Word as the absolute standard, he always considers his own thoughts and methods to be superior to those of God.

The word translated "receiveth" in this verse means "to accept or receive, to receive along side, or to welcome."[6] When a child's rebellion has been conquered by a loving parent's use of chastisement, he can be welcomed back into family fellowship. In yet another verse God specifically links the family relationship to chastisement:

Revelation 3:19a *"As many as I love, I rebuke and chasten;"*

The word translated "love" in this verse is not the same Greek word for love used most often in the Bible. Rather than a love that means "concern for the benefit of the object of love," this word means "rapport love."[7] It is the type of love that exists between people of common interests, thinking, or relationships — such as in a family. This verse in context reveals that God chastises His own rebellious children in order to bring them back into fellowship.

Human parents must also utilize chastisement to restore the break in family fellowship. In rebellion, the child is alienated from the parents, and they can neither bless him nor have fellowship with him. The only demonstration of love that is possible for parents to give a rebellious child is chastisement. In fact, when it is withheld, it demonstrates a lack of concern for the child's benefit:

Proverbs 13:24 *"He that spareth his rod hateth his son; but he that loveth him chasteneth him early."*

The Hebrew word translated "spareth" means "to restrain, or to hold back."[8] Parents who withhold the use of physical pain administered by a rod are said to hate their children. The Hebrew word translated "son" means "a child of special relationship."[9] It is used for the legal heir of the family. The word translated "early" means "to break forth — as a new day."[10] This pictorial word declares that parents who truly desire the best for their children will chastise them in the dawn of their lives.

The next passage indicates the abnormality of a parent who does not chastise his child:

Hebrews 12:7b *"for what son is he whom a father chasteneth not?"*

In this passage God states a timeless principle — that it is normal for a true son to be chastised by his father. Here we have the Greek word translated "son" that means "a child of special relationship"; "a legal heir."[11] The indication is that if a child is a true member of the family, it is only natural that his parents would care enough about him to use the physical pain of chastisement in the training process.

The next verse in its context even more graphically ties chastisement to family membership:

Hebrews 12:8 *"But if ye be without chastisement, of which all are partakers, then are ye bastards, and not sons."*

God does not mince words in His effort to communicate to men. Here He states that it is only the illegitimate child who does not receive chastisement. The father of an illegitimate child normally does not care for him. The child is not a legal heir to the father's name or inheritance. Such a child is rejected by his father as the unwanted product of his sin. It is no wonder that children who are not chastised by their parents have a sense of rejection.

No child is happy while he is in rebellion. Although he himself willfully caused the rebellion, he needs help to conquer it. When parents refuse to give a child the chastisement he needs to bring him back in control, he senses alienation from the family. He is miserable within himself, and his parents are angry with him. He is unacceptable into the family circle of fellowship and so is separated from his parents' love. The only way parents can demonstrate their love to the child in rebellion is to show him they care for him enough to make him acceptable to the family again. They must chastise him as one of their own, not ignore him as if he were a bastard child.

In conclusion, the foregoing verses reveal chastisement as the normal way parents are to control their child. God's Word also repeatedly declares that the physical pain of chastisement is an expression of parental love. Parents who are truly concerned for the benefit of their children will not restrain their use of the rod on a rebellious child. Its use is even a confirmation of family membership.

When a child is in rebellion, physical pain (chastisement) is the **only** pressure that will cause him to choose to accept parental direction and controls. A rebellious child has already rejected his parents' authority. He has already chosen to rule himself in accordance with what he wants. In other words, his will, dominated by his strong desires, has become his master. The only way parents can re-establish their challenged authority is to use the force of chastisement. It is also the only way to save the child from his evil master.

When rebellion is allowed to exist, it destroys the orderly arrangement of the family as ordained by God. The parents are not in control and so cannot fulfill their responsibility to teach their child. The child will not listen to or obey his rejected authorities since he has no respect for either their position or their person. The proper use of chastisement is the only way a child can be restored to family fellowship once the relationship has been estranged because of his rebellion.

Like any force, chastisement can be misused. The next chapter will deal with the correct way to use the force of chastisement.

AUTHOR NOTES TO THE 2ND EDITION

"Special Needs" children have a special need when it comes to chastisement. That need is **not** to be left out! One of America's top artist's son was congenitally deaf. He and his wife had done everything they could to express their love and acceptance for the boy. He attended a Montessori school where, at nine, he played all day long. They were fearful to discipline him although he became increasingly more rebellious each year. Finally, someone who had seen the boy's behavior and knew the parents' concern, gave them my book. They read it straight through one night and called me the next day. Their only question was, "Do you train a handicapped child in the same way that you do a non-handicapped child?" I explained that handicapped children have sin natures, their own wills, and a need to experience their parents' sacrificial love. If they are not chastised when required, they will sense the rejection of not being a regular member of the family and will not develop the external control needed to conquer their will and their flesh. The boy received his first of several spankings that next week. His parents said his anger and pouting soon turned to smiles and co-operation. This special needs child graduated at the top of his class from Pennsecola Christian College in 1993.

Treating special needs children as much as possible like any other child is vital to their acceptance and sense of normalcy. Of course, every child **must** be treated according to his ability to think and comprehend. A parents goal should be to train all of their children so that they will be mature adults; able to attain their maximum potential. A handicapped child may need special understanding when his efforts are more difficult than other children; and he also needs encouragement to keep trying to reach higher goals. When his limitations cause him to be frustrated, he may need extra comfort, but he must also learn not to feel sorry for himself. A special needs child should not be allowed to demand favoritism because of his handicap, and he must be taught consideration for others, like any child. He or she need not to see themselves as "handicapped" (i.e. not as accountable as other people), but they should strive to discover for what special purpose God has created them. Not much different than the non-handicapped child.

Testimony

"We are writing to thank you for your book and tapes.

Our son, Luke, was six-years-old (5/93), has cerebral palsy, and is essentially non-verbal. We are using the child training system you outline to benefit our son and his younger sister, Marie.

He has a fear of the rod (Note: not of the parents) and punishment (penalties) which help him gain self-control, peace, and joy. Luke loves his rules when we write them out, and he follows them.

I don't know how to describe the changes in Luke and Marie. Chastisement and punishments still happen, but much less, and when they are necessary there is an acceptance of them."

Ken and Judy Gerleman

FOOTNOTES

[1] *Oxford English Dictionary, s.v.* "chastise."

[2] Ibid., s.v. "discipline."

[3] Hebrew, verb *yasar,* noun *musar;* Greek, verb *paideuo,* noun *paideia* (Foundation for Biblical Research, "Child Training").

[4] The rod is defined as "A straight, slender shoot or wand, growing upon or cut from a tree, bush, etc....an instrument of punishment, either one straight stick, or a bundle of twigs bound together. . ." (Oxford *English Dictionary, s.v.* "rod").

[5] Greek, *mastigoo* "to scourge" (Foundation for Biblical Research, "Child Training").

[6] Greek, *paradechomai* "to accept, receive; to receive or embrace with favor, approve, love." (Ibid.)

[7] Greek, *phileo* "to love on the basis of compatibility; or the love of one person for another on the basis of something common between each other, like brothers or good friends." (Ibid.)

[8] Hebrew, *chasak* "to keep back, withhold." (Ibid.)

[9] Hebrew, *ben* son, offspring." This Hebrew word relates to the Greek word, *huios* "son, heir" (see Appendix C). (Ibid.)

[10] Hebrew, *shachar* "to go out early" (to anything), it does not here denote the early morning, but the morning of life. (Ibid.)

[11] Greek. *huios* "son. a legitimate son, legal heir" (see Appendix C). (Ibid.)

Chapter **17**

THE CORRECT USE OF CHASTISEMENT

God designed chastisement as the proper force to be used by parents to control the rebellion of their children. As is true with any human authority, force can be misused. As an authority under God's authority, parents are accountable for the way they handle this delegated power. Parents must be careful not to misuse chastisement. This chapter will cover the correct use of chastisement and the cautions against its misuse.

First, let us look again at the definition of chastisement. To chastise means "to inflict punishment or suffering upon, with a view to amendment; also simply, to punish, to inflict punishment (esp. corporal punishment) on."[1] When this definition is related to child training it means to use a rod to inflict pain sufficient to cause a child to correct his rebellion — or in other words, to restrain a child from willful disobedience.

When your child has willfully broken the standards you have set for him, he must be corrected by chastisement.

For example, you tell your son not to cross the street without your permission. He understands the standard and has been warned on several occasions as a reminder. He even forgot once and was rebuked verbally with a warning that any further occurrence would be rebellion and would earn a whipping. When he crosses the street again, he must be corrected by chastisement. The memory of the pain from the chastisement will help him to obey in the future and may save his life.

When your child defiantly resists your authority, harms or endangers another child, or is cruel to animals, he must be restrained by chastisement. For example, you try to give your child instructions, and he rebels by saying, "No," or ignores you and tries to get away when you hold him, or throws a temper tantrum. His rebellion must firmly and immediately be restrained by the use of the rod. The pain must be sufficient for him to choose to stop his rebellion right then and to accept your instructions.

The Importance of "The Rod"

Why must we use a rod to chastise our children? The first and only reason that should be necessary is because God's Word says to use a rod. God has specifically established the rod as the symbol of human authority.

The Hebrew word translated "rod"[2] in the Old Testament passages concerning the chastisement of children is a symbol of God's delegated authority to the human race. This rod refers to the right of human rulership of either government or parents. When the authority of a legitimate ruler is challenged, a rod is to be used to inflict pain sufficient to end the rebellion. Figuratively, the rod refers to military conquest by one nation against another that is being rebellious to God or His plan. Historically, the rod has been used in this manner on many such nations (Psalms 89:32; Isaiah 10:5, 24; Lamentations 3:1; Ezekiel 20:37; Micah 5:1). Literally, the rod is a narrow flexible stick used on a rebellious child by his parents (2 Samuel 7:14; Proverbs 13:24; 19:18; 22:15; 23:13 & 14; 29:15).

When parents utilize the instrument specifically designed by God as the symbol of His delegated authority, it triggers a response within the soul of the child. This natural response makes the minor pain experienced in chastisement take on special meaning. **No amount of spanking with the hand or hitting with any other instrument will have the same affect**. Just as it is natural for man to fear snakes or unfamiliar noises in the night, I believe it is ingrained in the child to identify the rod with an authority he should obey.

The use of the rod is best because it is a neutral object, not like the hand, which is a part of the person. Hands are not a symbol of authority; instead, they symbolize protection, comfort, and beckoning. The slap of a hand is an insult to which a child will react negatively. He will identify such use of the hand as personal rejection and either become passively alienated or overtly resistant to the parent personally. A belt can also be identified with the parent, but even it is not nearly as personal as the hand. Conversely, a rod is not identified with anything by the child but his own rebellion and the pain that results from his defiance of authority. When a child is chastised with a rod, his complete attention is focused on the instrument of pain, not the person using the rod.

The rod can be used equally well by the mother as by the father. Its use does not require physical strength. Unlike a paddle, whose pain varies with the strength of the user, a rod produces similar degrees of pain no matter who uses it.

The objective of chastisement is not to beat a child into submission by the use of brute force. The use of an instrument that can cause more than surface pain can actually hurt the child. This might cause the parent to resent his lack of control and perhaps even cease chastising altogether due to his feeling of guilt. Often when a paddle, board, or belt is used, it becomes a challenge to a male youth to prove his manhood by enduring the maximum force. Using a rod eliminates these problems. There is no pride in bearing up to a narrow rod, and it is less likely to cause any lasting injury.

The pain received from a rod is more humbling than harmful. There is no defense against it. The more a child braces himself, the more he tightens up and increases the sting. The most sensitive layer of skin is close to the surface where the nerve endings are located. The only way to stop the sting of a rod is to submit. That is exactly what a child will do — submit to his parents' will and thus end his rebellion.

God knows exactly what He is doing. His way is perfect whether He is designing the universe, the plan of salvation, or the rod as the instrument of authority to break the willful resistance of a child's rebellion. Parents would do well to teach their children about God's design of the rod as the symbol of their right to rule. The child should learn that his parents are as willing to obey God's Word as they expect him to be in obeying their word.

Each of the following Bible verses refers to parents' chastening their children and provides some important details about chastisement. Please study each of them carefully.

2 Samuel 7:14 *"I will be his father, and he shall be my son. If he commit iniquity, I will chasten him with the rod of men, and with the stripes of the children of men;"*

Proverbs 13:24 *"He that spareth his rod hateth his son; but he that loveth him chasteneth him early."*

Proverbs 19:18 *"Chasten thy son while there is hope, and let not they soul spare for his crying."*

Proverbs 22:15 *"Foolishness is bound in the heart of a child, but the rod of correction shall drive it far from him."*

Proverbs 23:13 *"Withhold not correction from the child; for if thou beatest him with the rod, he shall not die."*

Proverbs 23:14 *"Thou shalt beat him with the rod, and shalt deliver his soul from sheol."* 2

Proverbs 29:15 *"The rod and reproof give wisdom, but a child left to himself bringeth his mother shame."*

Hebrews 12: 6 & 7 *"For whom the Lord loveth he chasteneth, and scourgeth every son whom he receiveth. If ye endure chastening, God dealeth with you as with sons; for what son is he whom the father chasteneth not?"*

These verses illustrate that:

1. Parents are commanded to chasten their child early in life while there is hope for his reception to instruction (Proverbs 13:24; 19:18). The indication is that the earlier a child is brought under control, the more likely it is that he can be trained. Also indicated is the possibility that there is finally a time in a child's life when it is too late for the parents to be successful.

2. Parents are commanded not to withhold chastisement from their children and are warned of the negative consequences if they do (Proverbs 13:24; 23:13; 29:15).

3. The use of chastisement is revealed to be a necessary factor in the child's being trained away from foolishness and into wisdom (Proverbs 22:15; 29:15). These verses combine to indicate that the foolish self-confidence (cocky, know-it-all attitude) of a child must be driven out before he can be taught anything.

4. The rod that is to be used for chastisement has specific characteristics. It can cause stripes (thin marks like those left by a whip) and yet is small enough not to do permanent damage even if used strenuously (2 Samuel 7:14; Proverbs 23:13; Hebrews 12:6). Some children may scream as if they are dying, but striking a child with a narrow rod will not kill him. These verses indicate the rod is to be a thin wooden stick like a switch. Of course, the size of the rod should vary with the size of the child. A willow or peach tree branch may be fine for

a rebellious two-year-old, but a small hickory rod or dowel rod would be more fitting for a well-muscled teenage boy.

NOTE: A mother naturally cringes at the thought of switching her own child. The reality of intentionally inflicting pain, especially in using a rod that can make a mark (which will quickly go away), goes against the natural tendency to protect, comfort, and nurture her child. Uninformed mothers may even try to interfere with the father's proper use of a rod.

The only way a woman can become a godly mother is to combine the information found in God's Word with her own natural instincts. It is very difficult for a natural woman to control her emotional response toward a hurt or crying child. Although a mother has a natural concern for the immediate best interests of her child, she must learn how to love her children totally:

Titus 2:3, 4 *"The aged women likewise, that they be in behavior as becometh holiness, not false accusers, not given to much wine, teachers of good things, That they may teach the young women to be sober-minded, to love their husbands, to love their children."*

Biblical love for children is not instinctive for a woman. She must become farsighted in her thinking so that she can recognize chastisement as being necessary for the long-range benefit to her child.

A wise father can help his wife by understanding the woman's natural instincts and emotional make-up (I Peter 5:7). He can firmly set the standards for the child and chastise the child himself any time rebellion occurs while he is present. However, the mother of today is forced to handle most of the rebellion since it will happen while the father is gone and constitutes an attack against her authority. A mother should accept the fact that the little pain she must inflict for the moment will prevent her child from experiencing much worse pain in the future (Proverbs 23:14).

5. As we already saw in the last chapter, chastisement is an expression of true love and family membership (2 Samuel 7:14; Proverbs 13:24; Hebrews 12:6 & 7).

The use of a rod enables a controlled administration of pain to obtain submission and future obedience. If a child's rebellion has been to disobey an instruction willfully, the parent can stop after a sufficient number of strokes and ask the child if he will obey instructions in the future. The parent is the best judge of the correct number and intensity of strokes needed for a particular child. However, if the child repeatedly disobeys, the chastisement has not been painful enough.

If the child's rebellion has been the defiant resistance of his parents' authority, he should be chastised until he chooses to give in. The child can decide on his own when he wants the chastisement to cease. Whenever he is willing to submit to the parent's will, he can profess his willingness to obey. He should be given the opportunity for an honorable, but unconditional, surrender.

In either event, the child should be required to state verbally his willingness to comply with his parents' will. If he is mature enough to comprehend fully his own guilt, he also should be required to acknowledge his wrongdoing. The concepts of guilt and confession will be explained in a later chapter. The only issue in rebellion is the will; in other words, who is going to rule — the parent or the child? The major objective in chastisement is forcing the child's obedience to the will of his parents.

The rod should be used on the bare back, preferably on the buttocks, especially on younger children (Proverbs 10:13; 19:29; 26:3). The objective of chastisement is **not** to cause pain, stripes, tears, or sorrow, but to bring a rebellious child's will under control. It does not "break" a child's spirit or even his will to force him to obey. It only causes him to choose obedience over rebellion. Remember, God's Word commands that children are to obey their parents. It is the child who chooses to break God's law. The parents are merely enforcing God's law when they must chastise a rebellious child.

The Incorrect Use of Chastisement

Chastisement, as with any force, must be used wisely and with caution. The purpose of chastisement is **not:**

1. **to cause pain**. Although the use of a rod will certainly cause some pain, including a stinging reminder for a short time, causing pain should not be the objective. A whipping needs to last only as long as necessary for the child to acknowledge and accept his parents' right to rule him both then and in the future.

2. **to make stripes.** Children vary as to the number and intensity of strokes they require before they will submit. Some children are ready to give in when they first see the switch. These are usually the ones who have already come to trust that the parent really means business. A few strokes will suffice to help him remember better next time. However, the child who has not yet learned to trust his parent's commitment to his obedience, or who is exceptionally willful, will require more frequent and more intense whippings. Such a child is likely to require enough strokes to receive stripes or even welts. Some children have very sensitive skin that

will welt or even bruise quite easily. Parents should not be overly concerned if such minor injuries do result from their chastisement as it is perfectly normal (2 Samuel 7:14; Psalms 89:32; Proverbs 20:30). However, parents should be careful that their use of the rod is not excessive and that the size of the rod is reasonable. Making stripes on a child is not the objective of chastisement, but parents must realistically expect them to be a possible by-product of the child's rebellion on some occasions.

3. **to bring tears or sorrow.** Some children will begin to cry the instant they realize they are going to be chastised. Others will try to demonstrate apparent indifference as long as possible. The latter is a continued exertion of a child's will to prove that he is still in control of the situation. Parents should not establish the criterion that a child must cry or give some emotional demonstration of sorrow to end the whipping. Each child is sorry; that is, he is sorry he got caught. He is sorry he did not get away with doing what he wanted. He is even more sorry when the stripes sting. But, this type of sorrow will not produce obedience. Emotional sorrow is not the objective of chastisement.

True repentance is the voluntary change in thinking that must come from the inside and cannot be forced by external pressure. Only a child who truly desires to do the will of his parents will be mentally repentant when he realizes he is wrong. This attitude will only come later when a child has been trained to accept his own guilt for doing wrong without the use of force. The use of the rod is to re-establish the parent's position of authority over the child's will. The issue is his external conformance to the parent's will (obedience) not internal conformance (willing submission).

4. **to vent a parent's anger or frustrations.** Chastisement is the **controlled** use of force. It should never be administered by an angry or emotional parent. If a parent cannot control himself, he should send the child to his room to wait for his whipping. This action provides the parent time to "cool down," and it allows the child time to anticipate the coming consequences of his action.

Parents must be careful not to take out their own frustrations on their children. A child's rebellion is no excuse for a parent to unload on that child the pressures of a bad day at the office, financial problems, or any other personal failure in handling the stresses of life.

Occasionally a parent with a serious sin problem in his own life will truly abuse his child under the guise of chastisement. Such a parent has a soul problem that can only be permanently solved by spiritual means. That parent is usually tortured by guilt and desires help, at least subconsciously. In such a situation, the other parent needs to help this one see his spiritual need and try to isolate him from the stress of dealing with the children until the problem is solved. If the mother has the problem, the father could have the children cared for by someone else during the day. If the father has the problem, the mother must take special care to control the children herself. She can train the children not to give their father cause to express his anger against them. In either case, the more stable parent must maintain the children's respect of the other parent.

5. **to be used as punishment.** The penalties for broken standards should always match the deed. Physical pain as punishment should only be used to match the deed of the child's intentionally hurting another person or animal. Every other broken standard can be matched by an equal retribution. Chastisement should be generally reserved for open rejection of authority. Such rejection can include disrespect to authorities who are delegated by the parents (like teachers or baby sitters), or the willful destruction of property that represents authority (like a Bible, flag, church, school, or government property). Chastisement is to establish the right to rule and to restore respect for authority. It should seldom be used as a penalty.

Chastisement will be required often during the early "child" stage of development until the child becomes obedient. This should normally occur between eight and twelve years of age. During this period it should only be necessary to chastise a child occasionally when he tries to re-exert his own will against set standards. Most children can become obedient in their early training. However, if the parents have been lax during the child's early years, initially there will be heavy resistance to the new expectations of obedience.

There is no substitute for chastisement. Parents may wish for an "easier," more "humane" way, but chastisement is really the easiest way. Chastisement is not only "humane," it is Divine. Chastisement is God's method for parents to establish and maintain control of their children. How "humane" is it for a child **not** to learn a proper attitude toward authority and, therefore, become a criminal, a drug addict, or a homosexual?

The next chapter will conclude our study on the controlling facet of child training. It will explain some of the problems that parents may encounter in chastising their children. This chapter will also explain why control is essential in the training of children.

AUTHOR NOTES TO THE 2ND EDITION

Over the years of speaking to thousands of parents, more questions have been asked about chastisement than about all other areas combined. Parents want to know: How young to start, how old to continue, how many swats to give, what size of a rod to use, on bare bottoms or through how much clothing, in what position, what if chastisement doesn't seem to help, is there concern about breaking a child's spirit, and what about temper tantrums? The following comments will attempt to answer these reasonable questions:

1. **How young should chastisement begin?** Parents will usually only need to use a single swat with a small, flexible rod (balloon stick, willow or peach tree branch, blackboard pointer, or 1/8" dowel rod) with a toddler from the time he starts crawling to about 15 months old (age is no real criteria — how large and how stubborn the child is will be the real issue.) Mothers will often slap a toddler's hand for his getting into something he shouldn't. I see no problem with a single, warning slap for trying to touch the hot stove; or even for small infractions. This can take the place of formal chastisement as long as baby responds and mother doesn't hit too hard. I also don't think a baby will negatively respond to Mother's hand if used only occasionally.

2. **How old can a child be and still be chastised?** Several Christian psychologists have given their personal opinions in this area. One predominate opinion (apart from the authority of Scripture) advises parents not to use corporal punishment after 10 or 12 years old. There are no Bible verses to support this position. I agree that a properly trained child from infancy would

have little need for chastisement in his teens. However, a categorical statement that children shouldn't be chastised **anytime** throughout the child training period goes beyond, if not counter to, Scripture:

First of all, Scripture considers the entire non-adult stage up until 20-years-old subject to chastisement (the very Greek word for chastisement, *paideia* is derived from *pais* — the Greek word for the entire childhood period from infant to adult).

Secondly, the passage in Deuteronomy 21:18-21 about a drunkard son obviously has an older boy in view who had been chastised by his parents unsuccessfully before they turned him over as an incorrigible child to the elders for the death penalty. Also, the passages about a child striking or even cursing his parents (Exodus 21:15, 17; Matthew 15:4), thereby deserving the death penalty, was most likely referring to a youth in his late teens.

Thirdly, the opinion that chastisement shouldn't be used past 10 or 12 years old is unrealistic. Many parents today don't learn about Biblical child training until their children are already half-grown. Since they have never gained control of their children's wills and sin natures, ages 10 through perhaps 14 will be a period of intense struggle and require chastisement to establish the parents' authority.

I once taught a seminar to the "inmates" at Brother Roloff's home for girls at Corpus Christi, TX.. These 200 plus girls all came to the home from the streets or broken homes at ages of 12 to 16 years old. Most of them had never known a loving home and practically none of them had ever experienced loving chastisement, although some definitely had been abused. Brother Roloff and his staff of sacrificially serving believers, retrained these girls from scratch according to the Word of God. This included the use of corporal punishment on even the oldest girl, if she acted in rebellion to their clearly set standards. Some of these girls later worked for me at A.C.E.. They were beautiful girls inside and out. I would not like to have seen what these girls would have become had Brother Roloff's staff followed the advice of today's Christian psychologists.

Testimonies

Other parents meet our children and ask why they are so respectful and happy. We tell them, and then they start the excuses. "You can't spank a 12 or 16 or 18 year old, that would just turn them away." Now, I realize these people are not refusing your words or mine. They are refusing to hear and obey the Lord. I am consoled with the verse, *"As for me and my house, we will serve the Lord."*

Paul and Debra Reimer — OH

I'm still not 100% perfect or consistent with discipline, but my methods are 100% improved over my Dr. X days! I still can't forget a lady in Sunday School class stating that you can't spank a child over the age of 10 because Dr. X says you can't. Our ten-year-old son and I have regular meetings at the "Rod Station" — I got a late start with him. . . . The main thing that I want to say is that the rod does work!

Unsigned

3. **How many swats are necessary?** Only as many as are needed to re-establish your authority. My wife and I started a Christian school and enrolled 22 students our first year (including our three). By the third day our youngest student (the youngest brother of three boys — spoiled and with a cocky attitude) challenged my authority during opening exercises. I had warned him on the first day, and had reminded him on the second day, that I would spank him if he didn't straighten up. When opening exercises that day were over, I escorted him while he clopped his little cowboy boots across the room to my office. I shut the door, told him to bend over, and swatted him **once** on the jeans with a paddle (I didn't know about rods then). The sound of the air cushion exploding on the boys seat could be heard throughout

our one-room school. When the boy got over his shock and realized he wasn't hurt, he walked back to his desk in deafening silence. I never had to spank another child that year! When most children know you will, you won't need to.

Children have a tendency to live in the world of virtual reality. Sometimes, all you need to do is bring them back to the real world to cause them to change their behavior. "Are you two kids arguing again?" "Do I have to spank you?" "No!" both boys sing in unison. "Sorry, Bill." "Sorry, John." It's over without any swats being fired.

What if the problem is more serious? You've told the two boys previously that you won't tolerate any fighting between them. You overhear them arguing angrily in their bedroom. You confront them and they both reject your rebuke and start justifying their behavior by accusing the other with hateful language. "Well, the little creep started it first. He said my ears are too big." The other says, "I didn't either. I just said you look like Dumbo the elephant." This is when most parents would like to run from the situation and pretend these are someone else's kids.

Let's analyze the situation. Both boys have broken the standard of peace. The penalty for this will be a period of separation. They have both rebelled against authority by rejecting your rebuke. The penalty for this will be chastisement.

But, how many swats? You send the two boys to different rooms and you enter one with your rod in hand. You tell this boy that he **must** obey his parents' standards, that fighting is wrong, and that not accepting your authority is rebellion. Two or three swats with the appropriate rod should evoke a promise not to do "it" again from each of the boys. The boy who was cruel should also be required to apologize to his brother for making fun of him, and be warned that such behavior won't be tolerated in the future. The other boy could be taught to walk away from insults, or he could say, "This is the way God made me unique, and I accept it." Then, they should be separated for an hour or two. Parents should monitor their children's conversations as much as possible to help them be respectful to each other and to teach them how to resolve legitimate differences.

What if two or three swats won't work? To be effective make sure you have a rod of sufficient size; that a child isn't wearing jeans or other heavily padded clothing (or a phone book); and that you have the character to win the battle. I recommend stopping in between each set of three swats and give the child a chance to surrender. Tell him you're going to the other room, but that you'll be back in a few minutes. Explain that while you're gone he must decide if he needs another spanking, or if he is ready to admit his wrongdoing. This procedure can be repeated as necessary and should help break the resolve of even the most stubborn child.

4. **Size of the rod.** Don't use any heavier rod than is necessary. The rod should be flexible, but sturdy enough not to break. Use common sense. My wife and I sized and named a few rods **only** as a guide line for use with averaged sized children.

AGES

- 1-2   Tot Rod — 3/16" x 24" dowel
- 2-4   Mob Control — 1/4" x 24" dowel
- 4-8   Train or Consequences — 5/16" x 27" dowel
- 8-12   The Equalizer — 3/8" x 27" long dowel
- 12 & up Rebel Router — 1/2" x 33" dowel

(Of course, the Attention Getter for toddlers is defined under note 1.)

5. **The clothing issue.** Most parents would admit that it is a waste of effort to chastise through either a diaper or heavy pants, like jeans. But, we also don't want to embarrass our children any more than necessary. A rule of thumb might be that you can spank them bare-bottomed as long as you are still washing them in the tub or are otherwise seeing them nude anyway.

After then the child should be spanked wearing underwear at the least. When a child moves into puberty, a swim suit or similar clothing would be more suitable, if chastisement is still necessary. Obviously, it would be better to train your children as early as possible to avoid these difficulties.

6. **What position is best?** Over your lap for a one-year-old, laying on the bed for a two to four-year-old, or bent over holding the ankles for older children are just my suggestions. Be careful not to strike above the belt line on any child, or too low on boys.

7. **What if chastisement doesn't work?** Some parents would like to think that their child doesn't respond to spankings — he's laughed during one, puts his hand back to prevent one, won't acknowledge wrongdoing, or won't accept parents' authority. There are several reasons this happens:

   a. **Inconsistency**. The parent is arbitrary with the penalty. Sometimes the child gets away with the same infraction for which other times he is chastised.

   b **Parental Weakness**. The parent shows weakness to the child (tears, emotional trauma, etc.). He knows if he can hold out (making you pay the maximum pain), that he can break your will to continue.

   c. **Insufficient Pain**. The pain should be sufficient to cause the child to want it to stop, to remember it, and to not want it repeated.

   d. **New procedure**. Chastisement may not be effective with a ten-year-old who hasn't been spanked since he was in diapers. If chastisement is a new procedure it must be announced before hand with warnings given.

8. **Other Instruments**. Belts can whip around a child and be dangerous, boards can physically injure a child, and some parents might lose control while slapping a child with their hand.

Testimony

"I used a paddle, but I switched as soon as I began reading your book. We went out and bought two rods and I let my son saw them in half — he wanted to make arrows out of them! My two older children were quite excited about those rods and wondered what we were going to do with them. It didn't take long for them to find out. Thank you ! ! ! My children were to the point that the paddle didn't even bother them anymore. It was so baffling to me because I thought it hurt them, but they would walk away from a spanking without a cry or tear — not stunned at all. After a paddling, I would send them to their room and when I would come back to discuss it, they would always be rebellious to me. I would go through forgiveness with them and they would be so hateful to me. I knew very well that I was instilling rebellion in them and that it would definitely fester in later years, but I just didn't know what would be more effective.

I am a very strong-willed minister's kid who went through a lot of rebellion in my youth. All of my children have the strength of my will and I do want to prevent them from the mistakes I encountered because of open and unchallenged rebellion. My heart has been so burdened because I could see the open rebellion in them even after paddling and I couldn't figure out why. Thank you for answering."

Ron & Mary Tangeman — Ohio

9. **Privacy.** Chastisement should always be done in private, for the child's dignity and the parent's safety.

10. **What about breaking my child's spirit?** Proper chastisement will not break a child's spirit (desire to live, excitement for life). It won't even break his will. But, it will give him a reason for his will to choose obedience over self-centeredness. It also should break the hold pride has over your child, as he is humbled and forced to

choose to submit. Parents need to understand that before they use the power of chastisement, they must make sure they have the child dead-to-rights — especially if they intend to chastise until the child admits he is wrong. It is better to err on the side of the child than to chastise wrongly.

11. **What about temper tantrums?** When a child is already on the floor, banging his head on the cabinet, is not the time to chastise. He has gone so far as to lose all mental control and is hysterical. Chastisement can be administered before a temper tantrum begins, if you can see one coming. This helps the child develop self-control while he is still rational. A child who has already lost control can be brought to consciousness by splashing a couple of ounces of water in his face. This has the same effect of slapping a hysterical person to shock them back to reality. The second or third such treatment should cure future tantrums by causing a child to learn to control himself. If shock therapy is too traumatic for you, simply ignore his tantrum and walk away. At least this will teach him that he cannot control you.

FOOTNOTES

[1] *Oxford English Dictionary, s.v.* "chastisement."

[2] Rod. There are four distinct Hebrew words translated rod in the Old Testament. The most common word is *shebet*, "rod or tribe." It's most distinctive Biblical meaning is: delegated authority by God (like the twelve "tribes") or the "rod," the physical instrument for chastising rebellious children, or slaves, or fools or nations (figuratively). The second most used Hebrew word is *matteh,* Biblically: "the rod of God's authority on earth." This is the rod Moses and Aaron used to represent God before man. It was also used to establish God's authority over each of the twelve tribes. So, each tribe had a rod (*matteh*) as a symbol of being God's chosen representative on earth; and each was called a (*shebet*) a rod to be used to destroy the heathen nations. The other two words mistranslated "rod" are *choter*, which means sprout (like a plant); and *maqqel*, which means staff (to lean on).

[3] *Hebrew,* sheol "the underworld;" Biblically defined as a place where men (both righteous and unrighteous) descended after death during the Old Testament period (the grave) (Genesis 37:35; 42:38; 44:29,31; I Samuel 2:6; I Kings 2:6, 9; Job 7:9; Psalm 88:4). (Foundation for Biblical Research, "Child Training)

Chapter 18

CONTROL IS ESSENTIAL TO CHILD TRAINING

The proper use of chastisement is essential to controlling a child, and control is essential to being successful in child training. Controlling a child is definitely not all there is to child training, as we will see in the next section. However, a child who does not honor the authority of his parents will not accept their teaching and cannot be properly trained. Some parents will have problems in chastising their children. In this chapter, we will examine some of these problems and give their solutions.

Some children are much easier to train than others. They seem to desire to please their parents. They look forward to instructions, and control is seldom an issue. Naturally, these children are a delight to their parents. Most children will not fall into this category, and even the children who are the easiest to control will occasionally rebel at some point in their childhood. Parents need to be alert to the fact that a quiet child can be in rebellion passively. It is easy to overlook rebellion in a child who gives no direct opposition to control.

The other extreme is a child who apparently cannot be controlled. If a strong-willed child can seemingly withstand the rod with a grin on his face, he poses a difficult problem. His resistance to authority and strong will suggests that he could be a potential criminal (those same qualities may also indicate he is a potential leader with a high intelligence to match his strong will). One of several things is wrong when chastisement doesn't work: the rod is too small, a male child is already too big to be brought under control by his mother, or he is trying bravely to place his parents under his will.

If a child is too big for even his father to control (such as a teenage boy), it may be too late for his parents to train him. Appendix B, "Hope for the Failing Parent," may provide some answers.

If the child is very stubborn, he may not be beyond control, he may have just figured you out. Boys can do this to their mothers as early as ten years old. When the mother has shown signs of weakness (inconsistency, frustration, or emotional breakdown) during previous conflicts, this child calculates that he can eventually break her down. He makes a game out of resistance, hoping to play on the mother's weakness. His strategy is to use the mother's own weakness against her so that she will leave him alone to rule himself.

The solution to this problem is for the mother to realize what is happening, make up her mind to conquer her weakness for the child's sake, and steel herself for the conflict ahead. She must totally change the child's opinion about her and make him realize that she absolutely will not be intimidated. It would be extremely helpful for the father to step in and convince the child that the child **will**

not be allowed to win over the mother. The father's involvement will be essential if the child is a teenager, or has already conquered the mother. If the mother simply will not control the child, or if it is unreasonable to expect her to do so, the father must then assume the total responsibility to set the standards and make the child obedient. (The special provision God has made for the single parent will be explained later.)

Human Hindrances to God's Way

Often, even parents who fully understand how to control a child's rebellion will tend to try to find a way other than chastisement. Knowing the right thing to do and consistently applying it are two different things. It requires time and effort to train children properly. More than that, it requires parents who have character. They must be willing to put the child's need for training above their own personal wants. They must be willing to obey God's way rather than their own opinion.

Parents who are themselves in the sin of rebellion against God, His Word, or His established system of laws and authority, are likely to produce rebellious children. They will have great difficulty in setting and enforcing standards with their children since they are rebels themselves. Such parents will attempt to excuse their own disobedience to God by developing a "better way" to train their children. If an adult will not face his own rebellion before God, he will not consistently be able to apply the principles found in God's Word. He will be either permissive or too strict, or will swing between the two extremes because of his own instability.

Even parents who desire to do God's will must overcome their own sinful nature and opinions based on false philosophies. We are not only dependent on God's Word for the correct way to train our children, but we are also dependent on His power to practice that which we know. The following excuses and hindrances need to be recognized and avoided by parents who wish to be successful:

1. **Ignorance of God's way.** No one can do God's will unless he knows it; therefore, parents must master information on child training through study of the Bible and Biblical aids such as this book. Parents should teach their children what the Bible says about child training so the children will learn the source of parental authority and standards.

2. **Arrogance.** Human pride is the greatest hindrance to obeying God. Parents who are highly educated in human wisdom and philosophies (especially psychology) will need to exercise extreme caution against allowing their knowledge to exalt itself above God's Word (2 Corinthians 10:5 & 6). Pride is not a monopoly of the educated. Those who are uneducated can be arrogant in their lack of knowledge, refusing to accept information that differs from their opinions.

   Pride in one's own opinion expresses itself by rejecting God's truth and accepting human authorities in its place. Statements of this problem are typically like the following: "I can do it better my own way." "My child is different." "Every child is different and must be raised differently." "Everyone knows there is no one, right way." "Man in his wisdom has found a better way." "How could there be a simple solution to such a complex problem?" or even "Man has become too civilized to need to use force." and many others. Those who accept the fact that God has communicated timeless principles to man for his successful living must not allow themselves to be influenced by those who reject God's Word.

3. **The parent's own sinful nature.** Because the past several generations have not trained their children, most of us are self-centered. We tend to be lazy and selfish. We do not really want to train our children. We want to play or be entertained and avoid responsibilities when possible. Our laziness causes us to look for ways to avoid facing conflict. We hide behind excuses like, "Kids will be kids," or "He is just going through a stage."

   While it is true that kids will be kids, it is also true that they will stay that way if left untrained. This fact can be seen by the many untrained adults of today. Parents miss their training opportunities by just letting children grow through stages without any pruning. Probably the saddest of all parents are the Christian parents who use an incorrect definition of love or grace to excuse their children's permissiveness. Christian parents also deceive themselves when they think God is going to train their children for them. As long as a child is living under his parents' authority, his training is solely their responsibility.

All hindrances to controlling children by means of chastisement fall into three categories. The first hindrance is rejection of God. This rejection can be expressed either by a negative attitude toward learning His Word or by disobedience to that portion of His Word already learned. The only solution to this problem is a change of mind about who will rule. The decision is whether the individual will allow God, instead of his own prideful will, to rule. The second hindrance is simply ignorance of God's Word, which can be overcome by frequently attending a good Bible-teaching church and personal Bible study. The third hindrance is the nature of sin which always seeks to enslave man. The solution to this most difficult hindrance is to become mature in the knowledge of God's Word and consistently be submissive to His will as the Holy Spirit guides and directs.

There is no substitute for the use of chastisement by a rod to control a child's rebellion to parental authority.

What Chastisement is Not

Just as it is important to see what constitutes chastisement, it is also important to identify what chastisement is not. Chastisement is not:

1. **Verbal abuse.** Chastisement is not a tongue lashing, threats, or screaming fits of anger; in other words, adult temper tantrums. These things do nothing but support the child's disrespect for his parents' authority and demonstrate the parents' inability to rule. The parent is actually out of control himself. If a child can get his parent out of control, that child proves to himself that his parent does not possess the right to rule.

2. **Requesting or begging a rebellious child to submit.** Parents often use this approach: "Oh, Sonny, it makes Mommy feel so bad when you don't obey. **Please** do what I say." When a child is in rebellion, this type of approach only adds to his disrespect of authority. Words of instruction and rebuke have already been rejected; additional words are not chastisement. When parents plead and beg with a rebellious child, that child has his parents right where he wants them — under his will, negotiating for their rights.

3. **Punishment.** Chastisement is not equal to punishment. There are many types of punishment, but only one kind of chastisement. Any punishment, like isolating the child, restricting his privileges, or

any other approach that avoids the proper use of physical pain, will not conquer rebellion.

The use of punishment on a child who is in rebellion will only cause him to be more resolved in his rebellion and develop hatred toward authority. It is like trying to stop a charging lion with a water pistol. All it does is make him mad. Or, it is like sealing the release valve on a pressure cooker to stop the noise. Things may be quiet for a while, but eventually an explosion will occur. When the disobedience of a rebellious child is punished and the rebellion itself is not conquered, the pressure of his rebellion will build. A rebellious child who is dealt with in this manner will eventually explode like the pressure cooker.

4. **Psychological manipulation.** None of the techniques of manipulation are a substitute for chastisement. Techniques such as reasoning, bribes, redirecting of a child's attention, playing on his emotions or sinful nature, intimidation, or deception will not conquer rebellion. Their use may make things quiet for a while, but like the pressure cooker, the pressure of rebellion cannot be sealed off; instead, the fire must be extinguished.

A child who has been manipulated by his parents may never discover their deception, but he also will not become trained; and, as an adult, he will lack self-control. Some children do eventually catch on and are bright enough to turn the manipulation techniques back on the parents. Other children just lose all respect for their parents when they discover they have been manipulated.

None of these substitutes for chastisement will conquer a child's rebellion. They are each short-sighted attempts to treat the symptoms rather than solve the real problem. The use of verbal abuse, begging, punishment, or manipulation on a child in rebellion will only result in his negative response. He will develop hatred and lack of respect for all authority; suffer alienation from his parents; and practice self-pity, self-justification, and even martyrdom.

Parents who use these methods rather than chastisement never resolve the conflict. As a result, the parents are also adversely affected. They become estranged from the child and unable to demonstrate any true affection. In their frustration of not being in control, they transfer their guilt to the child. They often become vindictive toward the child, constantly showing disapproval and striking out in anger by trying to "get even."

When the conflict of rebellion is not resolved, harmony or fellowship can't exist between parent and child. There can only be temporary truces between outbreaks of the child's rebellion and the parents' frustrated attempts to direct and restrain him. Some parents will finally acquiesce to their little tyrants for the sake of "peace" and thus live a miserable existence virtually under his control. The diagram on the previous page visually represents this estranged condition:

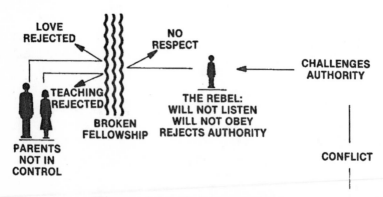

Figure 18.1 Estrangement

The only way parents can re-establish their challenged position of authority with a rebellious child is by the proper use of chastisement. It is the only way to end the alienation, frustration, and unhappiness that exists under the conditions of rebellion. It is the only way harmony, peace, and order can be returned to the family unit so that parents can continue to fulfill the responsibility to teach their children. The following diagram depicts a return to the correct position:

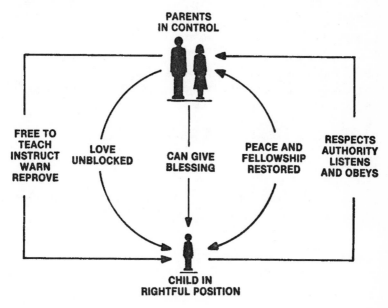

Figure 18.2 Harmony

The Results of Chastisement

Hebrews 12:11 b ". . . *afterward it* (chastisement) *yieldeth the peaceable fruit of righteousness unto them who are exercised by it.*"

With a return to normalcy the parents are again honored as authorities. They are in the position to teach their child through instructions, warnings, and reproofs. When the child is in his proper place, he will listen and obey. There is peace and harmony in the family based on the relationship of fellowship between parent and child. The parents' love can then be expressed in blessings to the child.

A child who has been properly trained will meet the Biblical requirement to "obey" and "honor" his parents. These objectives can be reached well before the child enters his teen years by parents who begin early and consistently to control their children. As crucial as obedience and honor are, they are not God's final goal for child training. They are the means that make it possible to reach that goal.

God's Goal for Parenting

Deuteronomy 6:6 & 7 *"And these words, which I command thee this day, shall be in thine heart; And thou shalt teach them diligently unto thy children, and shalt talk of them when thou sittest in thine house, and when thou walkest by the way, and when thou liest down, and when thou risest up."*

Proverbs 22:6 *"Train up a child in the way he should go and, when he is old, he will not depart from it."*

Ephesians 6:4 *"And, ye fathers, provoke not your children to wrath, but bring them up in the nurture and admonition of the Lord."*

God intends for children to be taught according to His Word so that they know how they should live their lives. The most important result of a child becoming obedient to, and respectful of, his parents is that he will then accept their instructions. The only way anyone will accept anothers' teaching is when he respects the other's position to teach. When a child honors his parents, he respects their word and is ready to be taught.

The child who has become obedient is also ready to develop the internal control of self-discipline. The parents' control up to this point has acted as an external control over his wants and strong desires. Chastisement has served as a painful warning that has helped him control himself. The threat of receiving physical pain has acted as an external control to counter-balance his temptations. Since he could depend on his parents' consistent use of chastisement when he rebelled, he was always faced with a choice. He could either submit to his desires and receive their chastisement, or he could suppress his desires and thereby avoid the pain. He must now learn why he should control himself without the threat of external controls.

Summary: Controlling Your Children

In this last section, we studied the "control" facet of child training. We should now have a clear understanding of what control means and why it is necessary with children. We have learned to expect conflict when we exercise the responsibility to direct or restrain our children and can now identify this conflict as rebellion which comes from the child's will. We have also studied God's natural solution to rebellion — chastisement. The following is a review of some of the major principles presented in this section:

- Control is the facet of child training by which parents obtain obedience and respect from their children.

- As long as a child accepts his parents' right to direct and restrain him, he is under their control.

- In controlling a child, parents can expect conflict to occur.

- When a child deliberately refuses to accept parental authority, he is in rebellion.

- Chastisement is God's method to end the rebellion and return the child under the parents' authority and control.

- Chastisement is the controlled administration of physical pain to cause the child to cease his rebelling and again accept his parents' authority.

- Parents are to chastise by using a rod, a narrow stick which can cause stripes.

- Parents are not to chastise in anger, for the purpose of hurting or causing stripes, to cause tears or sorrow, or to vent their own frustrations.

- Chastisement is the expression of true love and a demonstration of family membership.

- Chastisement is not verbal abuse, talking it over, punishment, or ignoring the conflict.

- The result of chastisement is the restoration of the proper relationship between child and parent. Only if this proper relationship exists can a parent fulfill God's objective to train the child.

- The ultimate purpose of control is to prepare the child for instruction from God's Word and for his development of self-discipline.

The next section will deal with the second facet of child training — teaching. It is by teaching that a child develops his standards. In the teaching stage of child training, a child learns the reasons behind his parents' directions and restraints. He is trained to become a mature adult who has purpose for his life. Teaching is only possible to a child who has come under his parents' control.

AUTHOR NOTES TO THE 2ND EDITION
The Child Abuse Issue

I personally believe **most** child abuse comes from parents' frustration with their children's uncontrolled rebellion, not from a desire to inflict pain on a helpless child. When parents avoid the proper use of chastisement, their children are likely to become more and more rebellious. Finally, their complacent or passive parents explode in an emotional rage. The proper use of chastisement would have eliminated most such emotional outbreaks.

Some truly sick, alcoholic, or drug crazed parents do physically, emotionally, and even sexually harm their own children or wards. These people should be prosecuted to the full extent of the law. However, because of a few of these misfits our nation has become obsessed with charges of child abuse. This obsession has been directed against even rational parents who properly use Biblical chastisement to deal with their child's rebellion.

The American public's attitude has changed drastically as each generation of untrained adults become decision makers. The May 15, 1994 Parade Magazine reported that in 1986, 84% of parents were in favor of corporal punishment; 67% in 1991; and 56% in 1994. At this rate almost two-thirds of the nation could be against corporal punishment by the year 2000. The Division of Child and Youth Services (DCYS) throughout the country operates outside of due process of law. They can obtain a court order (without any evidence) to enter your home, remove your children, require you to take psychological tests, and make your life miserable for years — all on the basis of one anonymous tipster (who might just have a grudge against you.) This could be your doctor, nurse, dentist, school teacher, neighbor, relative, or even your own children. Does this remind anyone of Nazi Germany? Mary Pride's book, *The Child Abuse Industry*, begins:

> "Last year, over one million North American families were falsely accused of child abuse. These families, people just like you and me, suffered in varying degrees. Some merely went through the humiliation of an investigation for child abuse and were 'cleared.' Although their names remain in

government files as suspected child abusers for a period ranging from five years to forever, these are the lucky ones. Others, not so fortunate, found themselves in compulsory counseling programs. Still others lost their houses and emptied their bank accounts fighting these unjust charges. Many lost their jobs. Others, the saddest of all, lost their children."

I believe that the issue of corporal punishment may be the test of Christian conviction in the next generation. American Christians have never had their beliefs tested by the threat of dying in the arena. Already, some Christians have had to testify their commitment to corporal punishment as their testimony to obey God rather than man (Acts 5:29). *What the Bible Says About . . Child Training* has been used in several court cases as these parents' Biblical reason and justification for corporal punishment. A professor who is writing a book **against** corporal punishment has stated that this book best presents the Christian position on corporal punishment:

"I have written a book which tries to argue the case against the use of physical punishment, both from the perspective of my research as a scholar and from my position as a person who cares deeply about the issue of punishment for children. I was most pleased by your assurance that it is not necessary to agree with you about corporal punishment in order to be given permission to quote extensively from your book, especially since I regard it as one of the most forthright and articulate defenses of corporal punishment from a Christian perspective that I have yet found."

Philip J. Greven, Jr.
Professor
History Department
Rutgers University

The Christian has two choices as I see it:

- He can fear what man and Satan might do to him for obeying God (See Matthew 10:28; and Hebrews 13:6 before you decide to go this way); or,

- He can attempt to keep his child training as private as possible, but still follow God and be willing to make this his testimony if necessary (Proverbs 22:3). To follow this route, spanking should never be done in public, or even around relatives of which you are not sure. If your child rebels in public, you can take them home to deal with the problem — even if it is inconvenient. Your child will feel important that you went to such effort, but won't want to repeat the experience.

* * *

TEACHING YOUR CHILDREN

Chapter 19

WHAT TEACHING MEANS

You cannot leave a child in a playpen forever. Eventually he must learn why he cannot play ball with the crystal heirloom or pull the cat's tail. The final objective of child training is not to control a child, but to teach him what is right so that he will control himself. Parents should not act as their child's external control any longer than necessary. As soon as a child becomes consistently obedient, he should be taught according to his ability to comprehend fully that teaching.

A very young child can be taught why not to touch hot items by holding his hand near a stove to feel the heat. A few lessons like this can be taught empirically (through the senses). However, most lessons will need to be taught through reason (logical thinking). Therefore, only a limited amount of teaching can be accomplished with a young child, even if he is completely obedient. Of course, there is virtually no limit to the amount of **data** a child can learn: the ABC's, rhymes, numbers, counting, Bible verses, and etc. – even if he doesn't understand what they mean. To learn with understanding, a child must be able to comprehend fully what you teach him. To comprehend instructions requires both vocabulary and concentration as well as a willingness to learn. Therefore, most teaching will not occur before a child both approaches the "youth" stage and honors his parents' authority.

Teaching as a part of child training is not simply a matter of giving instructions to be either accepted or rejected. Teaching provides the explanation for rules for which the child then becomes accountable. As with any teaching that is designed to reach the objective of inculcation (internalizing), the child must be required to demonstrate that he has learned the desired lesson; in other words, he must pass the test. Inculcation means "the action of impressing upon the mind by forcible admonition or frequent repetition; the emphatic or persistent teaching of something." [1] Since the teaching necessary in child training is primarily concerning proper conduct, the child's test is the way he behaves in conformity with his instructions.

The proper conduct parents are to teach their children ranges from manners to morality. Any value system could be taught to an obedient child, but God's Word is the only reliable source for a truly righteous system. For example, the Bible sets the absolute standard for honesty in speech and in deed. A child should be trained to neither lie nor steal. As soon as he is mature enough to comprehend exactly what constitutes a lie or a theft, he should be taught the standard of honesty and held accountable for any deviation. When honesty becomes his own way of life without any external pressure, then he has been trained to have an honest character.

God's Word reveals a perfect system (to be developed in the following chapters) by which a child can be trained successfully. This system consists of four basic steps for parents to follow. The first is "to set the standards." This step constitutes the giving of directions and serves as a warning of what is to be expected if the directions are not followed. The second is "to rebuke." This step is taken when a child breaks the established standard. The third is "to forgive." This step follows the child's acceptance of his wrong doing by admitting his guilt. The fourth and final step is "to punish." Punishment is the execution of justice to be administered by God's delegated authorities for broken standards. Punishment and chastisement are not equivalent, as will be fully explained.

Parents who follow this system correctly and consistently will be successful in training their children. Each child will learn and accept the standards that he or she is taught. The system is simple in structure and can be used with any child who submits to authority.

A child who is not obedient must be brought under control before this system can be used, since only an obedient child can be taught. The rebellious child has only one lesson to learn and that is who is in charge. Again, the principle to follow is: a child is to be controlled as long as he chooses to act like a child, and a child should be taught to the extent that he demonstrates obedience and respect.

When children are young, it is natural for parents to exercise maximum control. But, as a child grows older, the external controls should gradually be withdrawn. This withdrawal is possible only as he is progressively taught and demonstrates the willingness to control himself. It is important for a child to be trained before the parents lose their ability to control him. The child training chart we saw in Chapter 11 reflected the natural loss of parental control as a child grows older. That chart is hereby reproduced with an emphasis on this decreasing control.

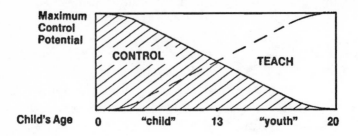

Figure 19.1 Decreasing Parental Control

This same chart could also be used to help understand the so-called "generation gap."

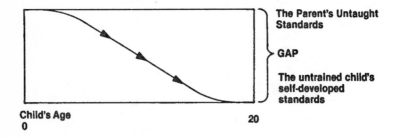

Figure 19.2 The Generation Gap

This gap exists only to the extent that parents do not inculcate their standards into their children. A child who is totally left to himself will develop a set of standards based on his own will and nature plus any outside influences he may have accepted. These influences are those whom he has accepted for his own authorities such as: teachers, celebrities, members of his peer group, or dynamic leaders of some cause. His self-imposed standards separate him from his parents and, as they gradually lose control, the gap widens.

The reverse curve of the same chart represents the potential parents have to teach an obedient child:

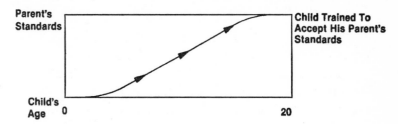

Figure 19.3 Increasing Teaching Potential

A well-trained child learns and accepts his parents' standards. He also develops internal controls to replace the need for his parents' external controls. Well before children reach physical adulthood they should be able to take complete care of themselves. No parent should still be awakening teenagers in the morning, picking up after them, or doing anything that they should be able to do on their own. When a child will responsibly care for himself and conduct himself according to his parents' teaching without any external pressure, parents have attained the objective of child training.

Parents should realize that they have something of value to give their children — the benefit of their experience. The wisdom parents have gained from living thirty or forty years can be passed on to their children through effective child training. When children have been properly trained during childhood, they are in a position to accept their parents' advice, even when they are adults. Who else is more qualified than parents to instill standards in children? No one else has been delegated the responsibility or authority to train children. No one else is accountable to God for a child's behavior and character molding.

To inculcate proper standards into a child is not brainwashing him. Brainwashing would be programming or indoctrinating a child by by-passing his will, and is an evil technique which will often backfire on its users. Instead of the child accepting the programming, he is likely to reject it altogether as soon as he can break free. Correct child training should always be aimed at the conscious mind of the child and be an open challenge to his will. Some parents attempt to indoctrinate their children by behavior modification techniques that are aimed at the subconscious mentality, thereby by-passing the will. These parents raise children who are limited in their ability to reason with, or apply, what they have been taught. When their standards are challenged later in life, they are unable to defend their position intelligently. Consequently, they are easily convinced to give up even correct standards.

Proper teaching requires substantiation of the accuracy of what is taught. In other words, what is taught must be accompanied by the reasons that confirm it to be true. Otherwise, the child has no information with which to answer the questions that will plague his thinking. The parents' standards, right or wrong, appear to be merely their opinions or traditions. Like the dramatization in the play, *Fiddler on the Roof*, children who are not taught the reasons for their parents' standards are likely to break away from the standards altogether. The parents are then left to wonder where they failed. Obviously, when parents have to give sensible reasons for their standards, those reasons must exist, and the parents must know them.

God's Word is the only trustworthy source for quality standards with sensible reasons to substantiate their correctness. Our current generation has a relatively limited knowledge of the Bible, although an estimated 45 million profess to be "born again" Christians in the United States alone.[2]   Even many of these Christians do not know the reasons for the standards of moral conduct taught in God's Word.   Naturally, most non-professing Christians reject even the standards themselves. Not only would most people be unable to explain why adultery is wrong, many would not even agree that it is wrong.

The present condition of a Biblically uneducated populace is due partly to the failure of parents in training their children. The past several generations of parents have generally been unsuccessful in training their children to have proper moral standards. The primary reason this decay has happened is because the parents have not given their children the reasons to substantiate the standards taught.

It is my personal opinion that this breakdown in child training occurs gradually over several generations. The first generation both knows and lives by God's righteous standards. They raise their children with strict controls and teach them those standards. However, because of apathy or laziness they fail to teach their children the reasons that support those standards.

The next generation of parents consists primarily of those same children who have no knowledge of why they think the way they do. In their insecurity, they become either dictatorial in their rulership or over tolerant and permissive. The dictators attempt to force their standards on their children without any reasons provided — "It is right because I say so." The other group of parents do not know for sure what is right to teach, so they just let the child go his own way. In their frustration they say, "What is a mother to do?" This type of parent hides behind the excuse, "I want my children to choose for themselves."

The next generation mostly consists of the children of dictatorial parents who either carry on the tradition or totally reject the standards that they were force-fed. The latter develop some sort of "do your own thing" system like universal love and brotherhood — I'm ok, you're ok;" pantheism; hedonism — "If it feels good, do it;" or eventually some discover the reasons behind the true system of morals. This generation also consists of the children who raised themselves. They also search for and settle on one of the types of systems described above.

The next generation consists basically of those who have rediscovered the truth as well as those who have settled on some humanistic system. If the majority of the people of a particular civilization follows the truth, that civilization receives the blessings that result from obedience to truth. Eventually, the whole cycle begins again. If the majority is humanistic, that civilization becomes decadent and is destroyed from within. Eventually, a decadent civilization is conquered by another civilization, unless it undergoes revival.

The only way a civilization can maintain a stable moral fiber is when each generation of parents bases its standards on those found in God's Word. It provides the only system of moral conduct that verifies itself by positive results in actual practice.

The following chart depicts the four-generation cycle:

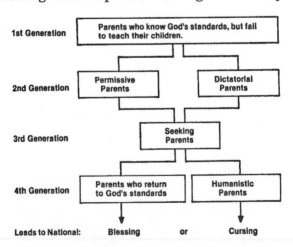

Figure 19.4 Four-Generation Cycle

Where on the chart does the Western Civilization stand now? Of course, traces of all four generations exist at any one time; but I believe we consist mostly of fourth generation adults. However, there are indications that many people are searching for a system of standards upon which to build stable lives. Our prayer is that enough parents with young children will learn God's standards and then teach them to their children in time to revive our civilization.

We have seen how to control our children so that we then can teach them. These two procedures — controlling and teaching — combine to constitute child training. But, without the teaching of righteous standards, God's purpose for child training cannot be accomplished. After all, children in Communist countries are trained — even more so than most other children. The difference is the quality of standards taught. If parents have nothing of value to teach, there is no good purpose in child training. Parents will then only teach their own unsupported opinions, prejudices, and confusions to the next generation. God's Word must be the standard for man's thinking and living.

The next chapter explains the fourth step in the teaching facet of the child training system — punishing the child. The reason for covering the last step first is to eliminate any confusion between chastisement and punishment.

FOOTNOTES

[1] *Oxford English Dictionary*, s.v. "inculcation."

[2] Jeremy Risken and Ted Howard, "Praise the Lord – Spread Evangelism." *Politics Today*, September-October, 1979, p. 53.

Chapter 20

PUNISHMENT

Punishment is not the same as chastisement; yet these two terms have become almost synonymous in the English language. This confusion in definition is unfortunate since each has lost its original, distinctive meaning. Equally unfortunate is the emotional connotation many people have about punishment. Generally, punishment is considered to be a cruel, harsh, and arbitrary penalty that is imposed on a helpless subject. However, punishment as defined by God's Word is always just.

As we have already seen, chastisement is the specific use of a rod to inflict pain. It is used to conquer rebellion and force submission to authority. Physical pain should be used as a punishment only for acts that demonstrate rebellion against authority; or for the intentional hurting of another person or a helpless animal. Acts that demonstrate a child's rebellion against authority include willful destruction of property which represents authority (like a Bible; a flag; or church, school, or government property), and open disrespect for authority figures (like parents, teachers, or others delegated by parents).

Normally, punishment is the just penalty for any type of wrong done. Its purpose is not to force submission or control rebellion. While chastisement can be withdrawn as soon as a child submits, punishment is the payment that must be made for a specific wrong committed. While chastisement acts as a warning of worse to come, punishment is the final payment. For example: If a child is about to throw a temper tantrum, he is chastised until he comes under control. But, if a child carelessly breaks a lamp, he is punished by paying the penalty for the wrong done; he cleans up the mess and buys a new lamp.

Punishment is "the action of punishing or the fact of being punished; the infliction of a penalty in retribution for an offense; a penalty imposed to ensure the application and enforcement of a law."[1] There is a correct amount, time, and way to administer punishment; it is a highly objective process. There is no reason why parents cannot be confident in establishing penalties and administering justice when necessary. Parents, as God's established authority over children, have the responsibility to execute justice when standards are broken.

God's Authorities are to Execute Justice

Romans 13:4 *"For he is the minister of God to thee for good. But if thou do that which is evil, be afraid; for he beareth not the sword in vain; for he is the minister of God, an avenger to execute wrath upon him that doeth evil."*

This verse is in the context of God's revelation concerning human institutions. When we studied Romans 13:1 in the chapter on authority (Chapter 4), we learned that no ruling power exists except through the will of God, that the positions of authority are ordained (instituted) by God and are under His control, and that every individual is to place himself willingly under the positions of rulership that exist above him. Romans 13:2 & 3 explain that whoever resists God's appointed authorities will receive judgment. Now we can see that verse four declares the responsibility of God's authorities to administer punishment.

Several words in this verse require explanation. "The minister of God" is the ordained authority who serves God; anyone who is placed in a position of rulership, including parents. The Greek word translated "avenger" means "an executor of justice."[2] Parents are to act as judges of their children's deeds and then to administer punishment to those who are guilty. The Greek word "wrath" is the Biblical word again for "punishment."[3] The word translated "doeth" is the Greek word for "to practice," and it is in the grammatical form that indicates "to habitually practice."[4] This form is very meaningful as we shall see. Finally, the word translated "do" in the phrase *"But if thou do that which is evil"* means "to make, form, construct or create,"[5] and the word translated "evil" means "that which is wrong or incorrect according to the standard."[6] In other words, this verse is saying that God's authorities serve Him when they administer justice by punishing the one who practices doing that which is against the standard of what is right.

This verse provides some encouraging information for parents. It indicates that authorities will eventually catch the habitual offender. Parents do not need to be a "giraffe," always spying on their children. If a child is practicing wrong doing, he will eventually get caught. This is one of the reasons human justice can be administered firmly. The one who is caught has probably gotten away without being noticed on other occasions. Since parents are not all-knowing or ever-present, they will not catch their child for his every offense. But, when they do catch him in the act, they can punish him to the fullest degree with confidence of being fair. The Bible bears out the fact that no one ever really gets away with anything:

Numbers 32:23b *"and be sure your sin will find you out"* (see also Isaiah 59:12)

The next question to be answered is, exactly what constitutes just punishment? What guidelines does a parent have to establish reasonable levels of punishment for each type of standard? God's Word provides the principles that establish how penalties are to be set. A penalty is the fixed amount of punishment corresponding to the wrong done. Therefore, a penalty is fair restitution, or the correct payment, to right a wrong. Restitution restores a righteous condition that has been destroyed through an unrighteous act.

In establishing standards of righteousness for man, God provides the principle for setting proper penalties:

Leviticus 24:17-22 *"And he who killeth any man shall surely be put to death. And he who killeth a beast shall make it good, beast for beast. And if a man cause a blemish in his neighbor; as he hath done, so shall it be done to him: Breach for breach, eye for eye, tooth for tooth: as he hath caused a blemish in a man, so shall it be done to him. And he who killeth a beast, he shall restore it; and he who killeth a man, he shall be put to death. Ye shall have one manner of law, as well for the sojourner as for one of your own country; for I am the Lord your God."* (See also Exodus 21:23-25 & Deuteronomy 19:15-21.)

It is clear that God intends for a wrong to be paid for by an equal penalty. This principle also applies to any accidental wrong occurring between individuals (Exodus 22:5, 6, 12 & 14). Parents, in setting penalties for their children, should utilize God's system of retribution when full accountability is in order. Excessive penalties should not be set as they would not be fair. If a child repeatedly breaks a particular standard, no amount of punishment is likely to prevent his disobedience. He is in rebellion, and the parents need to re-establish their authority with the rod.

Another way of explaining a proper penalty is by seeing it in relation to an absolute. First, the standard represents what is right (an absolute amount of righteousness). Second, the breaking of a standard represents what is wrong (a specific amount of unrighteousness). Third, the penalty is therefore the right amount of payment necessary to equal the wrong (to correct the unrighteousness). Pictorially it might be sketched:

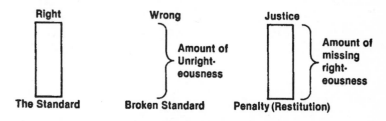

Figure 20.1 Penalty Equation

In the Greek language of the New Testament, both righteousness and justice are translated from the same word. In other words they are two sides of the same coin. What is right is just, and what is just is right. Penalties are not necessary as long as right is kept. When wrong is done, the penalty restores or pays an equal amount to make things right. The following three examples illustrate the concepts of just penalties (see Figure 20.2).

	THE STANDARD (RIGHTEOUSNESS)	WRONG (UNRIGHTEOUSNESS)	JUSTICE (PENALTY)	PUNISHMENT (EXECUTION OF JUSTICE)
	WHAT IS RIGHT AND FAIR	WHAT IS WRONG AND UNFAIR AS COMPARED WITH THE STANDARD	THE AMOUNT TO EQUAL OR CORRECT THE WRONG	APPLICATION OF THE PENALTY
EXAMPLE A	$5 PER HOUR PAY FOR FORTY HOURS PER WEEK	TO WORK ONLY 30 HOURS	¼ OF WEEKLY SALARY	DEDUCT $50 FROM PAYCHECK
EXAMPLE B	PROTECTION OF PROPERTY RIGHTS	TO DESTROY SOMEONE ELSE'S PROPERTY	COMPLETE RESTITUTION FOR DESTROYED PROPERTY INCLUDING ANY INCONVENIENCE SUFFERED	GUILTY PARTY FORCED TO PAY THE TOTAL COST OF RESTITUTION
EXAMPLE C	NO HARM TO HUMAN LIFE	TO TAKE ANOTHER PERSON'S LIFE	NO CORRECTION POSSIBLE LIFE REQUIRED FOR PAYMENT Life = Life	CAPITAL PUNISHMENT

Figure 20.2 Restoring Righteousness

Example A. If an employer agrees to hire someone to work forty hours for $200, a standard has been set. If the employee works only thirty hours, he does not meet the standard. Thirty hours is ten hours short of what is right. The penalty, therefore, is one-fourth of the weekly salary. When pay day arrives, the employer is right to deduct one-fourth of the agreed amount as the penalty for the employee not meeting the set standard.

Example B. God's Word establishes many laws to protect private property rights. No one has the right to destroy another person's property. Private property represents an extension of a person's life equal to how long the person had to work to pay for that property. If a man worked eight hours to purchase a radio, that radio represents one day of his life. This explains why God's laws allow a man to protect his property with force, if necessary. The destruction of someone's property is unrighteousness. Example B depicts a ball that has been thrown through a window. The wrong equals one broken window. Of course, balls do not break windows. Someone threw the ball through the window, and he is the guilty party. There is always personal responsibility in every "accident" caused by humans. It may have been unintentional, but the window is nonetheless broken.

In this example, the penalty is complete restoration of the broken window — cleaning up the broken glass, paying for the new glass, and doing all the work. To punish would be to make the guilty party pay full restitution so that after the penalty is paid, everything is returned to its original state.

Example C. Here the standard is the protection of human life. It is wrong to take a human life either intentionally with malice or accidentally through negligence. Murder is unrighteousness for which restoration is impossible. There is no way to make restitution for a life. The only just penalty is a payment of equal value-life for life. Capital punishment is the execution of justice appropriate for this wrong.

Now that we have seen the principles behind punishment, let us apply these principles to child training. Parents can establish penalties by employing the following guidelines:

Penalties for Children

1. **Respect for property**. Children can be taught that if they intentionally or carelessly damage property, they will have to pay for it. If they mark, tear, scratch, break, or otherwise damage property,

they should pay for restoration to the extent that they are accountable. This property should include even their own toys and clothes not bought with their own money. Children should learn respect for property as young as possible. Of course, if parents leave a two-year-old alone in grandmother's room of best china, they should expect the worst and be willing to pay the penalty themselves.

Proper warning should always be given (the standard set), and the child must have the necessary comprehension and physical ability to be held accountable. If you have an "accident-prone" child, he should be required to perform certain odd jobs for which he is paid. He will then be prepared to pay with his own money for his carelessness. No amount of warning, scolding, or verbal rebukes will train him to respect property like paying the penalty. If a child is out of money, he can always be required to work out the penalty by doing duties not normally required of him.

When children break something, they should usually be required to clean up the mess, even if it was an accident, or even if they are too young to be accountable for the full penalty. Their participation teaches them responsibility and caution. Every broken standard has a penalty; the question is, who pays the cost. Even when a child is too young to be held accountable, a broken vase must still be paid for and cleaned up by someone.

Children can learn to be responsible for their own actions quite early in life. For example, a small child breaks a window for which he should not be held totally accountable. He can be required to help his father clean up the mess, go to the store to buy the new pane, and hand his father the tools until the repair has been made. In this way he begins to learn that there is a cost of time for damaging property. When a child breaks his own toys, one penalty could be to go without the toy. However, if he is habitually careless or rough with his things, or especially if he destroys his toys in anger, he needs training in this area of weakness. He must pay the full cost.

2. **Manners and behavior toward others**. Children must learn to respect the rights of others. The penalty for being rude or crude can be an apology. However, if the offense is intentional or repeated, the penalty will need to be increased to isolation of the offending child from others. As in all other administrations of punishment, the parent must first make the child admit he was wrong before isolating him. If a child is a troublemaker, he needs to be separated from those he is bothering; he kept others from enjoying themselves, now only he is kept from enjoying himself. Here again the penalty can be increased for a repeated or intentional problem.

3. **Physical harm to others**. Children must learn the danger in causing pain to others. The penalty for causing others pain is to receive pain (chastisement). This penalty can even be imposed if a child engages in activities that are potentially dangerous — especially to children younger than he. An example is an older child who knows better trying to goad a naive younger child into catching a bumblebee with his bare hands. Older children should learn to protect those who are younger and to act responsibly around them.

4. **Self-control**. Children must learn to control themselves. The penalty for a child's lack of self-control would be denial of something wanted. If a child consistently exhibits laziness, he can be punished with additional duties; or if the problem is always trying to eat the wrong foods, he can be denied all candy or other junk food for a set period of time. Often, a child's specific weakness in the area of self control will require stricter measures. If a child has a problem with dishonesty, every act of lying, cheating, or stealing may need to be treated as rebellion for which he is chastised. However, ample warning should be clearly given before treating any disobedience with the penalty for rebellion.

These principles should help you understand the setting of penalties for disobedience. It is simply a process of common sense. Parents should determine the penalty at the time they set standards. fully expecting to carry out the punishment. In this way, the penalty will not be influenced by emotions at the time of disobedience. Knowing how to set penalties is not enough; parents must also know when to punish.

The Administration of Punishment

A child is held accountable for punishment only when the broken standard has been clearly set and communicated. If the penalty was not given, it could be less severe than normally called for, or even waived on the first offense. The old saying "ignorance is no excuse for breaking the law" does not come from the Bible:

Romans 4:15b *"for where no law is, there is no transgression."*

Romans 5:13b *"but sin is not imputed when there is no law."*

Punishment is a judicial sentence without partiality. Fathers are naturally soft on their daughters, and mothers are often too lenient with their sons. This is not just, nor is playing favorites between children in the family. No matter how convincingly a son promises his mother never to do it again, or how sweetly a daughter looks up at her father, punishment must be carried out consistently and fairly.

Deuteronomy 1:17a *"Ye shall not respect persons in judgment, but ye shall hear the small as well as the great; ye shall not be afraid of the face of man, for the judgment is God's;"*

God has given his laws to human judges to administer justice on earth between people. Parents are one of God's human judges. When parents punish their children, they are carrying out God's judgment. Because of this, parents can depend on God's power to help in the administration of punishment to even the largest child.

Punishment should normally be administered after a child has admitted his guilt (the fact that he was wrong), and after the parents have forgiven his disobedience. The principle of punishment after forgiveness is revealed in God's Word:

Psalms 99:8 *"Thou answeredst them, O Lord our God: Thou wast a God who forgavest them, though thou hast taken vengeance on their misdeeds."*

2 Chronicles 6:30a *"Then hear thou from heaven, thy dwelling place, and forgive, and render unto every man according unto all his ways,"*

Numbers 14:19 & 20 *"Pardon, I beseech thee, the iniquity of this people according unto the greatness of thy mercy, and as thou hast forgiven this people, from Egypt even until now. And the Lord said, I have pardoned according to thy word;"* **However . . .**

Numbers 14:23   *"Surely they shall not see the land which I swore to give unto their fathers, neither shall any of them that provoked me see it."*

Possibly the best Biblical example of this principle is David's multiple penalty for his adultery with Bathsheba and the murder of her husband (2 Samuel 12:9-14). His punishment continued over most of his life, long after he had confessed his sin (2 Samuel 12:13; Psalm 51), and even after God had forgiven him (2 Samuel 12:13). No amount of feeling sorry, crying, or fasting prevented the punishment from being carried out (2 Samuel 12:21, 22). The penalty for this great king's misuse of his powers was the death of his first son by Bathsheba and the future trouble in his household: incest among his children, revolution, and the violent death of three more sons (2 Samuel 12:14; 13:28; 18:14 & 15; 1 Kings 2:25).

Confession will cause the pressure of chastisement to stop and will allow forgiveness, but nothing prevents the just penalty from being required, except God's mercy. It is essential for parents to require that their children normally pay the penalty. Restitution is a part of cleansing the mentality from guilt.

Parents may occasionally decide that a child has paid sufficient penalty without formal punishment. This could be particularly true with a normally obedient child who even confessed his guilt before being rebuked. However, the penalty (broken glass, spilled milk, etc.) still exists, so the parents will have to absorb the cost. There is, however, a danger in making a habit of granting mercy. Only God has the right not to require an individual to pay for his guilt. Even then, someone must pay the cost. It is only because Christ paid the penalty for our sins that we can be pardoned   (Romans 5:9; 8:1; 2 Corinthians 5:21; Galatians 3:13; Colossians 2:14; Hebrews 9:26-28; 10:10, 14-17; 1 Peter 2:24).

When punishment occurs after confession and forgiveness, it can be administered by parents without anger. The conflict is over, and the penalty is just an objective fact of life. The child who has submitted to his parents' authority and truly accepted his guilt will also welcome punishment with a proper attitude. This does not mean that the child will laugh about having to clean up a mess, paying for something damaged, or apologizing. It does, however, mean that he should not resent or fight against the penalty.

If a child rebels against his parents about taking his punishment, it is likely that he did not truly accept responsibility for his guilt. His confession was probably not genuine. Parents will need to rebuke such a child for his attitude and may even need to use the rod, if he refuses to accept their authority.

The result of punishment is the establishment of a proper fear of justice and respect for the power of authority. It proves the sureness of judgment and prepares a child to accept the rule of government and God. It helps a child understand and believe the absolute reality of God's judgment. When a well-trained child hears the Word of God say, *"He that believeth on the Son hath everlasting life; and he that believeth not the Son shall not see life, but the wrath of God abideth on him."* (John 3:36), that child is much more likely to take it seriously than the child who has not learned about judgment.

The result of disregard for just punishment can be seen in adults. Many people have been raised in the last few generations who doubt the reality of God's eternal punishment. They have been raised by parents who threatened, but did not consistently carry through. They have observed the courts turn criminals loose who have broken established standards. It is no wonder people today question whether justice truly exists. Proper child training can help reverse this deceptive impression by instilling a respect for punishment of broken standards.

Now that we have studied the concept of punishment and have seen the difference between punishment and chastisement, we can develop the first three steps of the training system: setting the standards, rebuking the child, and forgiving the child. The next chapter will show how to establish and communicate standards to children. This important step is the basis for being a just parent.

AUTHOR NOTES TO THE 2ND EDITION

Since so many parents have great difficulty determining appropriate penalties for wrongs done, here are a number of disobediences matched with reasonable penalties.

1. What is the penalty for lying? Lying is a form of rebellion, not disobedience. Chastisement is in order and the child should be required to explain why he lied since the lie will be protecting the real problem.

2. When our son was about ten, one of his home responsibilities was to put out the garbage every Monday and Friday morning before the trucks came for the pick up. Week after week, Ron would forget one or the other days and we would have to put up with ripening garbage an extra three or four days. I finally determined that Ron just did not consider my command to do this task important enough to remember. I could have had him keep the garbage bags he forgot in his room until the next pick up, but I felt that was a bit extreme. So, I laid down the rule: remember the pick up days or bike the garbage to a convenience store dumpster (with the owner's permission, of course). About two times of paying this consequence and he became responsible about his duty. He also became more responsible about setting his own alarm and getting up on his own (he slept like a rock).

3. Our youngest daughter, JoAnn, locked herself in the bathroom when she was about five-years-old. Virginia knew something was wrong because she didn't hear her chirping around the house for awhile. When she tracked her down and used the special key to gain entry to our little cherub, she was happily finger painting the bathroom counter tops, mirror, and natural wood cabinets with . . . toothpaste. She knew she was doing something wrong (she locked the door and didn't answer Virginia's calls), but she didn't know exactly what the consequences would be. How could she know that toothpaste was capable of bleaching wood cabinets?

The Punishment. Our daughter was required to help her mom wash off the toothpaste and then re-stain the cabinet doors. She couldn't help much, but she did all that she was physically capable of and she was not allowed to play until the work was done. We never figured out why she did it, but she was very artistically prone. After this important lesson on the consequences of her actions, she never destroyed anyone's property again.

4. A nine-year-old boy won't come in the house and finish his homework. His mother repeatedly tries to coax him by reminding him that his teacher won't allow him to go with his class on the field trip if he doesn't finish his project. He finally comes in at dark, but it's too late to finish the work, so she helps him. WRONG! Because his mother didn't want him to feel left out, she took a key learning experience from him. Instead, after warning the boy once, it should have then become his responsibility. His penalty is built in when he fails the assignment and has to stay at school to finish the project while the other students go on the field trip. Parent's don't have to dream up a penalty when they just allow their children pay the consequences of their own actions.

5. Our oldest daughter, Kathy, used to talk with her hands, at least when she was thirteen. The faster she talked, the more exaggerated her hand motions would become.

When we moved to Colorado our cabin had an unforgiving porcelain sink (instead of the softer aluminum to which we were accustomed). This meant that she needed to be V-E-R-Y careful when she washed dishes, particularly with the very-thin, glass coffee pot. I explained that she would pay the consequences of replacing the $7.00 pot, if she broke it.

Within a few days, she was washing dishes and talking simultaneously and, as predicted, she broke the coffee pot — into the thousands of slivers that only tinsel-strength glass can shatter. She immediately said she was sorry and cleaned up the glass (showing she understood responsibility for her actions). Then she went up to her room, rattled her piggy bank, and brought me $7.50 to pay for a new pot, including the tax.

GREAT LESSON, but wait, she didn't pay the full penalty. I didn't have a pot for my coffee, just a handful of wadded up dollar bills and some loose change. I told her that she would have to go into town (30 miles away) and buy the pot herself before the penalty would be paid. She went with her mom and I on the weekly trip into town (taken early so I could have my coffee) and we took her to the local discount store. She went in, found the pot, paid for it herself, and danced out to the car. "Mama, Daddy, It was on sale. The Lord let me get the pot for only $4.50!" Praise God! He not only let her learn a valuable lesson in carefulness and personal accountability, but she learned something about the mercy of God that we all referred to for years afterward.

6. Several years later we were on vacation and all of the children took their own non-allergenic pillows. We warned them that they each were responsible for their own pillows. Our youngest daughter, JoAnn, (she too was about 13) realized that she had left hers behind at the last motel. It was only about 100 miles back, but she wouldn't have learned anything had I gone back for the pillow. Without a complaint, she offered to buy a replacement either on the trip or when we returned

home. No one had to remind her when we arrived home two weeks later. She handled the loss like an adult.

7. Kathy and JoAnn had the duty of washing supper dishes every other night. We tried to communicate to them what our standard of "clean" was. Mom and I started noticing pieces of food cemented on the plates and forks ever so often. We told the girls to be more careful in their pre-rinse before placing anything in the dishwasher. Still the dishes would have baked-on egg on the edges. We didn't know for sure which girl was doing the half-way job, but we had a good idea. We changed the girls schedule to one week on, one week off; and warned them if any more dirty dishes got through their shift, the guilty one would pay the consequences. The punishment would be: the removal of every dish and utensil from all kitchen shelves, washing and drying them carefully **by hand**, parental inspection, and then refilling the shelves.

After several days, we had found the culprit. It was Kathy, our oldest, who got to spend several hours making sure everything was clean in the kitchen. Four years after that she became a dental assistant and eight years later she married a dentist. Now, let me ask you, would you rather have the untrained girl cleaning the dental instruments that went into your mouth, or the trained one?

FOOTNOTES

[1]   *Oxford English Dictionary*, s.v. "punishment."

[2]   Greek, *ekdikos* "an avenger, one who punishes." Compound word consisting of the preposition *ek* "out of, from" and *dike* "righteousness, justice;" thus, "one who gives justice or vindicates." (Foundation for Biblical Research, "Child Training.")

[3]   Greek, *orge* "anger;" rendered in English by "wrath, anger" and "indignation." The use of the term is limited and reserved to God, or authorities ordained by God, for its right and proper use. (Luke 21:23; John 3:36; Romans 1:18; 2:5; 13:4; Revelation 6:17). *Orge* indicates the overt and consummative act and in most cases is best rendered "punishment." (Ibid.)

[4]   Greek, *prasso* "to do, practice." (Ibid.)

[5]   Greek, *poieo* "to do" an act or deed, "accomplish." *Poieo* is used to denote a single act; whereas prasso is used to denote a succession of acts, thus a practice or habit. (Ibid.)

[6]   Greek, *kakos* "bad, wrong," as in violation of a law given to man by God. (Ibid.)

Chapter 21

STANDARDS

Step one in the child training system is setting the standards. A standard is defined as "a rule, principle, or means of judgment or estimation; a criterion, measure."[1] A child must always know exactly what his parents expect of him. This principle is true for anyone who is under authority. The law of the land must be clearly stated before the citizens can be expected to follow it. When laws are not clearly set and objectively enforced, each man becomes his own authority and does only what he thinks is right in his own opinion.

Likewise, employers must set and consistently enforce company standards for their employees. Husbands must also clearly communicate what they expect from their wives. In this way, wives are able to follow the Biblical directive to submit to their husbands. Setting the standards is the responsibility of any person in a position of rulership, and it is necessary for the just treatment of subordinates. This chapter will describe how parents can set standards for their children and of what these standards should consist.

The Biblical principle behind setting standards is clear: there can be no personal accountability without the existence of law:

Romans 4:15 *"Because the law worketh wrath; for where no law is, there is no transgression."*

Again, the Greek word translated "wrath" means "punishment,"[2] and the word translated "transgression" means "the breaking of a known standard."[3] In other words, God is saying that punishment is the result of breaking a known law; if there is no law, there can be no punishment. The next verse bears out this fact:

Romans 5:13 *"For until the law sin was in the world; but sin is not imputed when there is no law."*

This verse states that man has always failed to measure up to the absolute standards of God, but that he is held personally accountable for only that portion of God's law that is revealed at any particular time. (The word translated "imputed" means "charged to one's account."[4]) For example, Adam was held accountable for only one law — not to eat the fruit of one specific tree in the garden of Eden (Genesis 2:17); but the Mosaic Law formally codified so many of God's standards that no man can avoid becoming personally accountable to the absolute ruler — God (Romans 3:19, 20, 23; Galatians 3:10).

In child training, parents must clearly state the directions or restrictions their children are expected to obey. Properly setting the standards is the foundation for fair rulership. A child has the right to know what his parents want him to do and not to do. The specific standards will vary from family to family depending on the parent's upbringing, education, and station in life. However, the basis for any purposeful child training should be the standards given to man by God.

The only authority parents possess is delegated by God. Therefore the standards by which parents control their children and then teach them should generally be in agreement with God's standards. Certainly, they should never conflict with God's Word. The correct standards will be re-enforced by the standards already instilled by God within the child's conscience. When parents train their children to obey and honor their rulership, to be honest, and to consider the rights and property of others, the child's conscience will confirm those standards. The child's conscience is also strengthened in the process of proper child training.

Children Must Comprehend Instructions

It is not enough to simply give a child instructions. Parents need to make certain their instructions are both heard and understood. This is sometimes difficult for parents because they fail to consider the child's immaturity. He is not inclined to concentrate on anything than what he wants to do, and he has a limited capacity to comprehend what he has been told, especially when he is young.

One way for parents to make sure they can expect their instructions to be followed is to insist that the child repeat each instruction. Parents can ask the child: "Now, what did I say?" "What does that mean?" or, "What will happen if you don't obey?" It is not necessary for a child to agree with an instruction — just that he understands.

Parents do not have to justify their instructions to their children. While parents have the responsibility to teach their children, teaching is to be done at the parent's timing, and only to children who are under control.

Instructions should be simple, especially for younger children. It is not necessary to try to get down on the child's level and try to reason with him in an attempt to get him to agree. The common expression, "KIS," "Keep It Simple," should become a parental guideline. Instructions should be as direct as possible. Children easily become confused when provided more explanation than necessary. When a child has been trained to ask the reason for every instruction, this insubordinate habit must be broken. If you believe it is beneficial to explain a particular instruction, always explain **after** requiring obedience.

Instructions should also be received with the right attitude. Children should be taught to respond to all instructions with respect and by showing a willingness to comply. It is not unreasonable to expect children to reply with: "Yes, sir," or "Yes, ma'am," as a demonstration of their respect for their parents' position. Such a response also indicates that the instructions have been acknowledged, and it is a courtesy to the parents. If a child will not accept instructions with the right attitude, he is being rebellious and chastisement is required.

With young children, chastisement is also necessary occasionally just to stop their playfulness and establish a serious attitude towards the situation. The following verse illustrates the concept:

Proverbs 22:15 *"Foolishness is bound in the heart of a child, but the rod of correction shall drive it far from him."*

Little children are often occupied with play and have difficulty bringing it to a halt. Parents must be sure not to give their instructions in a kidding manner or allow the child to think obedience is just a game. A good rule to follow is: do not kid with children when telling them what to do. If a child refuses to settle down after being firmly warned, his foolish behavior will have to be controlled.

Parents who have a playful, familiar relationship with

their little children actually promote their foolish behavior. This does not mean that parents should not play with their children, but rather that parents should be alert to the possibility of being part of the problem themselves. When father is playing "horsey" with his boy on the living room carpet, it is not the time to give the child instructions on carrying out the garbage. There needs to be a cooling off period after playtime to allow the return of the normal parent-child relationship before giving any instructions.

Children should not be "stirred-up" close to bedtime. It is almost impossible for them to turn off the excitement of a hardy romp and settle down for lying still in bed. The play itself should be controlled from getting out of hand. Children should not be allowed to do things in play that they cannot do normally. It requires wise parents to recognize when play ends and a breakdown in the child's respect for their authority begins.

Standards Should Include Warning

Setting standards should normally include a warning of the penalty for disobedience. God's Word, as always, provides us with this principle. When God sets a standard for man's obedience, He includes a warning of the punishment that can be expected. For example, God gave man the standard not to commit murder (intentional or negligent homicide):

Exodus 20:13 *"Thou shalt not kill."*

As a part of the standard. God also warned of the penalty for committing murder:

Exodus 21:12 *"He that smiteth a man, so that he die, shall be surely put to death."*

Other passages in Leviticus and Deuteronomy define the different degrees of homicide and provide additional information on how a government should administer the death penalty. Included in the discussions are the reasons for the penalty's necessity.

The warning of punishment for breaking a standard is only fair. Punishment should never be arbitrarily administered by an authority. Justice includes the warning of the penalty, as well as the giving of the standard, to those who are subject to obey. In His total fairness, God has warned man of the penalty for ignoring the most important standard ever given to man:

The Standard

John 3:36a *"He that believeth on the Son hath everlasting life;"*

The Penalty

John 3:36b *"and he that believeth not the Son shall not see life, but the wrath of God abideth on him."*

In this single verse, God not only clearly tells man the standard of salvation, but also warns of the punishment he will receive for disobedience of this all-important standard (see 2 Thessalonians 1:8, 9; Revelation 20:12-15).

Parents should follow God's example in setting standards for their children. First, they should make sure that the child understands what is expected of him. Then, they must make equally sure that the child understands the consequences for his disobedience. Both facets are parts of setting standards; however, parents will occasionally fail to set the penalty. This should not prevent their going through the other steps of the system, even punishing if the child should have known better.

Parents need to exercise wisdom in knowing what their child can comprehend. It would be foolish to tell a little child who had never been to a zoo that he could not go if he did not make his bed every day. The penalty is beyond his comprehension. Likewise, it would not be reasonable to expect a little child to meet a standard of quality in bathing, brushing his teeth, or washing the dishes on his own the first several times. In other words, both the standard and the penalty must match the child's mental and physical maturity.

A very young child can be taught that his instant obedience is expected when his parents tell him "no," "stop," or "come." He can also understand that his disobedience to these simple commands will not be tolerated and that he will be chastised as a result. Initially, the child can be physically restricted from doing what he is not to do as a demonstration of what the parents want. A baby can be taught not to squirm while his diapers are being changed, a toddler can be taught not to touch certain things in the house, and a young child can be taught not to play with his food. Willful disobedience to commands is always treated as rebellion.

Teaching a standard can be done either by example or by clear communication. To be sure that the child understands, he can be requested to demonstrate the example given or repeat the instructions in his own words. Some things parents teach their children will need to be repeated many times before a child will fully understand. No penalty should be established until the child can rightfully be held accountable.

Properly making a bed is an example of something that requires practice to learn. Demonstration and even parental assistance are needed at first. Telling a child to go clean his room is not setting a standard. He really does not know what "clean" means. Only after the child has seen what is expected and has the physical ability to meet the standard should he be held accountable. The principle is: when a child comprehends a standard and has the ability to comply, he then becomes fully accountable for his performance.

Once a child becomes accountable, the penalty can be set low at first. For not making his bed well, the penalty could be to have him unmake a poorly made bed and do it over again. If he still will not make it as well as he is able, then the penalty can be increased to a more significant punishment. If the child rebels against doing the job right or even refuses to do it at all, he is to be chastised and then still required to do the job right. Remember, rebellion can only be handled by chastisement. Punishment, by contrast, is the administration of a just penalty for a broken standard.

Five General Categories of Standards

Setting standards could be divided into five general categories. Listed in order of importance, they are: (1) obedience (doing what is told), (2) honor (respecting authority), (3) trustworthiness (requiring truthfulness and honesty in deed), (4) self-control (developing behavior toward others and self-discipline), and (5) following instructions (accepting parental advice based on personal respect). Obedience is the primary standard in child training since teaching all other standards depends on it. Even if a child is fifteen when his parents begin to train him, he must first be taught to obey. Obedience is the basis for respect of authority, and external control is the prerequisite for self-control.

The second most important standard in child training is for the child to honor both his father and his mother. Honor is the proper respect given to the parents' position of authority. It is natural for a small child to be awed by the mere size of his parents. As they demand his obedience by the use of the rod when necessary, he retains this awe. Eventually, he comes to respect the authority of their position and only fears the rightful punishment he will receive for disobedience. This honor will make it possible later for parents to influence a teenager beyond their physical ability to control him. It is the very basis for the child's acceptance of their teaching.

Trustworthiness is the next most important standard because it is the basis for developing integrity. A child should be required to be truthful at all times. Not only should he not be allowed to lie, but his word should be his bond. He should be taught that whatever he says he will do is a commitment that must be honored, regardless of personal cost. He should also be taught not to lie about someone else. As God's Word is the means by which we can trust Him, so also a man's word should be trustworthy.

A child should also learn honesty in deed. Parents should be able to trust their child not to take food or leave the house without permission. Of course, no cheating or stealing should be allowed. A child should be taught to do what he knows is expected of him without external pressure. He should learn to accept total responsibility for his own actions, words, and even thoughts. One test of a person's quality of character is what that person will do when he knows no one else will know. Dependability of word and deed is the expression of a trustworthy character.

The fourth category of standards consists of those standards that promote self-control. This category can be divided into two areas: behavior toward others and self-discipline. Children should be taught acceptable behavior such as manners. All manners emphasize consideration for others and require the child not to think only of his self-importance. Some of the standards that can be taught even to young children are: never to interrupt a conversation, especially of adults; to control the loudness of voice and other noises; to observe the privacy of others; to respect the rights and property of others; not to covet the possessions of others; to use correct table manners; not to fight or quarrel with other children — especially brothers or sisters; to show respect for parents and other adults; to be masculine boys or feminine girls in every way (in dress and behavior for each of the distinct masculine or feminine roles).

Initially, manners will need to be imposed by parents exercising their external control. Children do not come with volume controls or consideration of others before self. Some manners will need to be demonstrated and repeated many times before a child truly comprehends what is expected. Consideration must be given to the child's ability to meet the standard, but by eight to ten years of age a child should be able consistently to exercise acceptable behavior.

Self-discipline includes both restricting and forcing oneself to do those things that are not his choice by nature. Children should be required to control their desires in all areas of their life. Some areas where parents can train their children in self-discipline are: not to have temper tantrums; to control crying and whining; not to demand wants or attention; to do duties well; to eat only what and when allowed; to share possessions; to treat all property carefully; to control temper or anger; to control moodiness; and to follow directions promptly.

The fifth category of standards consists of all other instructions that are given by parents. These instructions will vary greatly between families and even between children within a single family. Parents should remember that their word is law. They not only have the right, but the responsibility to direct the activities of their children. Children are to obey their parents *"in all things."* This would include when to go to bed, when and what to eat, how to dress, what outside influences (friends, entertainment, church, school) are permitted, and what duties are required. It also includes the child's attitude. Parents must be alert to train their children in having a proper attitude toward the parents, God and other authorities, adults and children, school and work, and also themselves.

Children should be taught the uniqueness of the individual. They need to know that it is all right to be different from others — even from the majority. Parents who train their children properly will truly produce different children; therefore, those children need to be prepared for being different. The insecure child should be taught to accept himself for what he is and allow God to develop him into what he can be.

It is within this category of "instructions" that a child is taught about life, especially about those things in which he has had no experience. Instructions about the following can be given to a child who respects his parents: boy/girl relationships, marriage, finances, education, career possibilities, how to be people-wise, contentment, and living according to God's Word. When parents desire to teach their child about life in areas beyond the child's experience, they need more than obedience to and honor for their authority. Before a child is likely to follow this type of instruction, he must have respect for his parents' character.

Personal Respect

Respect can be impersonal, such as honor for a position of authority without consideration of the personal qualifications of the individual in that position; or respect can be personal, recognizing the worth of the person. An individual can be personally respected for his technical knowledge, his wisdom, or his quality of character. Personal respect must be earned and deserved; it cannot be taught or required.

Being a parent entitles you to honor for your position. However, to be totally successful in teaching your children you must earn their respect for you as a person. In other words, parents need to grow in character while their children are growing up. Parents who are respected by their children will not only be able to teach them as youths, but will be able to counsel them in adulthood.

A child who has been properly trained by parents whom he respects will accept their teaching as the basis for his adult life. Parents should not expect their children to accept their preferences, only the standards that are taught. Teenagers should begin to be allowed to express their individual likes and dislikes in food, dress, career, art, and so on, unless their choices directly violate God's Word. A youth should be allowed gradually to develop his own personality throughout his teen years as he establishes an identity unique to himself.

What Not to Do

Parents should avoid several negative factors in the process of setting standards. One thing to avoid is comparing one child unfavorably with another. Each child has his own strengths and weaknesses. It is unfair to use one child's strengths to shame another child. Chances are parents who use this tactic are not training either child.

Another thing to avoid is failure to follow through with a stated punishment for disobedience. Standards must be consistently enforced to be fair and effective. Parents have a tendency to avoid the unpleasantness of punishment when a child actually breaks a standard. It is very easy to say, "If you do that one more time, I am really going to punish you." Giving a child more than one chance to break a well established standard is not fair. No just law system works on a random basis. A child must learn to expect that each act of disobedience will be punished.

Sometimes parents are reluctant to punish because they have made the penalty too severe. The penalty should always match the standard. Parents need to exercise common sense in establishing penalties. To tell a child that if he doesn't come home by dinner time he will **never** get another meal would be ridiculous to enforce. The penalty can always be increased for repeated offenses until it reaches chastisement for willful disobedience. Parents must be firm in their instructions. Weak leadership receives no respect. Uncertain commands will not be followed. Parents who whine, "Oh, Johnny, I wish you would mind," will not be obeyed.

Probably the worst thing a parent can do to a child is to provoke him to anger or discourage him by belittling or teasing him. This type of indirect approach will infuriate a child, but it will not train him. Children, when being properly chastised, may become bitterly angry with their parents and even scream, "I hate you" (which is not tolerated, of course). But we are not discussing anger that results from **correct** child training. God commands parents not to irritate their children verbally:

Ephesians 6:4a *"And, ye fathers, provoke not your children unto wrath,"*

Colossians 3:21 *"Fathers, provoke not your children to anger, lest they be discouraged."*

The Greek word translated "provoke" in Colossians 3:21 means "to embitter, stir up, excite, provoke in a negative sense."[5] The father who irritates his children by verbal abuse is provoking the children to wrath. It is a sign of weak and insecure leadership for a parent to use cutting remarks intended to pressure a child.

Parents have said things like, "You fool, can't you ever do anything right," "I guess you will never learn," "I just don't know what to do with you, you're so bad," or "You will never amount to anything." This type of attack is the result of a parent's frustration and will do nothing but frustrate and discourage a child. If the authority is frustrated, the child is sure to be frustrated as well. A child has no protection against this kind of treatment, nor is he sure what he is to do since he has no clear directions to follow. The tragic result is for him to seethe internally, or come to consider himself as worthless.

The Greek word translated "provoke" in Ephesians 6:4, is different from the word used for "provoke" in Colossians 3:21, and means "to make one beside himself in anger."[6] Parents who needle their children may drive them right out of the home. While some children respond to verbal abuse by becoming discouraged, others respond with uncontrollable anger. Children become angered legitimately when their parents:

- Don't tell them what they expect (fail to set standards), but punish them unfairly ("Oh, Mary, you disappoint me so." or, "You should have known better." or, "You will have to miss the event because of that.")

- Do punish in anger and/or unjustly.

- Don't keep their word.

- Do have arbitrary or changing rules.

Parents have no excuse after reading this book to ever be frustrated and treat their children with cruel words. Knowing how properly to train children eliminates the reason for parental frustration and the resultant verbal abuse. It is necessary to declare a child's disobedience to be wrong as will be explained in the chapter on rebuke; however, it should be a deliberate step in the child training process, not a concealed effort to shame the child into the right conduct.

Notice that both of these Biblical commands are addressed to the father. One explanation is that the father, the head of the household, is the chief authority responsible for the proper training of his children. He is responsible even though the mother will execute most of the actual training. Another explanation could be that it is naturally more difficult for most women to assume the role of an authority, even over their own children. A mother will have a harder time being a firm leader and will tend to nag, snipe, or ridicule (especially with teens) and thereby "provoke" her children needlessly. The father will need to help her in this area.

With a thorough understanding of this most important step in the child training process, parents should find the rest of the system quite easy to understand. When parents know how to set standards properly and are willing to bring their children under control when necessary, they are well on their way to becoming successful parents. Therefore, let us review this section before studying the other steps.

Setting the Standard — Summary

- A standard is a rule or law to be kept.

- Standards must be established and clearly communicated before anyone subject to those standards can be held accountable to follow them.

- Children must be taught exactly what is expected of them.

- Since the parents' authority is delegated by God, the standards they set should generally be in agreement with God's standards.

- Parents must make sure their instructions are both heard and understood. Requiring a child to acknowledge the instructions and even to repeat them back will ensure reception and understanding.

- It is not necessary for a child to agree with the standard set, just to understand it.

- Instructions should be kept simple, especially for younger children.

- Children should be required to receive all instructions with a proper attitude of respect and willingness to comply.

- Parents must not kid with children when giving instructions. Giving instructions during play could be confusing to a child's respect for parental authority.

- Setting standards should also include a warning of the penalty for disobedience.

- The penalty should always match the standard and be one that the child can comprehend.

- Many standards must be taught by demonstration over a period of time.

- Only after a child both understands and has the physical ability to comply with a standard should he become fully accountable for his performance.

- Obedience is the primary standard for a child to learn. The teaching of all other standards is dependent on a child's obedience.

- Honor of parents, or respect for their right to rule, is the second most important standard to be learned. Honor is the natural result of firm but fair rulership.

- Training a child to be trustworthy in word and deed is the molding of a quality character. Learning to accept personal responsibility for one's own thoughts, words, and deeds is the mark of maturity.

- The next most important area of standards to teach a child is self-control. This area includes acceptable personal behavior and self-discipline.

- Training in acceptable behavior includes teaching manners that emphasize consideration for others and re-enforcing the natural masculine/feminine distinctions.

- Self-discipline is the restricting or forcing of oneself to do those things that are not one's choice by nature.

- The fifth category of standards parents are to teach their children consists of all instructions unique to each family.

- General instructions include the parents' decisions on bedtime, dress, cleanliness, food, duties, education, entertainment, associates, church, and attitude of the child.

- General instructions also include warnings and advice to the child about his life after childhood. These instructions will only be accepted by children who respect the persons of their parents.

- Parents do not have to earn or personally deserve the honor due to their position, but personal respect must be earned. To receive their child's personal respect, parents must develop a worthy character.

- Parents should not over influence their teenagers, but allow them to develop their own preferences within the bounds of God's Word.

- Parents should never compare one child against another unfavorably. They also must be consistent with the enforcement of all established standards.

- Above all, parents must not verbally provoke their child to anger or belittle him into frustration and discouragement.

Parents who set and consistently enforce quality standards will receive blessings beyond description through their trained children. Successful parenting has rewards like few other human endeavors. A woman can receive great satisfaction from a career well spent as a mother and a wife. A father not only receives inner joy from his well trained progeny, but he can also intensely appreciate his wife throughout the childless part of their lives because of her sacrifice that helped bring these results. The following verses are a reminder of the parents' blessing:

Proverbs 10:1a *"A wise son maketh a glad father,"*

Proverbs 23:24 & 25 *"The father of the righteous shall greatly rejoice, and he that begetteth a wise child shall have joy of him. Thy father and thy mother shall be glad, and she that bore thee shall rejoice."*

Proverbs 29:17 *"Correct thy son, and he shall give thee rest; yea, he shall give delight unto thy soul."*

Proverbs 31:28 *"Her children rise up, and call her blessed; her husband also, and he praiseth her."*

With the foundation of standards established, the parent can move to the next step, identifying what to do when these standards are not followed. If children would always obey, there would be no need for any further steps in child training. However, it is unreasonable to expect even the most docile child to obey all the time. Chastisement is not the response to every disobedience. Remember, chastisement is only necessary when a child is disobedient in willful rejection of your authority. The next chapter explains exactly what to do when your child disobeys, but is not being rebellious.

AUTHOR NOTES TO THE 2ND EDITION

Sibling Rivalry

Sibling rivalry is as **natural** as "the terrible twos" and "teenage rebellion." That is, it is part of the natural man (the sin nature) to be envious (covetous), greedy, even to war with each other (James 4:1 & 2). As always, parents are responsible to be the external control for their children until they develop internal controls. Parents, you have a responsibility to maintain peace for the subjects (children) in your kingdom (home) (I Timothy 2:2 & 3). You can't force your children to love each other, but you can make sure that they can lead quiet and peaceful lives.

You can teach your children that the Lord hates: *"A false witness that speaketh lies, and he that soweth discord among brethren"* (Proverbs 6:19). And, for the responder to an attack; *"Recompense to no man evil for evil"* (Romans 12:17a). And, the basis for all manners; *"Let nothing be done through strife or vainglory, but in lowliness of mind let each esteem others better than themselves"* (Phillipians 2:3).

Sharing

One of the reasons for sibling squabbles, as well as those with other children, is concerning possessions. Parents would like for their children to share their toys freely with others (of course, we don't offer our car, stereo outfit, new clothes, or other prize possessions to others). But, its not sharing unless it comes from the heart and forcing a little one to give up a prized possession to another won't change the heart. In fact, if the other child has been grabbing or whining for the prize, giving it to him supports stealing more than giving. It is the grabby child who is being selfish, not the one who owns the item. Russell Madden wrote in *The Freeman*, December, 1993, about forced sharing:

"Children grow into adults who accept the notion that those who demand the property of others are entitled to receive it, and those who defend their own property are immoral. The demands of the homeless, the uninsured, the student, the businessman, and the retiree, jealous of others who have what they do not, are echoes of the whining cries of those spoiled children who 'want' and 'need' the toys of their play-mates.

Parents should tell their children first that what is theirs is theirs: They need not share if they do not want to. By the same token, they cannot use the toys of other children — if those children prefer not to share. The idea of property is fundamental. Should a child wish to use another's toy the proper course for him to follow is to *ask*. If the other child declines, he should offer an exchange of some kind: this duck for that elephant. If the answer is still no, they should either increase their offer or be satisfied with what they already have. Under no circumstances should a child be allowed simply to seize the property of another. If another child should take a toy your child does not want to give up, the aggrieved party should feel free to come to you to rectify the problem, i.e., to return the toy, *not* to take the side of the thief against the innocent victim."

It is good for parents to encourage their children to share with those in need. Our children learned a lot about themselves, and others, by making up Christmas baskets and delivering them to other families, and by volunteering help to those in need. But, private property rights are important to teach as well.

Sophistication

I am extremely concerned about children becoming sophisticated in Christian families because they are allowed to have too many adult experiences before they are emotionally ready. A child is not an adult. By all accounts he is immature — physically and psychologically. If he becomes exposed to adult experiences prematurely it can actually harm his maturing process.

Sophistication: "The act of adulterating; a counterfeiting or debasing the purity of something by a foreign admixture; adulteration." *Noah Webster Dictionary*, 1828. "The use of specious, but fallacious reasoning." *Oxford English Dictionary*, 1971. Other factors of sophistication are: "An argument not based on sound reason; not pure or genuine; reasoning sound in appearance only, shallow, superficial." We might say a person is sophisticated when they can use a specialized vocabulary and convincingly argue their point, but who really doesn't have the depth of understanding to match their experience — a know-it-all who doesn't.

Children start to develop this attitude when parents allow or encourage them to "act adult" too early. For instance, a child of four to eleven calling his parents and other adults by their first names, or speaking in a familiar fashion to them, or asking adult (personal) questions, or making personal comments to them. It also occurs when a child is constantly made the center of attention in adult groupings. A child who is treated as if his opinions are of equal value with adults becomes puffed up in self-importance. This leads to frustration when he finds he really isn't allowed to live according to his own immature ideas. When parents promote premature adulthood in their children it produces an unhealthy **independence**, rather than a desired **self-sufficiency**. Self-sufficiency is based on personal responsibility; independence is based on a false sense of self-importance (conceit) and is usually accompanied with self-centeredness (being spoiled).

Over-familiarization may be cute for awhile, but it is also nauseating after short time; and it can destroy adult relationships. It also destroys the child's respect for his parents' authority and respect for adults overall. Timothy was no sophomore, but even he as an elder was commanded to show the respect of a son: *"Rebuke not an elder, but exhort him as a father; and the younger men, as brethren; The elder women, as mothers; the younger, as sisters, with all purity"* (1 Timothy 5:1 & 2). (See also Job 32:4 & 6; James 5:5a.) Children should be taught respect and honor for all adults. Familiarity is a privilege of common knowledge, rank, or class; not a right to be given children before their time.

Stimulation Addiction

Like sophistication, mental over-stimulation distorts a child's perception of reality. If allowed as a life style, a child can become bored and dissatisfied with normal life. I don't know if only those who naturally have a compulsive personality are affected by over-stimulation, or if over-stimulation produces compulsive behavior. I do know that boys/men are most susceptible to its addiction. The desire for mental stimulation, like any addiction, is insatiable and will lust for more quantity and increased levels as it continues un-checked.

Stimulation addiction can begin at two or three-years-old in children who are allowed to sit mesmerized (hypnotized; compelled by fascination) in front of a television for hours at a time. The colorful cartoons and other surrealistic entertainment (inanimate objects like plants, animals, and symbols that talk and move) create a world for the child with more mental stimulation than the real world can compete. Turning the sound up and sitting very close are ways of becoming more a part of the fantasy world, while shutting out distractions from the real world.

If parents are going to allow any such entertainment for their children, a few cautions are in order: ten or more feet away, sound no louder than a person speaking normally in the room would be, and limited time (like 15-30 minutes). Don't even start the must-complete-a-program habit. When it is time to eat or go somewhere, the program is turned off. Ideally, parents would sit with their child to discuss the content of any program they watch.

Anything that heightens the illusion, **increases** the mesmerizing effect (large screen, dark movie theater, surrealistic sound system, front row seats, and ear deafening volume). A Star Wars, Raiders, Jurassic Park, Tornado, or any other movie with special graphic and audio affects can be entertaining, or a "trip," depending on the mental maturity of the viewer. Some eight to twenty-year-old children will return many times to such movies for repeated trips (or fixes). They don't go back to study the plot or character development.

Notice that total involvement of the senses, especially sound, is a key element of stimulation addiction. Therefore, headphones play a vital role for children who wish to turn off the real world and escape into their fantasy world. I've never known a child to "trip" to easy-listening or classical music. It requires the loud, accented beat of rock, rap, or heavy metal to block the mind from reality and replace it with fantasy. Headphones allow a child to exist in a fantasy world of his own making where there are no rules, no work, and no adults.

Video games, either on the TV or on an arcade machine, can also induce stimulation addiction. I've known parents who have experienced extreme trauma in breaking their child from an addiction to Mario Brothers, Donkey Kong, or other equally exiting games. A child can play these games for H-O-U-R-S, and they become better than their parents over night (a side attraction). Even an adult can get hooked on video games or the computer with its infinite variety. Immature children don't have a chance against this level of mental stimulation. Parents would do well to limit their children's use of video games or on the computer to less than an hour-per-day; and only **after** all home duties, studies, and at least some form of physical exercises have been completed.

Video music is an even more intense experience. Many music videos add violence, sex, and the occult for heightened experiences. Children as young as twelve-years-old have been known to move into pornography, sexual experiences, and witchcraft under music video influence. Each of these areas is compulsively additive itself. When combined with the sensory stimulation of music videos they create an almost unbreakable hold on a child. The next logical step is to escape reality through drugs (suicide by degree) or by actual suicide (which is the number one killer of teens today). Children have no need for escape from reality. They haven't even experienced what reality is yet. Rock, rap, heavy metal, music videos; and games like Dungeons and Dragons or Magic — the Gathering, by Wizards of the Coast would be forbidden in my home.

A child can also become warped in regard to reality when he has **too many** adult experiences, **too young** for his emotional stability. When he has already been everywhere and done everything by the time he is fourteen or fifteen, it will be difficult for him to relate to the real world. School, family, church, and even his friends will appear dull to him. A pattern will have been set for him to always seek ever-increasing stimulation. There used to be an old saying that went something like this: "How are you going to keep them down on the farm after they've seen Pariee." A child becomes dissatisfied with the reality of life, if he experiences too much stimulation.

Character Development

There are some good resources available for teaching children of all ages about godly character.

WARNING: A lot of character development materials automatically cast the child as a child of God without his having consciously faced the issue. Another caution is not to make character standards the stepping stones to salvation. Don't allow a child to think that he will ever be accepted by God on the basis of his goodness (i.e. good character).

Teach character development to children as the way everyone should act toward each other. When the child becomes a Christian, these character traits can then take on spiritual significance as well.

Building Christian Character (Spiritual Character)
by Blair Adams
Published by Truth Forum
2433 N. 43rd Street
Waco, Tx 76710
(For adults to learn and teach)

Developing Character (Charismatic)
(How to Build Godly Character)
by Beverly Caruso, Ken Marks & Debbie Peterson
(Unit study of character traits with verses, songs, memory verses, books, games.)
Hands to Help
P.O. Box 3464
Orange, CA 92665

The Little Book of Christian Character and Manners   (Small, inexpensive)
by William and Colleen Detrick
Christian Tutorial Books
Goldfinch Lane
Port Angeles, Washington 98362

Write for current prices and availability.

FOOTNOTES

1 *Oxford English Dictionary*, s.v. "standard."

2 Greek, *orge* "anger;" rendered in English by "wrath, anger" and "indigation." The use of the term is limited and reserved to God, or authorities ordained by God, for its right and proper use. (Luke 21:23; John 3:36; Romans 1:18; 25; 13:4; Revelation 6:17). *Orge* indicates the overt and consummative act and in most cases is best rendered "punishment." (Ibid.)

3 Greek, *parabasis* "transgression, deviation." Compound word consisting of the preposition *para* "beside" and *basis* "a stepping" used for "the foot" or that with which one steps; thus, in a general sense, "a stepping beside." Used in an absolute sense, metaphorically for "a violation, a breaking of a standard or a breach of a law that has been ratified" (Romans 5:14; 1 Timothy 2:14). (Foundation for Biblical Research, "Child Training.")

4 Greek, *ellogeo* "to put on one's account, to impute." Compound word consisting of the preposition *en* "in" and *logeo* "word;" thus, "impute, charge to one's account." (Ibid.)

5 Greek, *erethizo* "embitter, stir up, excite, provoke in a negative sense;" connotes a turning in of anger. *Erethizo* is followed in context by *athumeo* "to be discouraged" or "inner wrath," emphasizing the results of such provocation. (Ibid.)

6 Greek, *parorgizo* "irritate, provoke." Compound word consisting of the preposition *para* "beside," and *orgizo* "anger." *Orgizo* is believed to have come from the root *orgao* "a vigorous upsurging of sap or thrusting upward of juice in a plant." In ancient literature *orgizo* was used in reference to that which blinded thought and manifested itself in uncontrollable action. *Parorgizo* might best be rendered "beside (oneself) with anger." The negative *me* with the second person plural present imperative of *parorgizo* should be rendered "Do not exasperate" or "Stop exasperating your children." (Ibid.)

Chapter 22

REBUKE

After parents have properly set a standard, the child is faced with a decision. He must either accept and submit to his parents' word, or reject their warning and disobey. Since every child is subject to his own sinful nature (especially in his particular area of weakness), he is more inclined to disobey than to obey. A conscious knowledge of the consequences for disobedience (fear of punishment) helps to counter balance his strong desire to go his own way. However, even the sure knowledge of punishment will not counteract a child's will and nature at all times.

Parents should be prepared for and expect their children to disobey; it would be unnatural if they did not. Each failure should be viewed as a training opportunity, not as a tragedy. Consider the standards that you set as being instructions in a course on soul training. The test for this course is obedience. When a child disobeys, he has failed the test and must receive the appropriate penalty as further instructions. Parents should look forward to each failure as an opportunity to teach their child a valuable lesson in personal responsibility. This chapter will explain how to evaluate a child's disobedience and why it is so important for parents to condemn every act of unrighteousness by their children.

When a parent's warning is ignored (the standard that was set has been broken) it is disobedience. There are three basic levels of disobedience. First, the child may honestly have disobeyed because of his natural childishness. It seems that a four-year-old wakes up to a new world every morning without remembering any of the instructions from the day before. Therefore, parents must repeat any important instructions that they want a very young child to follow. Parents must know their child and his ability to remember instructions. If a child legitimately cannot remember, he should simply be rebuked (told the action was wrong) and not be punished. However, children will often use the excuse that they forgot when they really just chose not to remember.   Children must be held accountable for their actions:

Proverbs 20:11 *"Even a child is known by his doings, whether his work be pure, and whether it be right."*

When a child is aware enough to remember the things he wants to remember (like what time his soccer game is) but forgets the instructions his parents give, he should be held accountable. In effect, such a child is declaring the word of his parents is simply not important enough to remember. If normal punishment for habitually forgetting to follow instructions does not solve the problem, the child may be in passive rebellion. When this is the case, he will also reject rebuking and be unwilling to admit he is wrong. He should be warned future forgetfulness of instructions will be considered intentional, and he will therefore be chastised. This warning should improve his memory rapidly.

The second level of disobedience is when a child breaks a standard through misunderstanding or not thinking. For example, you tell your child not to damage private property. He may not consider intentionally breaking a window in the house, but may carelessly toss a ball through a window during play in the front room. Assuming you had not already thought to set the standard of no ball playing in the house, his disobedience of damaging private property came from foolishness, not intent. However, a standard has been broken, so action must be taken. He must be rebuked, must admit the wrong done, and if he should have known better, must receive the appropriate punishment — clean-up, payment, and repair of the window.

Since no parent can think of all of the rules to set beforehand, there will be many standards broken that will result in the need of at least a rebuke. In these cases the rebuke itself becomes the setting of the standard for next time, but punishment is not necessary . For example, a child may cruelly make fun of a handicapped person before being told that it is wrong. The declaration of that as being unacceptable conduct (rebuke) will establish a rule for any future occurrence.

The third, and most severe, form of disobedience is outright rebellion. This occurs when the child fully comprehends the standard and is mature enough both to remember and to meet the standard.   For example, a child has been told not to eat between meals without specific permission. The first time he breaks the rule he is simply rebuked and warned that any future occurrence will be punishable. The next time he is discovered eating cookies before dinner, he will be rebuked, required to admit he is wrong, and then receive the promised punishment — like having no dessert for a week. Now he is without excuse. The standard has been made clear. When he again breaks the rule, he must be chastised for his willful rebellion and receive a more severe penalty as appropriate punishment.

An overview of the entire training system may help prevent any confusion at this point.

Step 1: Set the Standard

If a child keeps both the standards he has been taught and even those that have not yet been communicated, everything is unrealistically great. However, when a child does something that he should not have done, his parents must proceed to step two. This occurs when the child does something wrong that was (1) not communicated, (2) truly forgotten, (3) unintentionally done, (4) done after knowing better, or (5) done willfully.

Step 2: Rebuke the Child

Those things that a child does that are wrong (deeds, words, or attitudes) must be declared to be wrong by his parents. If a child is **not** to be held accountable for a particular wrong deed, he only needs to be told that the deed was wrong. Thus, the rebuke becomes his warning against any recurrence of such behavior. In these cases, confession is not necessary since the child did not realize he was doing anything wrong at the time. On the other hand, if a child is accountable (i.e., should have known better) he must be rebuked, acknowledge his guilt, and receive the appropriate punishment. (**Remember:** We are only discussing a child who mentally understands our instructions and the consequences of his disobedience; and who is not in active rebellion.) If a child has willfully broken a known standard, or if he refuses to accept the rebuke and admit his guilt, he must be chastised for his rebellion and also pay the penalty.

Step 3: Forgive the Child

After a non-rebellious child admits he wrongfully broke a standard, he should be forgiven. Forgiveness will be explained in detail in a following chapter.

Step 4: Punish the Child

A child who breaks a standard for which he is held accountable is to be finally punished with the appropriate penalty that matches the wrong done, as explained in the chapter on punishment (Chapter 20).

What Rebuke Means

Parents must act as judge of their child's actions, words, and attitudes. It is a part of the responsibility of anyone in a God-ordained position of rulership to judge every violation of God's law committed by those under their authority. Parents are clearly in a position of authority that not only gives them the right to make law, but also to judge wrong doing and to administer punishment.

The parents' authority is represented by their word. Their word is law as far as the child is concerned. When a child knowingly or unknowingly commits a wrong, his parents must declare the issue as being wrong. To rebuke means "to reprove, reprimand; to express blame or reprehension of (a quality, action, etc.)."[1] God's Word reveals that rebuking has two purposes: to expose the wrong (bring it to light) and to convict the guilty person.

John 3:20 *"For everyone that doeth evil hateth the light, neither cometh to the light, lest his deeds should be reproved."*

John 16:8 *"And when he is come, he will reprove the world of sin, and of righteousness, and of judgment:"*

Ephesians 5:13 *"But all things that are reproved are made manifest by the light; for whatever doth make manifest is light."*

Rebuking a child forces him to see that his action is unacceptable to his parents. He may not accept his guilt, but his parents' rebuke makes it clear that his authority considers him guilty. A child usually knows when he has done wrong, but the parents' rebuke makes him face the fact. When parents do not rebuke the wrong their children commit, they are actually condoning wrong doing. Authorities who tolerate unrighteous behavior promote unrighteousness and abdicate their responsibility. When authorities do not judge the wrongs committed, each person becomes his own judge.

Judges 21:25 *"In those days there was no king in Israel; every man did that which was right in his own eyes."*

Of course, when a child is allowed to be his own judge, he will not judge himself against his own will or desire. A person can justify almost anything he does as being right, even if his conscience initially condemns him.   The conscience can eventually become seared over so it no longer convicts a person of his most heinous actions (Romans 1:28-31; Ephesians 4:19; 1 Timothy 4:2; Titus 1:15).

Parents must rebuke their child to prevent his self-justification (the rationalization that he was right to do what is wrong) or his transfer of guilt (deceiving himself into thinking that it was really someone else's fault that he did wrong). The Bible gives the classic example of self-justification and guilt transfer in the account of the golden calf in Exodus 32.

In Exodus 32, Moses had been away from his position of leadership over the children of Israel for about forty days. He had been on Mount Sinai receiving additional commandments (standards) from God, while the people were left leaderless as a test. As usual when those who are immature are left to their own devices, they failed the test miserably. But the response of one man to his guilt is particularly significant.

Aaron, Moses' brother, was left in charge of the people, but he was weak in character and easily pressured to compromise God's standards. (Like so many of our leaders today, it was more important to Aaron to be appreciated and admired by the people than to do the right thing.)

While Moses was gone, the people came to Aaron and asked him to make an idol for a new leader to replace Moses who had been away so long. Instead of accepting his responsibility to direct the people correctly, Aaron commanded the people in accordance with their own evil desires. He told them to bring him a part of the treasure that God had given them when He brought them out of Egypt (Exodus 32:2). Of course, making an idol was a direct violation of the standard that God had already given to the people in the Ten Commandments:

Exodus 20:3, 4, 23 *"Thou shalt have no other gods before me. Thou shalt not make unto thee any carved image, or any likeness of anything that is in heaven above, or that is in the earth beneath, or that is in the water under the earth; Ye shall not make with me gods of silver, neither shall ye make unto you gods of gold."*

Therefore, Aaron knowingly broke one of God's primary standards. He actually collected the gold from the people, had it melted down, and he himself sculptured the image of an idol — a golden calf.

Exodus 32:4 *"And he received them at their hand, and fashioned it with an engraving tool, after he had made it a melted calf: and they said, These are thy gods, O Israel, which brought thee up out of the land of Egypt."*

When Moses returned to find the people engaged in a drunken orgy worshipping their new idol-god, he immediately went to Aaron and asked him for an excuse. Moses not only asked Aaron for an excuse, he suggested a patsy to blame in Aaron's place:

Exodus 32:21 *"And Moses said unto Aaron, What did this people unto thee, that thou hast brought so great a sin upon them?"*

This is not a rebuke, it is a solicitation for an excuse. A rebuke would have been "Aaron, you have done wrong and are responsible for bringing a great sin on the people." Instead, Moses set up a way for Aaron to escape responsibility for his fault by asking, "What did these people do to you?" Parents do this with their children when they try to find a justification for their children's wrong deeds. Parents may think that if a sufficient reason can be manufactured, perhaps no conflict will be necessary. Part of the motivation parents have in asking for an excuse is to avoid conflict. Of course, Aaron immediately took the opportunity Moses offered him:

Exodus 32:22 *"And Aaron said, Let not the anger of my lord [burn]: thou knowest the people, that they are set in mischief."*

Aaron asks Moses not to be angry with him because of the nature of the people and says, in effect: "You know how evil these people are. They are always doing something wrong." Aaron has now made a normal transfer of guilt. He has been able to shift his own responsibility and transfer the entire blame onto the people. The nature of children is naturally equipped with the ability to manufacture excuses and thereby avoid any reprisal for doing wrong. With just a little training by parents, children can become experts at shifting the blame to brothers and sisters, the kid down the block, or even their own parents.

Aaron next attempts to make Moses share part of the guilt for what happened:

Exodus 32:23 *"For they said unto me, Make us gods, which shall go before us; for as for this Moses, the man who brought us up out of the land of Egypt, we know not what is become of him."*

Aaron is saying that if Moses had not been gone so long, this would never have happened. Parents can get caught in this same type of entrapment. A child will soon learn to turn his parents' words or actions against them: "But, you said," or "You let Tommy do such and such."

Next, Aaron attempts the ultimate guilt transfer by attempting to transfer guilt to an inanimate object so that no one is really at fault. Thereby, the whole incident can be passed off as just an accident.

Exodus 32:24 *"And I said unto them, Whosoever hath any gold, let them break it off. So they gave it me: then I cast it into the fire, and there came out this calf."*

Aaron said, "All I did was ask the people for their gold, tossed it into the fire, and lo and behold, **out came this calf!**" This is the classic example of avoiding personal responsibility. First, Aaron justified his action by blaming it on the people. He then transferred his own guilt to them and even brought Moses in as being partly at fault. Ultimately, Aaron rejected any responsibility for the golden calf — the same calf that he himself had carefully molded and sculptured from the gold that he had melted. If Moses was willing to accept Aaron's fabrication, the people would not be at fault, Moses would not have to share in the guilt, and even Aaron would be "off-the-hook." No one would have been at fault if the golden calf had just jumped out of the fire on its own.

Parents experience similar no-fault situations frequently: "The glass tipped over," "The bottle broke," "The ball went through the window," and on and on. Transfer of guilt is common with children: "He pushed me," "All the other kids do it," "The teacher didn't tell me," "Mother said I could," "Johnny's mother said it would be all right," and so on. Parents must be careful not to be sidetracked by their child's attempt to avoid responsibility for his own actions. When parents act as judge of their child's wrong doing and clearly rebuke him for his personal guilt, many excuses can be eliminated. A proper rebuke causes a child to face when he is at fault and must stand accountable for his own actions.

The principle to follow is simple: never ask your children for an excuse — you will always get one. The reason a child breaks a standard — peer pressure, circumstances, or even severe soul disturbances — is not a legitimate excuse for wrong doing. Determining guilt is the true issue, not finding a reason to excuse guilt. (I told my children on several occasions that "No one can ever **make** you do something wrong. They can laugh at you, they can beat you, they could even kill you, but you always make the choice to do or not to do anything.")

Reproving a child should ordinarily be done in private. Embarrassment is not the objective; however, a child should never be allowed to get away with willful rebellion in public. If a child chooses to defy his parents' authority in front of others, he should be rebuked before them as an example. Example: "Son, you are not to tell me no. Go to your room and I'll be there in a minute."

Finally, a rebuke sets the stage for punishment. It is the open declaration by the authority that judges an act to be wrong and worthy of punishment. A child should never be punished without telling him what he did wrong and reminding him of the standard that was set. It is also essential for him to admit his guilt, as will be explained in the next chapter. A child needs to accept that he is to blame and truly deserves his punishment. A proper rebuke also re-enforces the conscience for the child's future guidance.

When a child has been rebuked, he again has a choice to make. He must either accept his parents' right to judge him, or he will reject their authority and be in rebellion. If he is in rebellion, chastisement is the only way to reestablish his parents' rejected position of authority. However, if a child accepts his guilt, the next step is for his parents to forgive him. Before we explore this step, let us discover what guilt and confession mean.

FOOTNOTES

[1] *Oxford English Dictionary*, s.v. "rebuke."

Chapter 23

GUILT AND CONFESSION

Guilt as a word and as a concept has had its original meaning distorted in contemporary use. Therefore, it is necessary to clarify its true meaning. Guilt is "the fact of having committed. . some specified or implied offense."[1] It is not an emotional feeling. Most people today, when asked to define "guilt," would say that it is the way they feel about something they did. This simply is not true.

A person is guilty because of what he has done, not because of the way he feels. It is possible for a person to be guilty, but not feel guilty. It is also possible for a person to feel guilty, but not be guilty. The reality of guilt needs to be understood apart from the emotional response. This chapter will describe true guilt and reveal the only solution to its devastating effects.

True guilt exists because right and wrong are absolutes. God is the source of all absolutes and has made man accountable for specific standards of right and wrong. God has instilled certain basic standards of right and wrong within the heart of man (Romans 2:15). When man breaks these standards, his mentality is convicted of guilt (the fact of having committed a wrong).

God has delegated authority to human institutions to punish those who are guilty (Romans 13:4). When an adult commits the crime of murder, for instance, he is guilty of committing a wrong. A judicial system based on the Bible would establish the fact of that guilt, declare the murderer to be guilty (rebuke), and sentence him to death (appropriate punishment). The guilty party's feelings about the crime are immaterial; he is guilty all the same. Likewise, when a child disobeys a standard established by his parents, he also is guilty of committing a wrong. He has broken God's standard:

Colossians 3:20a *"Children, obey your parents in all things;"*

After a child has committed a wrong, his conscience begins to convict him subconsciously of guilt. He is convicted of both the wrong itself and the need to right the wrong done. A child under conviction will normally hang his head and avoid looking his parents in the eyes. If a child's guilt is not cleansed from his soul, he is likely to become moody and bitter, condemning others around him in order to justify himself. Guilt continues to cause a mental conflict that can eventually result in emotional and physical problems if it is not resolved.

God has designed the only solution to the problem of guilt. This solution is confession and restitution for the wrong done. In the spiritual relationship between man and God, Jesus Christ is the only acceptable payment (restitution) for sins; therefore, man can only confess his guilt to God and accept Christ's payment. However, in the human realm when one party has injured another, he must admit his wrong action and attempt to repair the damage before guilt can be eliminated from his soul. For the child, this means he must admit to his parents that what he did was wrong and then willingly pay the proper penalty.

It is important for parents to remember that they are the symbol of God to their children and are to teach them about a spiritual relationship with God. It is also important for parents to realize the absolute necessity for their child to cleanse his soul from guilt. Parents, as God's delegated authority over their children, are to declare their children's disobedience to be wrong. Rebuke causes a child to think about what he has already been convicted of subconsciously. In other words, it makes him "face the issue" and also sets the stage for confession.

Confession

The definition of "confession" is "making known or acknowledging one's fault, wrong, crime, (or) weakness."[2] When a child is rebuked by his parents, he will be caused to face the issue of his guilt. His conscience may have already convicted him, but now his guilt is openly known. It is imperative for a child to admit his guilt as soon as possible after realizing he has done wrong.

A well-trained child will actually approach his parents when he realizes he has done something wrong. He will have learned it is better to "face the music," than to try to hide his guilt unsuccessfully. An untrained child will wait until he has been caught and rebuked before he will admit his guilt. A child who will not admit he was wrong even after being rebuked is being rebellious. Chastisement is again the only answer for rebellion. Any child who definitely understands he has done wrong should be required to admit his guilt.

Parents have several objectives for having their child confess. First, confession assists the child in cleansing his soul of unconfessed guilt. This process insures that unresolved guilt will not be gnawing at the child's mind and that he will be able to face his parents with a clear conscience. The second reason is that confession causes the child to recognize personal responsibility for all his actions and attitudes. The sooner a person learns he is personally responsible for everything he does, the better able he will be to face life. The third reason is that confession causes a child to accept his parents' authority — their right to set the standards and judge him.

It is not the parents' objective to force a child into having an emotional response like feeling guilty, feeling sorry, crying, begging, or performing some other act of penitence. Guilt is the fact of being wrong. It needs to be acknowledged mentally, not emotionally. A child may feel very sorry he was caught. He may emotionally regret the punishment he will receive. He may even want to cry because of the embarrassment. But the important thing is that he admits he was wrong. He must willingly agree with his authority's evaluation of his action and accept the rebuke. When a child admits his guilt of disobedience, he has acknowledged the wrong, owned up to his personal responsibility, and conceded to the rulership of his parents.

A child who has submitted to parental authority and truly accepted his guilt will also accept his punishment with a proper attitude. The Biblical pattern for this concept is revealed in the following passages:

Leviticus 26:40a *"If they should confess their iniquity,"*

Leviticus 26:41b *"if then their uncircumcised hearts be humbled, and they then accept of the punishment of their iniquity;"*

In the original Hebrew language of the Old Testament these passages mean, "If they will confess their guilt,. . .or rather their uncircumcised heart will humble itself, they will take pleasure in the punishment for their wrongdoing."[3] The Biblical pattern is first the admission of guilt, however, the admission must be genuine; and then punishment will be accepted as being what is deserved.

The truly repentant child (one who has mentally recognized his guilt and has admitted it to be wrong) should be willing to pay the penalty. Therefore, confession paves the way for the acceptance of punishment, which subsequently completes the cleansing of the mentality that has been convicted by guilt. Confessing cleanses the conscience of doing wrong, and paying the penalty relieves the conscience of the need to make things right.

On the other hand, a child who is punished without first admitting his guilt, will have great resentment toward his parents. Since he has not admitted his guilt, he will rationalize it or transfer it to someone else. If this happens, he will consider that he has been unjustly punished. Obviously, confession is an essential part of child training.

If a child will agree with his parents when they declare him wrong, he will not need the physical pressure of chastisement to face his guilt. All he needs to say is, "Yes, I was wrong," or "It was my fault." Whether a child is totally repentant internally is not the parents' responsibility to determine. They should accept any admission of guilt that is given with a proper attitude (not "Yeah, I'm wrong; so what?"). A child who agrees with his parents about his guilt has at least accepted their authority. If a child is "faking it," he will reveal his true attitude when it is time to receive his punishment. Then the parents can firmly handle what they may have suspected all along — rebellion.

True confession not only resolves the child's guilt, it also prevents any build-up of animosity between parent and child. The major reason parents are inclined to carry animosity toward their disobedient children is because the issue of disobedience is not resolved. When a child disobeys, he estranges himself from his parents. The parents feel rejected because the standard they set was not important enough to the child to keep. Consequently, they may wish to hurt the child or make him feel guilty. The child's confession tends to eliminate the parents' natural alienation and makes their forgiveness possible.

Now that we have an objective understanding of guilt and how a child is to admit when he is wrong, we can continue to step three in the child training process, forgiveness.

FOOTNOTES

[1] *Oxford English Dictionary*, s.v. "guilt."

[2] Ibid., "confession."

[3] Foundation for Biblical Research, "Child Training," s.v. "Leviticus 26:40 & 41 exegesis."

Chapter 24

FORGIVENESS

After a child disobeys one of his parents' standards (or at least after being rebuked), he feels alienated from them and desperately needs their forgiveness and acceptance. He may experience the "bad dog" syndrome; that is, he may act like a dog that tucks his tail between his legs after being scolded. A child who truly desires to please his parents (and all children want to be accepted and approved) is somewhat disoriented after his confession. He does not know if his parents are mad at him or what he should do next. Parents must forgive the child immediately and completely after his confession and reassure him of their full acceptance.

Forgiveness continues to remove the effects of guilt in a child's soul. The child should also be taught to accept the reality of forgiveness. God's Word reveals the standard for forgiveness:

1 John 1:9 *"If we confess our sins, he is faithful and just to forgive us our sins, and to cleanse us from all unrighteousness."*

Psalm 32:5 *"I acknowledged my sin unto thee, and mine iniquity have I not hidden. I said, I will confess my transgressions unto the Lord, and thou forgavest the iniquity of my sin. Selah."*

These verses reveal that forgiveness is available only **after** the confession of sin. The Greek word translated "confess" means "to agree or admit," and in a legal sense "to acknowledge guilt" (the fact of omitting a wrong); it means to agree with the charge.[1] In Palm 32:5, David says that he acknowledged his wrong action before God and did not hide his iniquity (guilt). Children are also to agree with their parents' judgment (rebuke) and admit their wrong doing before receiving forgiveness.

Forgiveness is to be immediate and unconditional upon confession. There is no indication that any restitution, penitence, promise of good behavior, or emotional experience, such as crying, is required for forgiveness. The issue is clearly the guilty party's agreement that he failed to meet the standard and is therefore wrong. He may or may not feel bad about his failure. An emotional person who strongly desires to be accepted will always feel bad when someone rebukes him, while an unemotional person seldom does. It requires a mature person to view mentally his own actions with the same disgust as does his authority. Parents, therefore, should not expect more from their immature children than is reasonable.

The Bible also reveals that forgiveness is to be complete; the wrong is to be completely forgotten:

Isaiah 43:25 *"I, even I, he who blotteth out thy transgressions for mine own sake, and will not remember thy sins."*

Jeremiah 31:34b *"for I will forgive their iniquity, and I will remember their sin no more."*

Parents must be willing to accept their child's legitimate confession. Disobedience that has been confessed is not to be brought up in the future and used against the child. It is to be forgotten, erased from the parent's mind so that the child starts with a new slate. Confession should be satisfactory to resolve any animosity the parents may have had because of the child's disobedience. Forgive and forget is the rule.

The result of forgiveness is that fellowship is restored between child and parents. This can be an emotional time when the child is relieved from the torment of guilt and alienation. The parents may also experience a release from the tension that the conflict produced. However, what is important is for the parents to assure the child that full fellowship and the normalization of family relations have occurred.

After a conflict has been resolved, especially if chastisement was necessary before the child would confess, the child will normally seek a sign of approval. He may bring something he has done and ask for his parents' comment, or he may just want to sit on their lap or hug their neck. It is important for the parents to demonstrate their love at this point and show that all is forgotten. This demonstration would be almost impossible without the child's confession and the parents' forgiveness. Another way a child can be reassured is for the parents to work with him in planning the restitution. They can help him figure out a time to go to the store to buy a replacement for a broken item or a way to make the money for its purchase.

This is a perfect time for teaching a child. He accepts parental authority at this point more than any other time. Parents can teach him the importance of standards and obedience; guilt, confession, and forgiveness; and the necessity of punishment for broken standards. Parents should capitalize on their child's interest in their word at times like these.

When parents must rebuke their child for doing something wrong for which he is not accountable, it is not necessary for him to confess. However, it is still necessary for the parents to assure him that everything is all right. The child who is not accountable is also not to be punished. However, all other disobedience is to be punished.

How many times are parents to forgive their children? The Biblical standard for forgiveness is 490 times (Matthew 18:21 & 22). Of course, forgiveness can only follow legitimate confession and willingness to make restoration.

The fourth and final step in the child training process is to punish the child. A review of Chapter 20 on punishment may be helpful at this time to re-establish the sequential order of the child training system. The final chapter will cover examples of the whole process and attempt to answer any unraised questions.

FOOTNOTES

[1] Greek, *homologeo* "to confess." Compound word consisting of *homos* "like, together" and *logeo* "a word;" thus "to speak together" or "acknowledge, admit, confess." (Foundation for Biblical Research, "Child Training.")

Chapter 25

EXAMPLES

We have now seen the entire system for child training as revealed in the Word of God. The concepts and principles have been presented throughout the book. This final chapter will attempt to draw the individual pieces together and demonstrate how to apply the principles to specific examples. Each parent will encounter different situations with his own unique creation from God. The important things to understand are the principles that can be applied to any situation. The following examples serve only as illustrations of the mechanics in applying these principles.

Study the chart on the next page which overviews the whole training system. Familiarity with this chart enables easy location of the parents' proper action for any type of situation. The chart has been placed on a page by itself so that it may be copied and placed in a prominent place until the training system becomes second nature.

CHILD TRAINING SYSTEM OVERVIEW

Training Situation	Controlling	Teaching
If a child's action is:	Parents are to:	Parents are to:
1. in conformity with his parents' will (even concerning those things not communicated).	give directions and set restrictions.	teach standards and express their love through providing blessing.
2. a refusal to accept his parents' directions, restrictions, or teachings (rebellion).	express their love through chastisement.	rebuke.
3. unknowingly contrary to his parents' will (unaccountable).		rebuke only to set the standard.
4. knowingly, but unintentionally contrary to set standards (accountable).		rebuke and require confession, then forgive and punish.
5. willfully contrary to set standards, or a refusal to accept his parents' rebuke or punishment.		rebuke and chastise until confession, then forgive and punish.

Figure 25.1   System Overview

The first situation shown on the chart will not often occur until after a child is already well trained. It is unusual for a child to do the right thing all of the time. Remember that every child is constantly being tempted by his sinful nature. He has a strong urge to satisfy his desire for attention, fleshly hunger, autonomy, or for anything else he wants at the moment. It is unreasonable for parents to expect their child to "be good" while his nature is promoting selfishness and crying "feed me, feed me, feed me!"

When a child is "being good" (in other words he is obeying the known standards and also doing nothing of which his parents disapprove) he can be taught further standards, given directions, and restricted from unacceptable behavior simply by command. A child who is acting in conformity with his parents' will can receive his parents' love through their blessings of fellowship, personal acceptance, peace, and provision.

The second situation on the chart is most likely to occur with an untrained child of any age when his parents begin to train him for the first time. This situation may also occur at intervals during a child's growth as he occasionally attempts to break away from parental control. A child who openly refuses to accept his parents' directions, restrictions, or teaching has little fear of judgment. Obviously, he has insufficient respect for the authority of his parents. Both respect for parental authority and a proper fear of judgment must be established by the parents when this condition exists.

For example, a father and mother both read this book and determine to begin following God's system for training their children. Perhaps they have a ten-year-old boy and a seven-year-old girl. They set both of the children down and explain that from now on standards will be fairly but firmly set, and that the children's immediate obedience will be expected. They also explain rebellion and what they will do about it. They also assure the children that their love is the motivation for properly training them.

Soon after this meeting, the boy decides to test the new procedure to see how much he can depend on his parents' word. When his mother tells him what time to come home from a friend's house, he argues, claims that she is not fair, and refuses to accept her instructions. The mother is frustrated and either emotionally wants to hit the child, or is tempted to give in and avoid the conflict altogether. However, now that she knows what to do, she instead declares her son's action to be wrong. She further warns him that a whipping is her only course of action unless he immediately changes his attitude.

Since the boy has not experienced this type of firm leadership in the past, he will probably continue testing his mother's commitment. Therefore, he continues to be unwilling to accept her instruction and ignores her warning. At this point his mother should send him to his room in order to prepare herself mentally. She does this by reviewing her responsibility to control her son, and by praying for God's strength. She then calmly proceeds to his room with a proper sized rod. To the boy's astonishment, his mother then gives him a whipping. She informs him that he can end the whipping whenever he chooses by declaring his willingness to follow her instructions both now and in the future.

The boy will probably change his mind and gain a new respect for his mother and her word. However, if he senses that she has a weak resolve and he thinks he can bluff her into believing that she cannot win, he may try to hold out. As soon as the mother realizes that he is going to be obstinate, she can stop the whipping and tell him to consider his rebellion while she calls his father.

While the boy remains in his room, his mother calls the father for moral support and advice. It may even be necessary on the first major conflict for the father to come home and put down his son's rebellion decisively. **The first conflict must be won by the parents**. It is imperative for the child to learn that his parents are serious about their rulership or all is lost. When a father has to come home from work to support his wife's authority, it should be a life-changing experience for his son.

If the boy refuses to go to his room or if his mother cannot physically handle him, the father will definitely need to be the one to bring the child under control. The father can even set the standard, if absolutely necessary, that the boy must obey his mother or he will have to answer directly to him. This provision should only be temporary since a mother needs to be able to handle the day-to-day acts of disobedience and rebellion against her standards.

After the boy finally agrees to follow the instructions of both his mother and father in the future, he needs to be reassured that all is forgiven. He may or may not be allowed to go to his friend's house depending on the extent of the confrontation, his attitude, and the circumstances at the time. When he attempts to reject parental directions in the future, the reminder of this chastisement should suffice as a warning. Parents should expect the need to handle their children very firmly when first introducing them to the reality of obedience and honor.

A child soon learns that his parents mean business and that they will not be intimidated by his cries, threats, or resistance of any kind. Only then can a child relax in the security of his parents' true love. He can trust that they care for him and will protect him, even from himself. He can trust in their word because he knows that they will do what they say.

The third situation on the chart, where the child unknowingly disobeys, will occur frequently in raising a young child. This situation will wear down a mother the most. She begins to think that her vocabulary consists only of "no," "stop that," and "don't." A young child will often act contrary to his parents' will before he has been told what standards to obey. In these cases, he is not accountable and only needs to be rebuked so that the standard will be set for the future. This situation will occur the first time a child does any unacceptable act for which there has been no prior instruction. Some examples would be when he brings his little tricycle into the house on a rainy day and begins to ride it around the living room, or the first time he discovers that he can bully another child, or when he comes home with a "new" word from grade school that his father has not heard since he was in the Army.

In the preceding instances, the child has not intentionally broken his parents' standards; however, parental correction is still required. The child is to be told that his specific action was wrong and that he is not to do it again. If he is mature enough to comprehend the reason, that also can be explained. However, a child will not remember a standard just because the reason was carefully explained. When a child is immature (either young or foolish), detailed explanations tend to confuse him and entice him into being difficult to handle. After rebuking a child, the parent must comfort him and assure him that everything is all right. It is just as important, if not even more important, to restore fellowship after a verbal reprimand as it is after a physical whipping.

The fourth situation on the chart, when a child knowingly but unintentionally acts contrary to standards which have already been clearly set by his parents, is the typical disobedience parents face throughout the entire child training period. It is the failure to follow directions or to observe restrictions on a first-time or occasional basis. In this situation the child is not defiantly disobeying the rules, but he is accountable for his wrong action.

An example of this type of disobedience is when a boy has been told to take out the garbage for collection on Tuesdays and Fridays. The parent who thinks that this instruction will be consistently followed is in for a surprise. As a general rule, Saturday is the only important day to a boy. Before a boy will remember to do an unwanted task on a mid week day, it will require considerable training. As long as he is truly attempting to remember and is constantly improving, his occasional failures need not be considered acts of disobedience. However, when he has had the task long enough to be held accountable, or if he is not improving and shows no concern when he forgets, corrective measures need to be taken.

As soon as the boy in this example becomes accountable, his parents should warn him of the penalty for future "forgetting." His parents suggest marking his calendar or writing a reminder and placing it in a prominent place. He should be cautioned that it all depends on him in the future. Dad will not take out the garbage when he forgets, and mother will not remind him beforehand.

Too often parents prevent their children from taking the required tests in life. It is necessary for parents to withdraw their assistance during times of testing, even when they think their children may fail. Children need to learn to face their failures and mistakes as one of the important lessons in becoming personally responsible.

After setting up this training experience, the boy's parents patiently wait for the inevitable disobedience. The boy may "forget" because he has a character weakness of being lazy, because he is a daydreamer who always is occupied with his own plans and projects, or because he just does not consider the duty important enough. In either case, he does not value his parents' desire or command enough to make it foremost in his mind.

When the boy eventually disobeys, his parents are mentally prepared to follow through. It is no surprise to them that he forgot so they are ready to train him. Mother notices that the garbage is still by the back door after the boy has already gone to school. When he returns from school, she tells him that he has disobeyed and is guilty of doing wrong. She will not accept any excuse and insists that he acknowledge his wrong. (It is very effective to ask a child, "What did you do?" before declaring his action wrong. This gives him the opportunity to judge himself before having his disobedience pointed out to him. However, it is not necessary to ask why he did it.)

For this example we will assume that he readily confesses and is willing to rectify the wrong. Mother then forgives him and requires him to pay the penalty of which he was warned. The penalty for a teenager with a driver's license could be to take the forgotten garbage to a public dump. The penalty for a younger child could be to take the garbage to a local convenience store and dump it in their trash bin (with the manager's approval, of course). Depending on the age of the child, father may want to go along to help explain the situation to the store manager. (My son learned what day the garbage truck visited our home after just two trips to the store carrying garbage bags in his basket.)

After the boy pays the proper penalty, his parents warn him that the penalty will be increased if he should disobey again. If disobedience continues through several levels of punishment, or if it is determined that a child is passively rebelling in his disobedience (quietly exerting his own will by refusing to obey), chastisement will then be necessary to obtain obedience.

The fifth situation on the chart, when a child willfully rebels by disobeying a set standard or refusing to accept his parents' rebuke or punishment, can be exemplified by the boy in the second situation. Refusing to follow his mother's instruction about what time to come home from a friend's house, he was chastised for his defiance and finally agreed to follow his parents' future instructions.

Several days later he wants to go to his friend's house to play. The standard has been clearly set he is never to leave the yard without permission. However, he wants to go and is sure mother will not let him if he asks; therefore, he sneaks off and willfully defies a known standard. Sometime later mother discovers he is gone and it is almost dinner time. She tracks him down and brings him home (no action is necessary in front of his friend since the defiance was not public). She again sends him to his room while she prepares for the intensity of conflict. She considers the importance of child training, and focuses on the future results to be gained from her present sacrifice.

While the boy is left alone he will think of the past whipping he received, excuses he might give, or any way he can get out of this dilemma. When mother enters the room with the rod, he may either begin crying, apologizing, promising never to disobey again, or he may volunteer excuses and adamantly protest his innocence. Mother correctly ignores the "camouflage" and proceeds directly to the Biblical system by asking, "Son, what did you do?" If he immediately judges himself by admitting his disobedience, his mother can forgive his rebellion and proceed to the punishment step.

Assuming that he will not face the fact of his guilt on his own, his mother then says, "Son, you were wrong to leave the yard without permission!" She asks him to admit that he knew the rule and knew that he was wrong to disobey.

This strong-willed boy still will not accept his mother's right to rule him and refuses to confess his guilt. At this point, he has again expressed his rebellion by rejecting his mother's rebuke. She now must chastise him until she breaks his resistance. If he does not submit after a reasonable whipping, she can leave him to consider his circumstances while she regains her composure for another round, if necessary. She says, "Son, I am going to rest for a few minutes while you reconsider admitting you were wrong. When I return, I will give you one more chance to confess before we continue with the whipping." Once the boy realizes that mother is determined to reach the objective, he will finally concede. (Proper chastisement is a controlled process to obtain a necessary result; it is not an angry attack to vent a parent's frustration.)

At whatever point the boy finally yields, his mother comforts and assures him that she still loves him. She can also take this opportunity to teach him about the necessity for rules (such as not leaving the yard) and teach him about her love shown in chastising him. She then assigns him a reasonable penalty, such as being confined to his own yard for a period of time. This boy should be well on his way to becoming obedient after these two lessons. (In this case, it is necessary to assume that a specific penalty was not established at the time the standard was set. Even though it is best to do so, parents often will not set specific penalties the first time they set a standard.)

Since disobedience in this situation occurred near dinner time, many mothers would be tempted to leave the problem for the father to handle. Unless the father is in full agreement with this procedure, it is definitely not advised. It is extremely difficult for a man to handle any problem when he first arrives home from work. It is also difficult for him to handle a conflict objectively when he was not personally involved. The father should enforce those standards which he himself establishes for the children. Even then, enforcement can be delegated to the mother to handle in his absence. However, the father should **always** back the mother. (My son told my wife, when he was about 30, that as a teen he felt like defying her on a couple of occasions, but he saw me in his mind and **knew** what I would do to him if he did.)

The preceding examples should help you to understand the mechanics of using God's system to train obedient and respectful children. If these examples are not sufficient, or if any portion of this book is unclear, please write and let me know. Be sure and give your home phone number.

To conclude this chapter, let us review the terms used to define both the parents' and the child's actions that relate to child training. You may wish to make a copy of this summary for your ready reference.

Child Training Summary

- Child training is the process used by parents that will cause a child to reach the objective for which he has been trained. Biblically, the process includes both restraining the child from following his natural inclination to sin and also teaching him the right way of life (Proverbs 22:6). The desired objective is for the child to learn God's Word, the knowledge of which can then direct him throughout his adult life. To reach this objective parents are commanded by God's Word to inculcate their children with God's standards (Deuteronomy 4:10; 6:6 & 7; 11:19). The properly trained child will develop a character of better quality than he would have developed had he been left to grow up according to his own sinful nature.

- The sinful nature with which each child is born seeks to enslave him by means of a constant temptation to fulfill his will and strong desires (Psalm 51:5; 58:3). Under control of this nature a child is totally self-centered. He desperately needs his parents' help in controlling his sinful nature (Proverbs 29:15; 1 Samuel 3:13).

- Controlling a child's natural tendencies requires exertion of parental power, force, or pressure sufficient to cause a child to follow his parents' directions (Proverbs 29:15; 1 Samuel 3:13). Parents must require their children to obey in order to control them effectively.

- Obedience is reality when a child consistently does what he is told, even when it is counter to his will or desire (Colossians 3:20). Obedience will help parents to protect their children from harm, both physically and psychologically. It is also the basis for a child's respect for his parents' authority (Ephesians 6:2).

- Parental authority is the God-delegated right to set the parents' will above that of the child and to command him to follow their rulership. It is the power that parents have to administer justice, to punish for disobedience and to reward for conformity to their commands. Parental authority includes the force necessary to resolve the inevitable conflict that occurs when a child rebels against being controlled. Some of the verses that support parental authority are: Exodus 21:15 & 17; Deuteronomy 21:18-21; 27:16; Proverbs 30:17; Matthew 15:4; Colossians 3:20; Ephesians 6:1.

- Rebellion is the act of open or determined defiance of, or resistance to, any authority or controlling power. A child rebels any time he knowingly and willingly places his will above the stated will of his parents. A child's rebellion can **only** be controlled by the force of chastisement.

- Chastisement, when related to child training, refers to the use of a rod to inflict pain sufficient to correct a child's rebellion or to restrain a child from willful disobedience (2 Samuel 7:14; Proverbs 3:24; 19:18; 22:15; 23:13 & 14; 29:15; Hebrews 12:6 & 7).

- The rod is God's designated instrument for parents to use in chastising their rebellious children. God has specifically established the rod as the symbol of human authority (2 Samuel 7:14; Proverbs 13:24; 19:18; 22:15; 23:13 & 14; 29:15). Parents will cause a child to become obedient and to respect their word by the proper use of the rod. A child must respect his parents' word before he can be taught.

- Teaching a child is the ultimate objective of child training. A child is to be taught to control himself. When this occurs, he no longer has a need for his parents' external control. He is also to be taught standards of acceptable behavior and the reasons behind those standards (Proverbs 22:6).

- Standards should be inculcated into children as soon as they are able to comprehend instructions. Since the parents' authority is delegated by God, the standards they set should not be contrary to God's standards (Deuteronomy 4:10; 6:6 & 7; 11:19). When a child breaks a standard, the wrong must be exposed by his parent's rebuke.

- Rebuking a child is when parents declare that a specific action is wrong and unacceptable. A rebuke exposes guilt and convicts the guilty person (John 3:20; 16:8; Ephesians 5:13).

- Guilt is the **fact** of having committed a wrong, not
  an emotional feeling. There are only three ways to
  handle guilt: justify the wrong done, transfer the
  guilt to someone or something else, or confess
  (admit to or agree with) the proper authority.
  Confession is necessary to eliminate the devastating effects of guilt. Children who knowingly have
  disobeyed feel alienated from their parents and
  desperately need to be restored to their fellowship
  and acceptance.

- Confession is the honest acknowledgment of guilt
  (Leviticus 26:40a; Psalm 32:5). When a child confesses his guilt and is forgiven by his parents, it
  begins to cleanse his soul and prepares him to accept
  his punishment. A child's confession also prevents
  any build-up of animosity on the parents' part and
  enables them to forgive the child's disobedience.

- Forgiveness of a child should be immediate and
  unconditional after the child's confession (Isaiah
  43:25; Jeremiah 31:34b; 1 John 1:9). He should be
  reassured by his parents of their love and restored
  acceptance. Forgiveness continues to remove the
  effects of guilt in the child's soul. He is now ready for
  the final step in the training process — punishment.

- Punishment is the infliction of a penalty in retribution for an offense. The correct penalty is the
  amount or kind of payment required to make equal
  restitution for the wrong done (Leviticus 24:17-22;
  Romans 13:4). When a child pays the penalty for a
  broken standard, he has completed the cleansing of
  his soul from guilt.

Conclusion

What the Bible Says About . . . Child Training has attempted to explain the Biblical concepts and principles of child training as thoroughly as possible. Much more could be written about child training, especially in such areas as: teaching positive moral instructions; teaching children about God; identifying the specific roles of father and mother; and setting parental priorities as they relate to church, marriage, and work. However, before such material can be discussed, the foundation must be laid on the basic techniques of controlling and teaching children.

Much of this material may have been new, as well as dramatically different from most of the theories taught today. Do not be discouraged if you do not grasp all of the material at this point. Read the book again and the whole system should become more clear to you. Some readers would benefit from studying the book in a study group under the leadership of a mature, Christian parent who has been successful in training his own children to adulthood. Those parents who have reread the book every year or two seem to have been the most successful in their child training.   Children grow and change every year.   What you don't see the purpose for today may become clear to you next year.

The knowledge you have obtained should provide you with a great deal of confidence in dealing with your children. You should be more comfortable in your position of authority than ever before. You should also be able to express a balanced love to your children based correctly on standards of righteousness and justice. You now know how to express your love even through restrictions and chastisement.

The following appendices provide further information valuable in child training. As has been stated in the Introduction, Appendix A provides the basic premise for accepting the Bible as man's best source of information on child training. Appendix B offers suggestions for the parent who thinks he has failed, and it is also practical information for any parent who faces a difficult child training task. Appendix C gives a sample of the research that was the basis for this book. Appendix D, special information concerning teenagers, has been added as part of the 2nd edition changes.

APPENDICES

Appendix **A**

THE BIBLE AS A SOURCE OF INFORMATION FOR MAN

The following development sets forth why the author looks to the Bible for the truth man should live by, and this discussion establishes the Bible as the basic premise for this book.

God Exists

Genesis 1:1 *"In the beginning God created the heaven and the earth."*

Psalm 90:2 *"Before the mountains were brought forth, or ever thou hadst formed the earth and the world, even from everlasting to everlasting, thou art God."*

The Bible never attempts to prove or explain God's existence. It simply declares it to be true. This book, therefore, begins with this absolute: God's existence is certain truth. The Bible further states that no man can escape the recognition of the fact that God does exist:

Romans 1:19 & 20 *"Because that which may be known of God is manifest in them; for God hath shown it unto them. For the invisible things of him from the creation of the world are clearly seen, being understood by the things that are made, even his eternal power and Godhead, so that they are without excuse;"*

Man may attempt to reject God, but man can never honestly deny his knowledge of God's existence. This passage reveals that God has made Himself known to man both rationally and empirically. The knowledge of the existence of God has been placed by God within the rational perception of man's mind. Creation, through its order and consistency, clearly presents the empirical proof of God the Creator. Acceptance of the knowledge of the existence of God as Creator will lead to the next logical assumption.

Mankind Exists as a Creation of God

Genesis 1:27 *"So God created man in his own image, in the image of God created he him; male and female created he them."*

Man as a creature is dependent on his Creator, God. As Creator, God is responsible for His creation. To bring a creature into existence, but to fail to provide for the needs of that creature would be an act of irresponsibility. Because God cares for His creatures and takes full responsibility for His creation, He has provided for man's needs.

God Has Provided for Mankind's Physical Needs

Genesis 1:28 & 29 *"And God blessed them, and God said unto them, Be fruitful, and multiply, and fill the earth, and subdue it; and have dominion over the fish of the sea, and over the fowl of the air, and over every living thing that moveth upon the earth. And God said, Behold, I have given you every herb bearing seed, which is upon the face of all the earth, and*

*every tree, in which is the fruit of a tree yielding
seed; to you it shall be for food."*

The Hebrew word translated "to subdue" means "to tread
down with the feet, to dominate"; [1] and the word translated "dominion" means "to rule." [2] Man was given the command to rule all earth's living creatures. He was given the
command to control and use all earth's resources. God's
provision for man's physical needs is the entire physical
universe including air, water, land, plants, living creatures, and the climactic range required for man's existence. Physical science recognizes the extremely narrow
range of environment in which man can survive and how
perfectly it has been arranged to support all man's physical requirements.

Man is not merely a physical creation that exists in only a
physical universe. He is also a creation of soul and spirit.
As such, he has needs of the soul and the spirit, not just
physical needs. In taking full responsibility for His creation, God has also provided for all man's soul and spiritual needs just as completely as He has for the physical.

God Has Provided for Mankind's Soul
and Spiritual Needs

Matthew 4:4 *"But he answered and said, It is written, Man
shall not live by bread alone, but by every word that
proceedeth out of the mouth of God."*

Bread is the example of God's physical provision, while
God's Word is God's provision for man's soul and spiritual
life. God's Word has been provided for man's benefit. It has
been recorded and preserved according to the faithfulness
and justice of God. Because God cares for His creation, He
has provided all that man needs to live; not only to survive
physically, but to live abundantly in both soul and spirit.

Man was given the ability by God to subdue the physical universe and to rule the living things. Man was given strength and dexterity, but above all he was given mentality. With this mentality man could, on his own, discover the principles by which God governs the physical universe. Man has gradually obtained knowledge of the physical universe by observation of these natural laws, in other words, by science. Geology, astronomy, physiology, and mathematics are examples of true science. By contrast, the principles that govern the soul and spirit of man are not of a physical nature and cannot be discovered through the mentality of man.

Man has the need to understand his own soul, to know how to relate to other human beings, and to know his proper relationship with the physical universe. When man attempts to discover soul information by means of his own mentality apart from God's revelation, he is limited to his ability to observe and to reason. He therefore invents the pseudo-sciences of psychology, sociology, and anthropology in an attempt to answer man's soul questions and to solve man's soul problems.

Man also has the need to understand his spiritual relationship to His Creator, God. He needs to know where he came from, where he is going, who he is, and why he exists. Without knowing his own origin, destiny, make-up, and purpose, man is disoriented to life — even though he is physically alive. When man attempts to discover spiritual information by means of his own intellect apart from God's revelation, he develops various types of pseudo knowledge such as philosophy and religion, both of which are man-centered.

For soul and spiritual knowledge, man is totally dependent on God. Man cannot discover the principles that govern the soul or the spirit apart from the information that

God has provided. God's Word is infinitely superior to any thought man could possibly have.

God's Thinking is Superior to Man's

Isaiah 55:8 & 9 *"For my thoughts are not your thoughts, neither are your ways my ways, saith the Lord. For as the heavens are higher than the earth, so are my ways higher than your ways, and my thoughts than your thoughts."*

God's thinking is far beyond the ability of man. It is foolish for man in his arrogance to question God's Word by means of his own viewpoint. As God declares:

Proverbs 28:26a *"He that trusteth in his own heart is a fool,"*

When God presents information on any subject, it will naturally conflict with the human systems of thinking. Human philosophy, psychology, sociology, or religion apart from God's Word is the attempt of mere man to organize thoughts that are inferior to God's thoughts. These systems of thinking must be evaluated by God's Word, not God's Word by them.

Each person's opinions are a combination of these human systems of thinking plus their own experiences. As the Biblical position is presented, it will be necessary for the reader to evaluate objectively his existing opinion by God's Word.

The Bible is God's Word

The Bible declares itself to be God's Word:

2 Timothy 3:16 *"All scripture is given by inspiration of God, and is profitable for doctrine, for reproof, for correction, for instruction in righteousness,"*

2 Peter 1:20 & 21 *"Knowing this first, that no prophecy of the scripture is of any private interpretation. For*

the prophecy came not at any time by the will of man, but holy men of God spoke as they were moved by the Holy Spirit."

God did not cause His Word to be recorded for His own benefit, but to benefit mankind. It is a complete instruction manual containing soul and spiritual principles; therefore, mankind can look to the Bible for the information he needs on any moral or spiritual issue. The Bible has the answer for all of man's non-physical questions from eternal salvation to every practical matter in life. It is the only true source of moral and spiritual information by which man can successfully live each day. Since God's Word is to benefit man, it is meant to be understood.

Mankind is Meant to Understand God's Word

Deuteronomy 29:29 *"the secret things belong unto the Lord our God; but those things which are revealed belong unto us and to our children forever, that we may do all the words of this law."*

God is infinite and omniscient. He has not revealed all His knowledge to finite man, but what He has revealed can both be understood and utilized. God's information is available to those who diligently search out its meaning and can be used successfully by those who accept its teaching. God has not hidden His soul and spiritual provision from mankind. God's Word is dependable and verifiably true.

God's Word Equals Truth

John 17:17b *"thy word is truth."*

It is impossible for God to lie (Hebrews 6:18). The Bible presents true principles (or laws) which can be applied in practice with predictable results. There are natural, fixed consequences for either observing or violating the soul and spiritual laws just as surely as for violating the physical laws. No man would expect to violate the law of gravity and not pay the consequences, but he will often foolishly violate soul and spiritual principles with total abandon. When physical laws are properly observed, the results are predictable and beneficial to man. Proper observance of the soul and spiritual principles will also produce consistent, beneficial results. God's Word declares the natural consequences of either observing or violating truth.

Observing Truth Results in Blessing
Violating Truth Results in Cursing

Deuteronomy 28:1 & 2 *"And it shall come to pass, if thou shalt hearken diligently unto the voice of the Lord thy God, to observe and to do all his commandments which I command thee this day, that the Lord thy God will set thee on high above all nations of the earth; And all these blessings shall come on thee, and overtake thee, if thou shalt hearken unto the voice of the Lord thy God."*

Deuteronomy 28:15 *"But it shall come to pass, if thou wilt not hearken unto the voice of the Lord thy God, to observe to do all his commandments and his statutes which I command thee this day, that all these curses shall come upon thee, and overtake thee."*

Deuteronomy 30:19b *"I have set before you life and death, blessing and cursing; therefore, choose life, that both thou and thy seed may live,"*

Joshua 1:8 *"This book of the law shall not depart out of thy mouth, but thou shalt meditate therein day and night, that thou mayest observe to do according to all that is written therein; for then thou shalt make thy way prosperous, and then thou shalt have good success."*

These verses clearly declare that it is to man's benefit to learn and to follow God's Word. *What the Bible Says About . . . Child Training* presents the principles that the Bible reveals concerning child training so that both parents and their children may experience the blessings promised by God. Child training is soul training, and therefore the Bible is man's only reliable source of truth on this subject.

FOOTNOTES

¹ Hebrew, *kabash* "subdue, bring into bondage, tread down with the feet;" thus "to dominate" (Zechariah 9:15; Micah 7:19; Jeremiah 34:11, 16; 2 Chronicles 28:10; Nehemiah 5:5). In Genesis 1:28 the aspect of "control" is evident and *kabash* is in the imperative mood of command. (Foundation for Biblical Research, "Child Training.")

² Hebrew, *radah* "have dominion, rule, dominate" over someone or something; used here to indicate a position of dominance once the subduing has been accomplished. Like *kabash, radah* is a command. God commands man to "subdue" and then "rule" over that which has been subdued. (Ibid.)

Appendix B

HOPE FOR THE FAILING PARENT

This book was written from the perspective of training a child from infancy. God's guidelines on child training are designed as a perfect system to be used by two parents who are both willing to obey God's Word from the very beginning with their children. Unfortunately, many parents do not realize that they need this information until their children are teenagers.

But what if your children are already grown and you now recognize your past mistakes? How can you cope with the knowledge you now possess that you could have done a better job? What if you are a single parent who is left with the task of training a child on your own; or what if your child is already a rebellious, unmanageable teenager and time is slipping away? Is there any hope for parents in these situations?

The answer to these questions can be found in knowing the character of God and His plan of grace for man. When the natural laws of God are violated, God's supernatural intervention alone can avoid the natural consequences. If a person were to jump off a ten-story building, he would not expect to be spared the results except by a miracle. Fortunately for man, God is in the miracle business. He alone can heal a broken heart or answer a mother's prayer for her lost son. God is a God of grace who can restore a family and repair the damage done through many years of negative child training. A variety of examples explain the options.

The situation of the untrained child who has already left home and is reaping the fruit of his selfish existence appears hopeless. The father or mother of such a child will surely suffer the cursing that results as the natural consequence of their not observing God's laws (Proverbs 10:1b; 17-21; 29:15b). The child also suffers for his parents' failure to train him properly:

Jeremiah 31:29b *"The fathers have eaten a sour grape, and the children's teeth are set on edge."*

However, once a child leaves his parents' authority, he becomes totally accountable for his own actions:

Jeremiah 31:30 *"But every one shall die for his own iniquity; every man that eateth the sour grape, his teeth shall be set on edge."*

Parents who have failed can continue to have hope because God is just. They can trust that after the untrained child leaves home, God will deal with him as an individual, responsible for his own actions. God will take over the training of the untrained child through human authorities (other than the parents), and by means of the pressures of life. The parents who are in this situation can confess to God any true guilt they may have concerning their failure in child training and receive His complete forgiveness. They can also pray that their child will turn to God and will accept His training. After I had left home, my own dear mother prayed for me for ten long years before I finally responded to God's pressure and allowed Him to change my wasted life.

The next example is the single parent who must train a child alone. This parent must rely heavily on God's supernatural assistance in addition to constantly following the principles for child training which God designed for the normal family. Many single parents have been able to train their children successfully even under such a severe handicap.

A parent who is in such a situation, like all parents, should be attending a solid Bible-teaching church, learning about God's character, and growing to spiritual maturity. A single parent can place his or her children in a school that has firm rules of conduct which are consistently enforced, such as some private schools. The single mother should seek out a school and a church that have strong masculine leadership to offset the missing father's influence. Above all, such a parent must follow God's child training system and depend on God to fill the gap. His Word promises that He will be a father to the fatherless (Psalm 10:14; 68:5; 146:9). His grace is sufficient to provide power for the single parent's weaknesses (2 Corinthians 12:9).

Finally, parents sometimes recognize that they are failing, but the child is still at home. He may be a wild, apparently uncontrollable child of eight. (Many such children have been labeled "hyper-active" and yet have no physiological problem. Most of these children are simply running rampant under the control of their sin natures.) On the other hand, he may be a rebellious teenager who has never been under control and who may possibly leave home if his parents attempt to implement this system.

Several years ago I was the principal of a small Christian

school. Among the twenty-one students, there was a seven-year-old boy who had been diagnosed as being hyper-active, and a twelve-year-old girl who was seeing a child psychologist as well as being subdued by tranquilizers. After two months of consistent application of God's principles at school, the boy became calm and manageable in the classroom, and the psychologist took the girl off the tranquilizers and told her parents that he no longer needed to see her. Even with this and other successful experiences, 1 soon realized that only the parents can properly train their children. A school can only support what is taught at home; it cannot replace the parent.

Parents of untrained pre-teenagers still have time to bring their children under control and then to teach them. However, it will be necessary to intensify the training process. Parents of such children should learn the material in this book thoroughly, then prepare themselves for the inevitable conflicts that must ensue. They must firmly and consistently gain total control over their children by causing them to become obedient as quickly as possible.

As encouragement to parents in this predicament, let me give you a real life example. My wife and I were blessed and challenged by God with an intelligent and strong-willed boy. He was the one at two-years-old who liked to pull all the trash out of the trash cans. Of course, this was unacceptable behavior to his mother, so she instructed him not to do it. However, he was so stubborn that when he was seen doing his mischief, he would begin feverishly pulling out the trash before he could be stopped. He would even grasp the can, screaming as his mother picked him up.

His rebellion continued until he was eight years old. By this time he had become an accomplished liar to cover his rebellion and to avoid getting caught. We tried everything for punishment that any other parent might consider. He was confined to his room, had his privileges taken away, and was threatened repeatedly — all the wrong things to do. Nothing seemed to work, he just became more and more resolved not to submit. At this time we knew nothing about Biblical child training.

Finally, a situation arose at school. He decided he did not want to write the book reports his teacher assigned. He hid his assignments in his locker, told us he had no homework, and told his teacher that he had forgotten the reports and left them at home. Eventually, the teacher informed us of the problem. By this time he had three reports past due. We did not know God's Word at that time, but knew our boy could not be allowed to continue to be lazy and to lie.

Finally, in desperation, we decided to chastise him for his lies and laziness and also to punish him by making him write excellent, longer than necessary reports. No matter how long it took, he was not allowed to do **anything** that he wanted to do until his three reports were finished and approved by us. We asked his teacher to inform us of any new assignments. Our son was instructed to work after school until bedtime, and every weekend until all reports were done. This was strictly enforced. After two intense weeks of his crying and attempting to make us feel guilty, he finally submitted. He completed all the reports, and in addition, he even discovered that he enjoyed the research and writing of reports. He then wrote the following letter:

To my dear Mother and Father whom I love very much because they love, care, and punish me because they love me

Sincerely,

Ron

P.S. I love them! Why shouldn't I.

After this conflict, our son was very obedient; not perfect, but normally under our will. He is now an extremely honest man, graduated from high school and college with exceptional grades, and is the manager of a computer programming department.

There is no such thing as a "bad seed." If you are committed to gaining control of your child, willing to utilize God's power, and consistent in applying God's training principles for as long as it takes, you will be able to subdue the will of the rebellious child. However, parents of a hardened teenager (who is old enough to leave home when the pressure becomes intense), may not be able to bring him under control. In fact, if parents cannot get a rebellious teenager to submit to parental authority, they may have to turn him over to God for chastising.

Parents who must take the drastic action of forcing their child either to obey or leave home should make sure that he knows what he is facing. They should warn him that the trials he will face will be from God so that he will properly identify his future pain as chastisement. An example of this type of warning is given in the unedited edition of *Robinson Crusoe*.

In the first chapter, Crusoe's father warned him not to go to sea.

> "He told me I had my elder brother for an example, to whom he had used the same earnest persuasion to keep him from going into the Low Country wars, but could not prevail, my brother's young desires prompting him

to run into the army, where he was killed. Though my father said he would not cease to pray for me, yet he ventured to say to me that if I did take this foolish step, God would not bless me. I would have leisure to reflect upon having neglected his counsel, when there might be none to assist in my recovery."[1]

The chapter heading for the second chapter says "...The action of Providence for disobedience to parents now overtakes me — Taken by a Sallee River Rover, and all sold as slaves. . ."[2] The entire book tells the story of a man who suffers great pressures as a result of rebelling against his parents. It also shows how God turned these sufferings into blessings after Crusoe turned to God.

The following letters to Ann Landers also reflect positive results from tragic circumstances in the home:

DEAR ANN: I must answer the letter from "Heartbroken Parents," and I really qualify because I'm the kid who needed to be thrown out.

It began when I was 12 — always in fights and starting trouble. At 16 I was arrested for the first time. Seven arrests followed. I refused to go to school, drank like a fish, did drugs and caused my family plenty of heartache.

Many times I came knuckle-to-knuckle with my brother over my wishing our mother was dead and swearing at her like she was a dog in the street.

Then it happened. Mom said, "GET OUT!" When I kissed her good bye she cried her eyes out. l realized then how I had been tearing her apart.

I had to eat so I got myself a job. I soon discovered I couldn't work spaced out, so I went to a drug-abuse center and got off the junk. Those people were really terrific.

It took a while before I got up the nerve to go see my folks. My heart melted when Mom and my brother told me they were proud I was part of their family again. Dad gave me the best compliment of all when he said I turned out to be a real man after all.

All this happened because Mom forced me to grow up. It took 18 years of tears and heartache, one day to pack up and get out, one year of suffering (for both my Mom and myself) and three years to build the beautiful life we now share. — Love, Respect and Thanks.

DEAR ANN: In March, 1976, we threw our son out of the house on his 18th birthday. We had spent six years watching him self-destruct. He put in a year at college — majoring in poker. (Tuition: $6,200.) We finally decided he had a right to ruin his life if he wanted to but we didn't have to support him while he did it.

We faced his anger (and abuse) and refused to give him money while he stayed with friends. We even refused to sign the forms when he wanted to apply for food stamps and welfare.

We were once called from a hospital 30 miles away. Someone had slipped a hallucinogen into his coffee. It frightened us to death but we refused to go see him. Instead we told the friend who phoned he had chosen a lifestyle that was foolish and dangerous and we weren't going to run to him every time he got into trouble.

God was with us. It took only six months of panhandling and sleeping on subways before our son came to his senses.

After a few weeks of reflection on the last half-year of

his life (during which everything he owned had been stolen several times), the loss of his pride and the absence of all security, our son decided he wanted no more of that kind of life.

All this happened 21/2 years ago. He joined the military and really loves the discipline and security. Today he's a fine, happy, productive man who feels good about himself. And I am — Thanking God We Had The Courage To Throw Him Out. [3]

These examples demonstrate that there is always hope for the failing parent. There is hope in the miracle that can result when parents utilize God's Word. There is hope for parents who will depend on God's power and who will trust Him to overcome their weaknesses. There also is hope in the fact that God's love will pursue a lost youth and treat him in absolute justice. I suggest that both parents of an out-of-control teen attend a couple of meetings of their local Toughlove Chapter*. Even though this is a secular organization, they understand what it takes to deal with a teen (or older) with whom parents have no physical authority.

   * (Call 215/348-7090 or send a stamped, self-addressed envelope to:
      Toughlove, Box 1069
      Doylestown, PA 18901
      for the address of a group near you.)

Parents who find themselves facing a difficult period of conflict before they can bring their untrained children under control should:

   1. Master the information in this book and read the context of all Bible verses that have been quoted.

   2. Make a commitment together to consistently apply

these principles in the training of their children until they reach the objective.

3. Pray to God for His miraculous power and His personal guidance in applying His principles correctly.

4. Explain to their children exactly what they intend to do. They should admit their own guilt to the children for not following God's will, and then inform them of their responsibility and commitment before God.

5. DO IT!

God promises blessings to parents who are successful:

Proverbs 10:1 a *"A wise son maketh a glad father,"*

Proverbs 23:24 & 25 *"The father of the righteous shall greatly rejoice, and he that begetteth a wise child shall have joy of him. Thy father and thy mother shall be glad, and she that bore thee shall rejoice."*

Proverbs 29:17 *"Correct thy son, and he shall give thee rest; yea, he shall give delight unto thy soul."*

Proverbs 31:28 *"Her children rise up, and call her blessed; her husband also, and he praiseth her."*

FOOTNOTES

[1] Daniel Defoe, *Robinson Crusoe* (Chicago: Moody Press, 1965), p. 10.

[2] Ibid., p. 16.

[3] *Austin* (Texas) *American Statesman*, (date unknown).

Appendix C

GREEK WORDS RELATING TO CHILDREN

A summary of the approach utilized by Foundation for Biblical Research (FBR) in determining Biblical word meanings is all that will be covered in this appendix. Not all of the steps are shown.

First, a list of words from the English Bible (King James Version) were selected that fell within the semantic domain of the subject area pertaining to children.

Second, a cross list of Greek and Hebrew words for the English words in step one was made. (Only the Greek development is contained herein.)

Third, a word study was performed on each individual word and its use in all contexts. Every occurrence of the word was checked. Morphology, syntax, use of the article, comparison/contrasts with other words were noted.

Fourth, a hypothesis was drawn based upon the data.

Fifth, unresolved problems were noted for future analysis.

Sixth, a specific analysis was made of more than one of the words within the semantic domain where they occurred together in the same context.

Seventh, the resultant data was compared to the hypothesis which was altered accordingly (when needed).

Eighth, lexicons were studied for each word's etymology and extra Biblical usage. The results of this step were compared to the hypothesis mentioned in step four. This was done to evaluate lexical data by Biblical data. (The lexical data was dealt with subsequent to the Biblical data to ensure that the veil of previous human studies did not cloud what the Bible had to say about the use of the word.)

Ninth, the hypothetical meaning (or derived Biblical meaning) was checked against lexical data and deviations were evaluated and noted.

Tenth, a conclusion was then arrived at with regard to specific Biblical meanings of each word.

Eleventh, a chart was then drawn to denote the relationships between the words in the semantic domain of children.

This procedure was devised in order to assist the serious student in better understanding what God's Word precisely communicates. The following chart shows forty-four English words used in the New Testament to translate the eleven unique Greek words relating to children.

WORDS IN THE SEMANTIC RANGE
OF "CHILDREN"

Greek Transliteration	English Translation (KJV)
brephos	child, embryo, infant, babe
nepios	not speaking, babe, infant, child, minor, simple, unlearned.
teknon	child, son or daughter, descendants, people
teknion	little child, dear children
huios	son, descendant, disciple
pais	child, boy, youth, girl, servant, slave, minister
paidarion	little boy, child, boy, lad
paidion	infant, baby, dear children
paidiske	girl, damsel, maiden, female
korasion	girl, damsel, maiden
neaniskos	young man, youth, soldiers, prime of life

Related Words

aner	male adult, husband, human being, individual
teleios	brought to completion, fully accomplished, fully developed, complete, entire, full grown, ripe age, perfect, consummate, higher excellence

As you can see from this chart, it would be impossible for the English reader to determine which Greek word was used in the original. It is also difficult to distinguish each

Greek word's specific meaning. FBR has been able to apply the procedures summarized in this appendix to determine the distinctions between these words. The following chart pictorially shows the relationship of all eleven Greek words for children.

These meanings reflect the most specific nuance of each word. In actual Biblical usage, the meaning may not be emphasized and the word may even be used in its most general sense in a particular context.

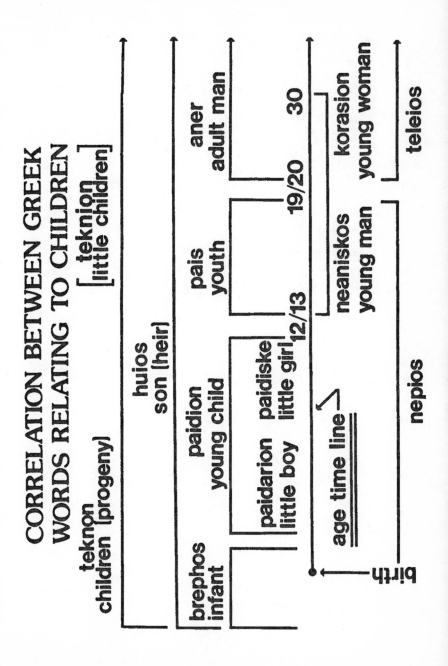

CORRELATION BETWEEN GREEK
WORDS RELATING TO CHILDREN

teknon
children [progeny]

[teknion
little children]

huios
son [heir]

brephos
infant

paidion
young child

paidarion
little boy

paidiske
little girl

aner
adult man

pais
youth

neaniskos
young man

korasion
young woman

nepios

teleios

birth

age time line

12/13   19/20   30

Appendix D

Teenagers

The very word teenager implies an in-between age, neither child nor adult. It is no wonder that teens feel isolated during this extremely awkward age. Let's call them **young adults** from now on. This implies that they are going somewhere — to adulthood.

The following are my personal thoughts for parents of young adults. I hope they are helpful:

How to Develop Maturity

1. Allow your children enough room to fail. Don't make their world fail proof. Let a young adult make some mistakes and suffer the natural consequences for those mistakes (as long as it isn't dangerous of course). Let a lazy child fail a math test; let a proud child make a fool of herself because she boasts in front of her friends; or, let a willful boy have enough rope to trip himself. Parents who constantly "coddle their children," (i.e., keeping them from ever failing, paying the consequences for them when they do, or making excuses for the sin

that might have caused a failure, actually promote their child's perpetual immaturity. I think we have enough adults today who won't accept responsibility for their own actions.

2. The father **must** take an active role in the training of young adults, especially the boys. They desperately need the guidance and acceptance of the Father. He must not deal with only the correction problems. Dads, try to arrange your business career so as not to move your young adults **if at all possible**. If your teens have to uproot from their friends, adjust to a new church group, and (God forbid) attend a new public school, they are almost certain to become disoriented (especially with their hormones screaming at the same time).

3. Don't harangue (repetitive warnings) or try to intimidate your young adults to accept your position. Don't be critical or belittle your children. If they disobey, punish them, but don't brow beat them.

4. Talk **with** your young adults. Discuss tough issues with them (alcohol, drugs, dating vs courtship,[1] entertainment, dress, etc.). Allow them to say what they think or feel about anything without your immediate criticisms or corrections. You don't have to agree with every strange opinion your young adults might have, just let them express themselves as with a friend. Guidance, not control is your goal. Rather than always teaching, practice asking questions that cause your young adults to think through their stated opinion to its logical conclusion. Better to have your standards questioned now than after the young adult leaves home.

5. Don't always speak negatively or ridicule every-

thing the **world** says and produces (even though
you are correct). Ask your children to tell you what
they see wrong with a humanistic statement on
the news or what is wrong with the values a particular movie exhibits. Teach young adults to analyze things for themselves. Guide, don't preach or
even tell.

6. Every young man should be trained for becoming
totally self-sufficient from his parents — economi-
cally, physically, and emotionally. This doesn't
require that they push him away, it only requires
leading him toward his life-role as a man. God's
design for the distinct role of the man to lead, protect, and provide for his family; and to cherish his
wife needs to be emulated by the father and
respected by the mother.

Boys should be doing meaningful work by 12 or 13
years of age — yard work, paper route, grocery
store, etc. A young man of 16 or 17 should have the
experience of having worked for several bosses, at
least over the summers. (A young man can learn in
a hurry what he **doesn't** want to do for a lifetime!)
Ideally, he should be working toward paying for
part or even all of his college education. If your son
is going to college, I would recommend that he first
attend a Jr. College in your town to earn an associates degree; and that he continue to live at home
(especially if this is his first real experience with
the world). This is preferable over his leaving town
for even a Christian college.

If a young man stays at home after coming of age
(20), and is not in school full time, he should be
required to pay room and board, thus reinforcing his
responsibility and developing his self-sufficiency.

7. Every young woman should be trained to fulfill her
    Biblical role (as is thoroughly defined in my wife's book,
    *On the Other Side of the Garden — Biblical Womanhood
    for Today's World*.) A young woman, raised on the
    principles in this book, will not be anxious to pursue
    the world's standards for womanhood. Instead, she
    will be sensitive to her father's leadership and
    discovering God's will for her life. We do not
    recommend that girls leave home to attend college
    unless they have been called to celibacy and a career,
    and even then the college should be carefully chosen.
    Colossians 2:8 *"Beware lest any man spoil you through
    philosophy and vain deceit, after the tradition of men,
    after the rudiments of the world, and not after Christ."*

Comment: A recent nationwide poll of teenagers[2] found that
86% of the girls said they expect to work when they are married,
only 7% said they expect to stay home. Among the boys, 58%
said they expect their wives to work outside the home. Only
19% expected them to stay home.

It is interesting that even with all the women's liberation and
"politically correct" attack against traditional male and female
roles, and although the majority of the boys in this survey
expected their wives to work, they still believed the 1950's
marriage should be the natural order. Sadly, the girls were
overwhelmingly committed to having careers, and far less so
to making and maintaining a marriage. The girls in this survey
have obviously been spoiled already by the "philosophy and
vian deceit, after the tradition of men, after the rudiments of
the world."

8. Both girls and boys should be required to do every-
    thing for themselves for which they are capable as

they mature. This includes caring for their room and clothing (wash, fold, iron, and put away), clean up after themselves (and others), helping with home repair and maintenance as required, and possibly even assisting with family finances in time of dire need. By the time a child reaches the young adult years, he should not expect anyone to "take care" of him. A boy should be able to cook and mend; a girl should be able to balance a check book and operate a household budget. Neither sex should feel pressure to marry just to get someone who can care for their mundane needs. By early teens, a boy should have his life direction tentatively planned and be actively working toward his goals through his education. This plan creates a self-motivation to help push through the tedious or difficult areas of education.

9. If you have done your child training job successfully, your young adults won't fit with the rest of the world's untrained teenagers (in between agers, aimless youth without purpose or goals except for self-gratification). But, they will fit well with adults and will **be fit** for their mates.

   Your children will have been trained to be what some people may consider weird. They need to be taught that they are different, special, unique. Teach them that they **will** be misunderstood by their peers. Study together famous people in history who didn't fit the mold of society either.

10. Before any young adult leaves home for the first time, he should be prepared for the culture shock he will encounter. After living in the home environment and socializing with only Christians, a young person often experiences trauma when he

enters a secular college or the secular work place. **Please** take the time to explain and even to show the young people what it is really like "out there." They need a crash course on Proverbs: about the vile woman (prostitute or promiscuous man or woman); about the foolish (one who is ignorant of God's truth), the scorner (the one who knows about God and openly rejects Him and His Word), and the liars, slanderers, backbiters, thieves, proud, and lazy indulgent ones (especially among professing Christians).

FOOTNOTES

[1] Dating and Courtship Resources:
Passion and Purity, by Elisabeth Elliot
(Excellent for Mothers and Daughters)

Preparing Your Children for Courtship and Marriage, by Reb Bradley
(Excellent for parents)
Family Ministries
P.O. Box 1412
Fair Oaks, CA 95628
800/545-1729

I Kissed Dating Goodbye
(Multnomah Press)
by Josh Harris
(Excellent for teens)

[2] *The New York Times* and *CBS News,* June 1, 1994

Afterward

Over twenty years have passed since I wrote this book. Many things have changed in just a short time. The morality of our nation's people worsens as evidenced by the television programs and movies they watch, and worse yet, allow their children to watch. The curse of AIDS is now here to plague us for our national tolerance of immorality. Drugs are flooding the U.S. in answer to our adult children's cry for escape from responsibility. All in all this is a pretty dark picture.

Of course, there is one thing that hasn't changed and never will – God's Word and all the principles for living that it sets forth. The light of the world, Jesus Christ, and His Word shines even more brightly in this perverse and evil world. It gives me extreme gratification to hear from the scores of parents who have applied God's principles of child training, as outlined in this book. They have testimonies of victory in their families and are committed to pass on a Godly heritage to succeeding generations.

There is one other bright spot in our country today that provides me tremendous encouragement – the home school movement. Already about twenty years old, this movement is growing in strength each year. The reasons I see home schooling as such a bright hope are multiple:

- Home schools can help parents become more mature as they learn to overcome their own childhood deficiencies. Parents naturally become better organized, more industrious, more humble, and more knowledgeable about their world, their children, and themselves.

  Children are trained properly because parents can't successfully home school for any period of time without being caused to train their children. When children are required to do school work and to learn, it often conflicts with their immaturity. A child's nature may exhibit willfulness, pride, or laziness under the pressure of even reasonably moderate school work. Therefore, a multitude of training opportunities present themselves daily.

- Home school families are drawn closer together – like in the days when the home was truly the center of a family's life. As a result, these children are influenced by the standards of their parents rather than by those of their peers. In other words, the competition for the minds of the children is greatly reduced.

I believe home schooling can provide the ideal opportunity to apply God's principles of child training. It requires a great deal of commitment and dedication, but the rewards can be tremendous and eternal. Let me encourage you to investigate home schooling. If you decide to take on this endeavor, I promise that the opportunity for soul and spiritual growth will be enormous for the entire family. If you persevere through the tests the rewards will be indescribable. Even if you home school for only a year, it can be the single most important year of your lives. The several years my wife and I home taught our three children were the most meaningful to our entire family. But, whether you decide to home school or not, please commit yourselves to . . . train up your children in the way they should go.

Bibliography

Austin (Texas) *American Statesman*, May 4, 1980.

Defoe, Daniel. *Robinson Crusoe*. Chicago: Moody Press, 1965.

Foundation for Biblical Research. "Child Training." Austin, Texas, 1979.*

Risken, Jeremy, and Howard, Ted. "Praise the Lord – Spread Evangelism." *Politics Today*, September-October, 1979, p. 53.

Scofield, C.I., ed. *Holy Bible* (Authorized King James Version). New York: Oxford University Press, 1967.

The Compact Edition of the Oxford English Dictionary, 1971.

* The Foundation for Biblical Research utilized the following resource books in their research. (This is only a selected list.)

Abbott-Smith, G. A. *A Manual Greek Lexicon of the New Testament*. Edinburgh: T. & T. Clark, 1937.

Alsop, John R. I*ndex to the Bauer-Arndt-Gingrich Greek Lexicon*. Grand Rapids: Zondervan Publishing House, 1968.

Arndt, William F. and Gingrich, F. Wilbur. *A Greek-English Lexicon of the New Testament*. Chicago: University of Chicago Press, 1957.

Botterweck, G., and Ringgren, H., ed. *Theological Dictionary of the Old Testament*. Grand Rapids: Wm. B. Eerdmans

Publishing Co. Vol. I & II (revised edition) 1977; Vol. III, 1978.

Brown, Francis; Driver, S.R.; and Briggs, Charles A., eds. *A Hebrew and English Lexicon of the Old Testament*, 1929. Reprint. Oxford: At the Clarendon Press, 1974

The New Testament (Textus Receptus). London: Trinitarian Bible Society, 1977.

Einspahr, Bruce. *Index to Brown, Driver & Briggs*. Chicago: Moody Press, 1976.

Gesenius, William. *Hebrew-Chaldee Lexicon to the Old Testament*. Trans. Samuel P. Tregelles. Grand Rapids: Wm. B. Eerdmans Publishing Co., 1949.

Girdlestone, Robert B. *Synonyms of the Old Testament*. 2nd ed. 1897. Reprint. Grand Rapids: Wm. B. Eerdmans Publishing Co, 1956.

Kittel, R. *Biblia Hebraica*, 3rd Ed. Stuttgart: Wurtetembergische Bibelanstalt, 1961.

Kittel, R. *Theological Dictionary of the New Testament*. 10 vols. Grand Rapids: Wm. B. Eerdmans Publishing Co., 1964

Liddell, Henry George and Scott, Robert. *A Greek-English Lexicon*. Oxford: Oxford University Press, 1940.

Moulton, James Hope and Milligan, George. *The Vocabulary of the Greek Testament*. Grand Rapids: Wm. B. Eerdmans Publishing Co., 1952.

Thayer, Joseph Henry. *Greek-English Lexicon of the New Testament*. Grand Rapids: Zondervan Publishing House, 1976.

The Greek New Testament, 3rd ed. London: The United Bible Societies, 1975.

Trench, Richard C. *Synonyms of the New Testament*. Grand Rapids: Wm. B. Eerdmans Publishing Co., 1880.

MAIL TO: Foundation for Biblical Research
J. Richard and Virginia Fugate
P. O. Box 1412
Fair Oaks, CA 95628

For wholesale quantities call or fax:
916-729-6993
www.rfugate.org
email: cbg@rfugate.org

HOWEVER, PLEASE SUPPORT YOUR LOCAL CHRISTIAN BOOKSTORE. CALL THEM WITH THE FOLLOWING ISBN'S TO SEE IF THEY STOCK THE ITEM YOU WANT BEFORE ORDERING BY MAIL.

ISBN	Description	Qty	Price	Total

Second Edition
What the Bible Says About...Child Training

1-889700-13-4	Book	_____	$12.95	_____
1-889700-15-0	Video Set	_____	$99.00	_____
1-889700-22-3	Audio Set	_____	$42.00	_____
1-889700-29-0	*What the Bible Says About...Being a Man*	_____	$11.95	_____
1-889700-35-5	*What the Bible Says About...Suffering*		$12.00	_____

*On the Other Side of the Garden
- Biblical Womanhood in Today's World*

0-86717-008-05	Book	_____	$10.00	_____
0-86717-010-7	Workbook	_____	$13.00	_____

VICTORIOUS WOMEN On the Other Side of the Garden

1-889700-25-8	Book	_____	$10.95	_____

Subtotal $_____

Shipping & Handling $___4.00___

ORDER TOTAL $_____

**PLEASE REMIT CHECK OR MONEY ORDER
WITH COPY OF THIS FORM.
ALL PRODUCTS CARRY A FULL,
MONEY BACK GUARANTEE!**

Product Description

What the Bible Says About...Child Training is the title of a best selling Christian book (250,000 copies) and of a film nominated "Best Film Series" by the Christian Film Distributors in 1981. This material is unique in that the subject is handled solely from the Biblical viewpoint. The author, J. Richard Fugate, accepts the Bible as absolute truth and as infinitely superior to any human system of thinking. There has been no attempt to modify God's Word to make it compatible with human philosophies, psychology, sociology, religious views, or public opinion. *What the Bible Says About...Child Training* has been accepted by most Bible-believing churches as the standard text on child training for over 20 years. NOW, this classic work has been released as a 2nd edition with the same chapters plus author's comments, examples, and anecdotes added. The popular four-hour film series, which has been shown in many churches throughout the country, has also been improved in speaker presentation, graphics, and content to six, one-hour videos on VHS.

Biblical Marriage. All of the products in this category are based on the popular book by Virginia Fugate, *On the Other Side of the Garden; Biblical Womanhood for Today's World*, and Mr. Fugate's new book, *What the Bible Says About...Being A Man.* The Biblical manhood book teaches God's absolute responsibility to men for their family's leadership, not just for their provision and protection. It also explains why men of the past three or so generations have been raised *either* emasculated, or totally insensitive toward women; so that neither can fulfill the Biblical command to cherish their wives. These books also deal with the uniqueness of God's creation of mankind – male and female, and their permanent uniting into one through marriage.